M

The Rough

Chr

Fran

credits

Text editor: Joe Staines
Rough Guides series editor: Mark Ellingham
Production: Julia Bovis and Link Hall
Cartography: Ed Wright
Proofreading: Carole Mansur

cover credits

Front – Statue of Napoléon on his death bed by Vincenzo Vela
Back – Gargoyle on Notre-Dame Cathedral, Paris

publishing information

This edition published October 2002 by
Rough Guides Ltd, 80 Strand, London WC2R ORL

distributed by the Penguin group

Penguin Books Ltd, 80 Strand, London WC2R ORL
Penguin Putnam, Inc, 375 Hudson Street, New York 10014, USA
Penguin Books Australia Ltd, 487 Maroondah Highway,
PO Box 257, Ringwood, Victoria 3134, Australia
Penguin Books Canada Ltd, 10 Alcorn Avenue,
Toronto, Ontario M4V 1E4, Canada
Penguin Books (NZ) Ltd, 182–190 Wairau Road,
Auckland 10, New Zealand

Typeset to an original design by Henry Iles
Picture research by Eleanor Hill of Lovely

Printed in Spain by Graphy Cems

416 pages includes index

A catalogue record for this book is
available from the British Library.
ISBN 1-85828-826-6

The Rough Guide
Chronicle

France

by
Ian Littlewood

Chronicles series editor
Justin Wintle

acknowledgements

I would like to thank the series editor, Justin Wintle, and my editor at Rough Guides, Joe Staines. Both of them have contributed a lot, and done so with great tact. I've been very lucky to have their help. Special thanks to my wife Ayumi, to whom, as always, I owe the biggest debt.

Ian Littlewood
Sussex 2002

contents

introduction

France had wood, water and stone. To its early inhabitants these were the essential raw materials, and the land offered them in abundance. Less rich in mineral resources, it proved in time to have scattered deposits of coal, iron ore and bauxite. More important, its mixture of soils, climatic zones and different kinds of landscape provided the basis for a variety of agriculture that has been the mainstay of its economy. In shape a rough hexagon about a thousand kilometres long and the same across, France stretches from the North Sea to the Mediterranean, giving it a blend of northern and southern characteristics that can sometimes disconcert its neighbours. For centuries, the more stolid English have looked across the Channel with alternating envy and disapproval at this unpredictable, seductive country, with its flair for style, its dubious taste for the speculative and theoretical, its alarming penchant for revolutions.

Where does its history begin? Popular tradition long ago fixed on Clovis. It was he who dispatched the last representative of Roman power in Gaul and went on to piece together a Frankish kingdom that had at least the rough outlines of what later became France. But only after five ragged centuries of Merovingian and Carolingian rule do we really begin to see the emergence of modern France. Once the Capetian monarchs have established their sovereignty, we can talk with more assurance about the history of a nation. The Hundred Years' War against England left it drained but intact, and before long it was looking towards Italy for foreign conquests. At the end of the 16th century, after decades of religious civil war, the Bourbon dynasty came to the throne. Within a generation, it had set France on a course of expansion abroad and absolutism at home which led at last to the financial chaos, political exclusion and social inequity that precipitated the Revolution. Napoléon's rapidly acquired empire was as rapidly dismantled, leaving France to weave its way through a chequered century of restoration, revolution, empire and republic towards the cataclysm of 1914. In spite of the trauma of two devastating world wars and bitter colonial troubles, the end of the 20th century saw France in confident mood. Its millennium celebrations, by common consent among the best in the world, reflected a country that was still, as it had been for centuries, at the forefront of European powers.

For those living at the time, it is the political history of a nation that looms largest – the wars, the laws, the governments, the national triumphs and disasters. For those who come after, the perspective changes. In the middle of the bloody horrors of the Seven Years' War, Voltaire published *Candide*. Its words of provocation still ripple across the world; but who cares now about the victories and defeats that in 1759 seemed so much more important? In truth, the impact of a nation's history often has less to do with battles than with books. Measured in terms of the unspectacular events that create a cultural heritage, the significance of France's history is immense. From the poetry of the troubadours and the architecture of the great medieval cathedrals to the dominant artistic and intellectual movements of the 20th century, France has exercised a cultural influence unrivalled by any other country in Europe. If we look for the forces that shaped our way of thinking today, it is to the writers of the French Enlightenment – to Montesquieu, Diderot, Voltaire, Rousseau and the rest – that we must return, and beyond them to Pascal and Descartes.

The French themselves have rarely been in doubt about their cultural pre-eminence, which is perhaps one reason why, at a time when the west has in general been eager to

FRANCE

UNITED KINGDOM · Calais · BELGIUM · GERMANY

ENGLISH CHANNEL

LUX.

Cherbourg · Amiens · Laon · ARDENNE · Moselle

Compiègne

Bayeux · Rouen · Soissons · Reims · Metz

PARIS

Seine · Strasbourg · VOSGES · Rhine

Brest

Chartres · Bassin Parisien

BRITTANY · Rennes · Le Mans · Fontainebleau

Orléans · Loire · Dijon · Saône · JURA · SWITZER-LAND

Blois

Loire · Bourges · MORVAN

Nantes · VENDÉE · Cher

Poitiers · Vienne

La Rochelle · LIMOUSIN · Vichy · Lyon · Sillon Rhodanien

Limoges · MASSIF · ALPS · ITALY

ATLANTIC OCEAN

CENTRAL

Dordogne · Allier · Rhône

Bordeaux · Lot · Durance

Bassin Aquitain

Garonne · Albi · Tarn · Avignon

Montpellier

Toulouse · Marseille

Lourdes · MEDITERRANEAN SEA

PYRENEES

SPAIN · ANDORRA

metres
4000
3000
2000
1500
1000
500
200
100
0

N

0   100 km

shelter under America's umbrella and share its culture, France has tended to stand aloof. A healthy suspicion of American influence has marked French policy on a range of issues from its attitude to NATO to its stance on the Middle East, from pursuit of nuclear weapons to protection of the national film industry. France goes its own way. And this irritating, admirable confidence in the superiority of its own arrangements comes ultimately from a pride in its past. No one demonstrated this more clearly than General de Gaulle. France, he explained at the start of his war memoirs, had always seemed to him to have a special destiny: 'France could not be France without greatness.' The conviction came to him from his father in a manner that de Gaulle sums up in a single, brief sentence. Quite simply, 'Il m'en a découvert l'Histoire' – He revealed to me its History.

1
From the beginnings
up to 476 AD

The prehistory of a nation is by definition elusive. We can estimate roughly the chronology that led from *homo erectus* to our immediate ancestors, but this tells us little that is specific to the geographical region we now call France. Even when we reach *homo sapiens*, we are reliant on the occasional shafts of light provided by random discoveries such as that of the **Lascaux caves**. Fragments are all that exist to guide us, sparse hints that indicate, for example, the beginnings of agriculture and cattle-rearing in the Neolithic period.

As the Stone Age gives way to the ages of Bronze and Iron, surviving artefacts multiply and human impact on the environment begins to leave a discernible historical trail. Towards the end of the third millennium BC, tribes move in from the east and make their mark. Objects in metal and clay, discovered at a range of sites, bear witness to commerce, hierarchy and ritual. From the 6th century BC, a trading colony established on the Mediterranean coast yields further evidence of the tribal groups that have settled in the area: they build fortified towns, they use coins, they drink wine. But always what is lacking is a coherent written record.

And then came the **Romans**. By this time, the **Gauls**, though still an assortment of diverse tribes, had evolved a relatively advanced civilisation of their own, centred on urban strongholds known as *oppida*. The comparative ease with which they accommodated themselves to Roman customs and institutions – in contrast to the Germanic tribes beyond the Rhine – can be seen as a measure of their sophistication. For **Julius Caesar** the conquest of Gaul was ostensibly about protecting Rome's allies, securing Roman frontiers and advancing Roman interests; in reality, it was largely about establishing himself as a contender for the Roman imperium. Having dealt swiftly with the modest threat represented by the **Helvetii**, he then moved on to the piecemeal subjugation of the rest of the Gallic tribes. Within eight years the outlines of Roman Gaul had been set. It was left to **Augustus** to organize the administrative provinces that gave this new territory its final shape.

The next three centuries saw the development of a **Gallo-Roman** civilization whose prosperity was reflected, particularly in the south, in its buildings, social institutions, cultural artefacts and general style of life. There were periodic troubles – uprisings against Rome and their cruel aftermath – but it was only in the second half of the 3rd century AD that Gaul really began to suffer the full effects of the empire's social and economic decline. By this time, moreover, the weakness of Roman frontiers had been exploited by the watchful barbarian tribes on the far side of the Rhine. The **Franks** and **Alamanni** were penetrating deeper and deeper into Gaul. It was partly in response to these incursions that an independent Gallic empire was proclaimed in 260 AD: its supporters were not nationalist rebels, they actually wanted to preserve Roman Gaul, which Rome itself – distracted by growing internal problems – was leaving vulnerable. After fourteen years the emperor **Aurelian** succeeded in bringing the breakaway empire to heel and restoring Roman authority, but the process was harsh. By the end of the third century the face of Gaul was changing: the economy was in decline, open towns were shrinking back into fortified strongholds, abandoned villas were being quarried for materials to build defensive walls.

For a hundred years the imperial armies struggled with some success to defend the northern frontier, shifting the capital from **Lyon** to **Trier** and fighting repeated engagements with the Alamanni and the Franks. It was an expensive, draining enterprise that imposed heavier and heavier burdens on the Gauls themselves. Finally, at the beginning of the 5th century, the frontier crumbled. Waves of barbarian tribes swept across the Rhine, some to force a passage through Gaul into Italy, Spain and North Africa, others to find a place where they could settle. The old order could not survive: Roman Gaul and the civilization it had produced were coming to an end.

c.1,000,000–700,000 BC The area of France, along with the rest of Europe, is occupied by *homo erectus*.

c.400,000 BC Near **Tautavel** in southern France a cave-dwelling community leaves evidence that suggests tool-using hominids in transition from *homo erectus* to a form of Neanderthal. Among the remains discovered here, in the cave of Arago, is a partial human skull.

c.100,000 BC **Neanderthal** peoples begin to inhabit France during the last interglacial period of the **Pleistocene Age**. The Neanderthals are cave-dwellers and hunters who use fire, make stone and wooden tools, and bury their dead. Important evidence about their mode of life comes from the cave of **Le Moustier** in the Dordogne, inhabited around 50,000 years ago.

c.35,000–30,000 BC **Cro-Magnons**, so-called from the site discovered in the Dordogne in 1868, begin to displace the Neanderthals. Early representatives of *homo sapiens sapiens*, the Cro-Magnons have more intricate tools and a culture that expresses artistic and religious concerns.

c.20,000 BC An **Upper Palaeolithic** community at Solutré-Pouilly (near modern Mâcon) develops stone-working techniques that produce finely flaked blades in the

The Lascaux caves

On 12 September, 1940 four schoolboys, out walking in the Dordogne, decided to investigate a hole in the ground left by an uprooted pine. They enlarged it, crawled through and found themselves in what is still the largest site of prehistoric wall paintings ever discovered. Executed in about 15,000 BC, the **Lascaux** paintings offer an extraordinary glimpse of the Stone Age world. A variety of animals, including deer, horses and aurochs (a type of wild ox), are depicted in shades of red, yellow, brown and black. Among them a single human figure, not much more than a matchstick-man in this pageant of magnificent, breathing beasts, finds his way on to the scene.

Made up of a central cavern and a number of connecting galleries, the caves were probably used as the site for rituals related to the hunt. Scattered through them were fragments of tools, lamps, minerals used for colouring, even vestiges of the wooden scaffolding on which the artists had worked. When the Lascaux Grotto was opened to the public in 1948, the attention it received, along with the measures taken to pump out water, quickly led to a degradation of the site. Since 1963 the caves have been closed to all but occasional researchers. A facsimile of part of them was set up nearby and opened to the public in 1983.

Painting of two great aurochs in the 'Great Hall of the Bulls' at Lascaux

pattern of laurel and willow leaves. Other tools, such as bone needles, indicate the use of stitched animal skins for protection against the cold. This site, which is apparently used for the slaughter of horses to provide meat, gives its name to **Solutrean** culture.

Early 6th millennium BC **Neolithic** wanderers reach the south of France along the Mediterranean coast. Around the beginning of the 5th millennium BC others from across the Rhine find their way to the Parisian basin. This period sees the introduction of agriculture and the construction of villages. It is also the period of the great megalithic monuments such as the **Carnac menhirs** in Brittany.

From 2300 BC Tribes from central Europe settle in France. Soon afterwards, partly through the influence of **bell-beaker culture** (so-called from its characteristic bell-shaped goblets), the use of metal is introduced. Small domestic items in copper appear from the end of the third millennium, but the production of sophisticated weapons and tools does not become common until the mid- to late **Bronze Age**.

c.1500–750 BC **Proto-Celts** settle in Gaul.

c.725–450 BC **Iron Age** culture passes through the later Hallstatt period, named after the archeological site in Upper Austria. Its achievements can be seen in the **Vix tomb** in Burgundy, discovered in 1953 and dating from about 500 BC. The contents of the tomb include pieces of finely worked jewellery in gold and bronze as well as examples of the ornate drinking equipment favoured by the Gallic aristocracy of the time. Among other objects that indicate the extent of contemporary trade links, the grave contains a colossal bronze wine krater from southern Italy, five-foot high and capable of holding over 1000 litres.

c.600 BC The colony of **Massalia** (Marseille) is founded.

Massalia: the Mediterranean connection

This colony, set up in about 600 BC by **Phocean Greeks** on the site of present-day Marseille, was an important trading centre in pre-Christian Gaul. Objects from Etruria, Corinth, Athens, Rhodes and elsewhere, discovered in archeological digs, suggest the range of its contacts. Perfectly situated to take advantage of Mediterranean trade routes, it funnelled goods into and out of southern Gaul, establishing a network of subsidiary trading posts along the coast at places such as Nice and Antibes. Luxury items, often connected with wine-drinking, were passed on to the barbarian chieftains in exchange for slaves, food and raw materials. A wise decision to side with Rome against **Hannibal** at the end of the 3rd century BC ensured valuable help from Rome in defending its interests against pirates and the encroachment of hostile tribes. Less astutely, it opted for **Pompey** rather than Caesar in the Civil War and in consequence found its sphere of influence much curtailed in favour of Nîmes and Arles. Although it retained its status as a free city and remained for some time a centre of Greek learning, Massalia thereafter dwindled in importance until its revival in the Middle Ages.

450–50 BC In the late Iron Age, **La Tène** culture (called after the site of that name in Switzerland) emerges from the Celtic encounter with Greek and Etruscan influences.

c.390 BC Brennus, a Gallic leader, defeats the Roman army and sacks Rome. Only the defenders on the Capitoline hill hold out (alerted, according to legend, by the cackling of the temple geese). Brennus is finally persuaded to withdraw on receipt of a huge ransom, but fearful memories of him will have a lasting effect on Roman attitudes to Gaul and the Gallic tribes.

300–250 BC Celtic tribes reach southern Gaul. Once more or less permanent settlements are established, they begin to concentrate in *oppida*, strongholds of about 100 hectares (somewhat less in the south), surrounded by wood and earth walls. These are the focus of manufacture, trade and politics. Religious practice is controlled by the caste of **Druids**, whose influence is indicated by the fact that Augustus later bans them.

218 BC The Gauls support **Hannibal** in his onslaught on Italy during the Punic War.

180 BC The first **Roman army** crosses the Alps into Gaul, though no concerted effort of conquest is made for another half century.

154 BC Massalia calls on Rome for protection against neighbouring tribes, in particular the **Salluvii**.

125–121 BC Massalia again calls for help from Rome, but this time the Romans stay. Having defeated the Salluvii, they then go on to conquer southern France, founding the city of **Aquae Sextiae** (Aix-en-Provence) and establishing the province of Gallia Transalpina. The Aedui tribe are declared 'friends and brothers of the Roman people'.

118 BC **Narbo Martius** (Narbonne) is founded as the western capital of Rome's new possession.

> ❝ The Druids officiate at the worship of the gods, regulate public and private sacrifices, and give rulings on all religious questions. Large numbers of young men flock to them for instruction, and they are held in great honour by the people. They act as judges in practically all disputes, whether between tribes or between individuals... Any individual or tribe failing to accept their award is banned from taking part in sacrifice – the heaviest punishment that can be inflicted upon a Gaul. ❞
>
> Julius Caesar, *De Bello Gallico*, trans. S. A. Handford

109–101 BC The appearance of the Germanic **Cimbri** and their allies, who have pushed down from the north, heralds a period of unrest, intensified by uprisings among some of the conquered tribes. Roman forces are defeated near Agen in 107BC and again at Orange in 107BC, but **Gaius Marius** crushes the opposition in two decisive battles at Aquae Sextiae (102BC) against the Teutones and at Vercellae (101BC) against the Cimbri.

62–61 BC A rebellion by the Allobroges is put down after fierce fighting.

58–53 BC A year after he becomes Consul (59 BC), **Julius Caesar** is appointed governor of Cisalpine Gaul.

Vercingetorix and the Gallic revolt

A chieftain of the Arverni, **Vercingetorix** owes his fame to Julius Caesar's account of the Gallic Wars. At the beginning of 52 BC, an uprising against Roman rule had begun with the massacre of Roman traders in Cenabum (Orléans) by warriors of the Carnutes tribe. Vercingetorix saw his moment. By a mixture of rabble-rousing and terrorism, he whipped together a coalition of hostile Gallic tribes. It was to be the one serious challenge to Rome's pacification of Gaul. In a pitched battle the odds would always be on the side of the highly disciplined and well-equipped Roman army. Vercingetorix realized this and accordingly developed something much closer to

Gold coin depicting Vercingetorix

On the pretext of protecting Rome's allies among the Gallic tribes from the incursions of the Helvetii and the Suevi, he initiates the **Gallic War**. After defeating the Helvetii at Bibracte, and the Suevi, led by Ariovistus, at Mühlhausen, he marches north in 57BC to campaign against the Nervii and then pushes south and west against the Veneti, before turning north again to invade Britain (55BC and 54BC), to suppress uprisings among the northern tribes (54BC) and to campaign across the Rhine (55BC and 53BC). The conquest has its own momentum, with each stage requiring a further move in order to secure it, but it is also driven by the political ambitions of Caesar himself.

a guerrilla strategy, which he combined with a scorched earth policy intended to leave Caesar's army without supplies.

By the middle of 52 BC the revolt had swelled to include even the Aedui, Rome's most trusted allies among the tribes. Caesar's army was in retreat. At this point Vercingetorix made the double error that was his downfall: after holding the hill fort of **Gergovia** against Caesar and inflicting heavy losses, he abandoned his usual tactics and attacked the Roman army in the open field. The result was a defeat which he compounded by falling back on the town of Alésia, where he could be boxed in by the Roman legions. Caesar set in place an array of siege works, saw off the army that came to relieve the town, and then starved it into submission. Vercingetorix called a last assembly and offered to be handed over to the Romans alive or dead. More interested in a living trophy, Caesar sent him back to Rome where he languished in prison for six years before following the general's chariot in a triumph. Having served his purpose, he was strangled. Forgotten for many years, he was resurrected in the 19th century to act as a convenient, if anachronistic, symbol of French nationalism and resistance to foreign oppression.

52 BC A major Gallic revolt under **Vercingetorix** is crushed by Caesar.

50 BC The Gallic War is brought to a close. At the cost of much slaughter and destruction among the Gauls, it has increased the extent of the Roman empire by about a third. There continue to be periodic revolts, one in Aquitaine in 39BC and others by the Treveri in 29BC, but Roman control is not seriously contested for the rest of the century. Rome consolidates its conquest by providing incentives that encourage both individuals and tribes to accommodate themselves to Roman rule. The condition of different cities ranges from those laid under tribute to those, like Orange and Arles, that are granted the status of 'colony'.

49 BC Massalia is annexed by Rome after a siege.

43 BC **Lugdunum** (Lyon) is founded. Sited at the point where the three parts of Gaul more or less converge, it will become the capital of Roman Gaul.

c.39 BC **Marcus Vipsanius Agrippa**, probably Rome's greatest military organizer, lays out the framework of Gaul's road system.

27 BC Having established himself as Rome's first emperor, **Augustus** goes to Gaul to oversee a series of administrative changes. In conjunction with his later reforms carried out in 16–13 BC, they determine Gaul's structure within the empire. The Romanized south enjoys special status as the province of **Gallia Narbonensis**, while the rest of Transalpine Gaul, still known disdainfully to many Romans as **Gallia Comata** (long-haired Gaul, as opposed to Cisalpine Gaul on the Italian side of the Alps), is divided into the three provinces of **Aquitania**, **Lugdunensis** and **Belgica**.

25–16 BC Augustus oversees the conquest of the northern Alpine tribes, whom Julius Caesar had not engaged. The central region of the Alps is conquered some ten years later from 9 to 6 BC.

ROMAN GAUL & THE
GALLIC TRIBES, c.10 BC

0   100 km

BRITANNIA

BELGICA

NERVII

BELLOVACI   REMI   Augusta
                     Treverorum   TREVERI
                     (Trier)

VENETI   L U G D U N E N S I S

Lutetia
(Paris)
CARNUTES

LINGONES

Portus Namnetum
(Nantes)   PICTONES   BITURIGES
                        CUBI   AEDUI   Augustodunum
                                         (Autun)   SEQUANI

                                         Lugdunum
                                         (Lyon)   HELVETII

N   SANTONES   AQUITANIA   ARVERNI   ALLOBROGES

BITURIGES
VIVISCI

Burdigala
(Bordeaux)   RUTENI   GALLIA NARBONENSIS

                        Nemausus
                        (Nîmes)   LIGURES

                        Massilia
                        (Marseille)

HISPANIA

c.20 BC At about the same time as the construction of the
temple in **Nîmes**, known today as the Maison carrée, the
aqueduct of the Pont-du-Gard is built to bring water to the
town.

c.10 BC The manufacture of red-glazed samian pottery (*terra
sigillata* ware) is introduced from Arretium in Italy to Lugdunum. About thirty years later production is moved to **La
Graufesenque** (near Millau) and from there spreads out to
other centres. An extremely important industry for Roman
Gaul, samian pottery is widely exported to other parts of
the empire, providing valuable information about

> In secret conferences to which the fiercest spirits were admitted, or any to whom poverty or the fear of guilt was an irresistible stimulus to crime, they arranged that Florus was to rouse the Belgae, Sacrovir the Gauls nearer home. These men accordingly talked sedition before small gatherings and popular assemblies, about the perpetual tributes, the oppressive usury, the cruelty and arrogance of their governors, hinting too that there was disaffection among our soldiers...

Tacitus, The Annals, trans. Alfred John Church and William Jackson Brodribb

patterns of trade across the period.

21 AD An uprising led by **Julius Florus** and **Julius Sacrovir**, both of them Roman citizens and army officers, ends in their defeat and suicide.

c.25 The amphitheatre at **Arles** is built.

48 The emperor **Claudius** procures the admission of Gauls to the Senate in Rome.

c.60 Work begins on the amphitheatre at Nîmes.

65 A great fire destroys much of Lugdunum.

68 Gaius Julius Vindex, the governor of Gallia Lugdunensis, leads a revolt against the rule of the emperor **Nero**. Defeated by the Roman army of the Rhine, which remains loyal to Nero, Vindex kills himself.

69 The revolt of Vindex proves a catalyst to more extensive uprisings, facilitated by civil war in the empire at large and demoralization among the legions of the Rhine.

70 The attempt to establish a Gallic empire is finally defeated by the forces of the emperor **Vespasian** at the battle of **Trier**.

92 The emperor **Domitian** severely curtails wine-growing in Gaul, partly to reduce competition with Italy, partly to encourage the cultivation of cereal crops.

98 **Trajan** becomes Roman emperor. The period of Gallic prosperity already initiated by the Flavian emperors continues under Trajan, **Hadrian** and the **Antonines**. Trade increases, towns grow bigger, and there is a surge in public and private building.

177 A number of **Christians** are martyred at Lugdunum, among them the slave girl **Blandina**.

186–87 **Maternus**, an army deserter, organizes bands of brigands that pillage towns and countryside. His force overruns Gaul and part of Hispania (present-day Spain) before the revolt is finally suppressed and Maternus himself killed. The huge following he attracts suggests widespread resentment of Roman rule under the emperor **Commodus**.

ROBERT HARDING/EXPLORER

The Roman amphitheatre at Arles (Arelate)

196–67 The revolt of the governor of Britain, **Clodius Albinus**, is partially supported in Gaul. His army is defeated at Lugdunum by the emperor **Septimius Severus**.

212 The emperor **Caracalla** gives Roman citizenship to all freemen throughout the empire.

253–60 The **Franks** and **Alamanni** begin to penetrate the Roman frontier in the north, more sparsely defended now that troops are being drawn away by Rome's internal conflicts.

260 The capture of the emperor **Valerian** by the Persians throws the Roman world into turmoil. The Franks take advantage of the confusion to cross the lower Rhine into Gaul.

c.260 The Roman governor of Lower Germany, **Latinius Postumus**, proclaims a Gallic empire and successfully resists efforts by Valerian's son and successor, the emperor **Gallienus**, to restore Roman rule.

274 The emperor **Aurelian** regains control of Gaul.

274–75 Franks and Alamanni invade southern Gaul.

277 The emperor **Probus** defeats the Alamanni.

c.280 Probus authorises **viniculture** throughout Gaul.

284–311 Heavy taxes imposed by the emperor **Diocletian** to pay for the army lead to rebellion among many peasants and small landowners, especially in the north and east, who create armed bands known as *bagaudae*. This form of brigandage is suppressed only after a number of military campaigns, and it reappears with particular violence in the first half of the 5th century.

303–04 Christians are persecuted on the orders of Diocletian.

313 The emperor Constantine's **Edict of Milan** enjoins religious toleration.

The spreading vine

The Gauls were wine drinkers long before they became wine producers. Accustomed to eat their grapes and import their wine from Italy, they were not introduced to viniculture until the Roman conquest. But they were quick to learn. By the end of the first century AD wine was flowing back from Gaul into Italy at such a rate that the emperor Domitian ordered the destruction of half the vines in the Gallic provinces. The new **wine industry**, however, continued to thrive; Pliny the Elder commends in particular the wine produced just south of Lyon by the tribe of the **Allobroges**. Viniculture was further boosted by the spread of Christianity, which demanded a supply of wine for its central ritual.

From the Middle Ages the pattern of wine production was largely determined by a mixture of commerce and politics. In the early 13th century, for example, control of the ports in the Poitou region passed to the king of France, so the English merchants shifted their centre of operations to **Bordeaux**, which was still part of the king of England's Angevin empire. Fashion too played its part. For a long time white wine was considered healthier and more refined than red and commanded correspondingly higher prices.

The greatest crisis in two thousand years of French wine-growing occurred in the 19th century when a series of plant diseases, of which the worst was **phylloxera** in the 1880s, devastated the industry. A solution was eventually found by grafting French grapes on to disease-resistant American stock, but by then many of the smaller producers had gone out of business. It was only in the second half of the 20th century, when over-production led to restrictions on wine-growing and a new emphasis on higher-quality grapes, that the native stock regained its dominance.

357–58 After defeating the Alamanni at Strasbourg, the Roman general **Julian** goes on to defeat the Franks.

360 Julian winters in **Lutetia** (Paris), to which he has given renewed importance as a military base, and where his troops proclaim him emperor.

> **Therefore, your Worship should know that it has pleased us to remove all conditions whatsoever, which were in the rescripts formerly given to you officially, concerning the Christians and now any one of these who wishes to observe Christian religion may do so freely and openly, without molestation.**
>
> From the *Edict of Milan*

371 **St Martin** becomes bishop of Tours. Until his death in 397 he works to spread Christianity through the surrounding region. Responsible for establishing **monasticism** in Gaul, he earns a special a place in popular esteem through his ascetic life, becoming the patron saint of France.

378 The emperor **Gratian** defeats the Alamanni.

Lutetia: the birth of the capital

Originally a town of the **Parisii**, from whom it took its modern name in the 4th century, **Lutetia** came to prominence in 52 BC.

Recognising the strategic advantages of a site that commanded the crossing of the Seine, Julius Caesar ordered his lieutenant Labienus to take possession of it. The Gauls set fire to the **Île de la Cité**, but the Romans occupied what was left and set about creating a Gallo-Roman town. The Île de la Cité provided a fortified base which could be defended against aggressors, while on the left bank of the Seine the amenities of Roman life – baths, amphitheatre, forum – occupied the slopes of **Mont St-Geneviève**. With the barbarian invasions of the mid-3rd century, Lutetia shrank back to the Île de la Cité before enjoying a revival of importance under the emperor **Julian**. What settled its future destiny was the decision by the Frankish king Clovis in the early 6th century to establish his court there. The town that Julian referred to affectionately as his 'dear Lutetia' had taken its first step towards becoming the capital of France.

c.394 Death of the poet and teacher Ausonius. Tutor of the future emperor Gratian and later a consul, Ausonius has been living in comfortable retirement on his estates bordering the Garonne, a celebrated member of the Gallo-Roman elite.

395 With the death of the emperor **Theodosius** a definitive split takes place between the empire of the west and the empire of the east (later known as the Byzantine empire).

406 On 31 December Vandals, Alans, Burgondes and Suevi cross the frozen Rhine and overrun the garrisons that defend the so-called *limes* (the boundary that marks the northern frontiers of the Roman world).

410 Alaric the Visigoth sacks Rome.

c.418 The **Visigoths** settle by treaty in **Aquitaine**. Like the agreements made later with the Burgondes and the Franks, this arrangement contradicts the notion that they were no more than rampaging barbarians bent on destroying the Roman empire. To a significant extent their goal is integration, or at least a form of peaceful coexistence.

c.430 The **Franks** settle in northern Gaul.

c.440 The Burgondes settle in Savoy and then the valleys of the Rhône and Saône.

c.450 The **Bretons** begin to settle in the Armorican peninsula, which later becomes Brittany.

> **❝** For from the topmost ridge to the foot of the slope the riverside is thickly planted with green vines… Here the wayfarer tramping along the low-lying bank, and there the bargeman floating by, call out their rude jests at the loitering vine-dressers; and all the hill, and shivering woods, and channelled river, ring with their cries. **❞**
>
> Ausonius on the Moselle, trans. Hugh White

The Visigoths in Gaul

A Germanic tribe driven south by the Huns, the **Visigoths** sacked Rome in 410 AD and then wandered north again before settling in the Bordeaux region two years later. The treaty they made with the Romans in 418 granted them vast territories between Toulouse and the Atlantic. This was the basis of a kingdom that by the end of the century included southwest France as far east as the Rhône, and most of the Iberian peninsula. Its laws were codified by King **Euric**, who had hopes of achieving a fusion between barbarian and Gallo-Roman traditions. The Visigoths, however, had been converted to **Arian Christianity,** which denied the divinity of Christ and was condemned as heretical by the Council of Nicea in 325, whereas the Gallo-Romans were **Nicean Catholics.** **Alaric II** made some attempt to forge a compromise but he was outmanoeuvred by the Frankish king **Clovis,** who presented himself as the champion of the Nicean Christians. The defeat of Alaric II by Clovis at the battle of Vouillé (near Poitiers) in 507 marked the effective end of the Visigoths in Gaul. They withdrew to consolidate their kingdom in Spain.

451 **Attila the Hun** invades Gaul. Inspired by **St Geneviève**, the Parisii hold out against him. At the battle of the Catalaunian Plains he is defeated by the Roman general **Aetius** and the Visigoth **Theodoric**. The nature of this battle, which sees Germans fighting alongside Romans against other Germans, indicates a political reality that has evolved far beyond the simple opposition between Roman and barbarian.

c.455–70 The **Alamanni** settle in Alsace.

476 The last Roman emperor is deposed, bringing to an end the Roman empire in the west.

2
From Clovis to the Carolingians
476–987

The Frankish king **Clovis** (465–511) came to power as the ruler of one kingdom among a patchwork of territories that had been carved out of Roman Gaul by several different groups. The Franks themselves occupied the northeast; to the south, in the region of Alsace, were the Alamanni, and to the west was the kingdom of the last Roman ruler, Syagrius; further south were the Visigoths and the Burgundians. Starting with Syagrius, Clovis worked steadily to eliminate neighbouring rivals. By the end of his reign the barbarian chief had become the Christian king of a realm that covered a large part of Gaul. The Burgundians in the southeast and the Ostrogoths in Provence retained their independence, but otherwise only the Armorican peninsula (Brittany) was outside Frankish control. Supported by an increasingly powerful Church and the old Gallo-Roman elite, Clovis had created a massive inheritance.

It was a mixed blessing. For much of the next five centuries French history presents the recurring pattern of a kingdom painstakingly stitched together by one ruler only to be torn apart by his feuding descendants. Neither the **Merovingians** nor the **Carolingians** could find a way out of this murderous cycle. Through luck and lack of scruple, **Chlotar I**, Clovis's youngest son, managed to re-establish the integrity of his father's kingdom in 558, but this was only the prelude to another and more savage period of family conflict between his own sons and their wives, which continued through the generations until for a brief period (629–39) **Dagobert I** ruled as sole king of the three Frankish kingdoms of **Neustria**, **Burgundy** and **Austrasia**. On his death the realm was again divided, and by now the character of the monarchy was beginning to change. Rivalry for the crown had strengthened the hand of the aristocratic power-brokers to the point where real authority increasingly resided with the heads of the royal household (de facto prime ministers), known as **mayors of the palace**. It was one of them, **Charles Martel**, who stage-managed the end of the Merovingian dynasty, leaving the way open for his son **Pepin the Short** to inaugurate the new dynasty of **Carolingians** in 751.

Throughout this period, warfare was endemic. When the Frankish rulers were not fighting each other, they were fighting to expand their kingdom or secure its borders in campaigns against the Arabs, Gascons, Frisians, Alamanni and others. From these beginnings, the second of the Carolingians, Charles I (**Charlemagne**), founded an empire that by the time of his death in 814 stretched from the Atlantic to the Elbe and south to Rome. To this period of relative stability belong the main cultural achievements of the early Middle Ages in France: the development of an easily legible script, the production and dissemination of manuscript books, the promotion of schools of ivory sculpture and painting on parchment, the birth of a new ecclesiastical architecture. Meanwhile, social and administrative reforms contributed to a markedly more unified and centrally ordered state.

The imperial crown passed to Charlemagne's son, **Louis I**, but within a generation the old question of inheritance was again tearing the empire apart. Its disintegration was confirmed by the **treaty of Verdun** in 843, which created the separate kingdoms of West, Middle and East Francia. To add to troubles at home, there was now an external threat. As the 9th century progressed, the Viking invaders cast an ever longer shadow, until finally an accommodation was reached that allowed them to settle and become part of the kingdom they had set out to pillage (see p.39). From the divergent histories of West and East Francia were gradually emerging the outlines of the future France and Germany, but for the moment it was a story of dissolution. By the time the last of the Carolingians was succeeded by **Hugues Capet**, the western half of Charlemagne's former empire was little more than a collection of independent fiefdoms.

c.481 Childeric I, king of the Salian Franks, is succeeded by his son **Clovis**, whose grandfather **Merovech** gives his name to the **Merovingian** dynasty.

c.486 At the **battle of Soissons** Clovis defeats **Syagrius**, the last representative of Roman power in Gaul.

c.493 Clovis marries the Burgundian princess **Clotilda**, a Christian.

c.496 Clovis goes to the aid of the Rhenish Franks and stops the westward thrust of the Alamanni, defeating them at the **battle of Tolbiac**.

498 Campaigning against the Visigoths in Aquitaine, Clovis takes **Bordeaux**. It is probably in the same year, on Christmas Day, that he is baptised a Christian.

c.500 Clovis campaigns against the **Burgundians**, but the alliance of the Burgundian king Gundobad with the Visigoths forces him to withdraw.

c.502 The customary law of the Burgundians is set down by **Gundobad**.

c.506 The Roman law of the Visigoths is set down in a form that comes to be known as the **Breviary of Alaric**.

Clovis I: creator of a kingdom

For details of the life of **Clovis** (465–511) we are largely dependent on **Gregory of Tours**, who was writing well over half a century after Clovis's death. What is clear, however, is that in 481 or 482 Clovis succeeded his father as king of the Salian Franks and that in the course of the next thirty years he welded a large part of divided Gaul into a unified kingdom. His policy was executed by means of a ruthless series of military campaigns. In c.486 he defeated the Roman army of northern Gaul, led by **Syagrius**, making himself master of territories that reached as far as the Loire. Later campaigns against the Alamanni, the Visigoths and potential rivals among the other Frankish chieftains steadily increased his power. In particular, his defeat of the Visigoths at the **battle of Vouillé** (507) extended the kingdom of the Franks for the first time south of the Loire.

Clovis's marriage to the Christian Burgundian princess **Clotilda** in c.493 consolidated his position and probably also influenced his acceptance of **Christianity**. This conversion, whatever its religious promptings, had the effect of boosting his support among the generally Catholic Gallo-Roman population. The inheritance he bequeathed was soon in fragments, but Clovis had pointed the way forward: he had created, albeit briefly, a more or less unified kingdom, and he had chosen Paris as his capital.

507 Clovis defeats the Visigoths at the **battle of Vouillé**, killing their king Alaric II and opening the way to the annexation of **Aquitaine**.

508 After capturing the Visigoths' capital **Toulouse** and bringing their kingdom in Gaul to an end, Clovis decides on Paris for his own capital.

508–11 The legal code of the Franks is drawn up in 65 chapters, known as the **Salic Law** (*Pactus legis salicae*).

c.509 Recognized by the **Rhenish Franks**, Clovis becomes sole king of the Franks.

511 In the summer Clovis convenes the first **Council of Frankish bishops** at Orléans.

On 27 November Clovis dies and Clotilda retires to a monastery. The kingdom is divided between their four sons: **Theodoric** gets the eastern portion, consisting of an area between the Loire and the Rhine and all the territory beyond the Rhine; **Clodomir**, the Loire basin, with Orléans as his capital; **Childebert**, present-day Normandy and Paris; **Chlotar**, the kingdom of Soissons. Aquitaine is shared among all four.

Salic Law

A body of legal texts drawn up towards the end of the reign of Clovis, the *Pactus legis salicae*, or **Salic Law**, was primarily intended as a mechanism for keeping the peace rather than for defining a social consensus on criminal behaviour. By establishing a record of customary law, that stipulated penalties and compensations for a range of delinquencies from calling someone a fox to stealing their cattle or murdering them, it was hoped to prevent people from having recourse to private justice and clan feuds.

The importance of Salic Law to later French history was a single clause specifying that 'in the case of salic land [probably meaning ancestral land], no part of the inheritance must be transmitted to a woman but the whole must pass to the male sex'. Resurrected in the 14th century, this article became, by some adroit manipulation, a fundamental law governing the succession to the French throne. Not only could no woman inherit the crown, but no claim to it could be made through the female line. This was of particular importance in 1593 in blocking the claim of the Spanish infanta, Isabella, who was the granddaughter of Henri II.

523 The brothers, with the exception of Theodoric, open a campaign against **Burgundy**.

524 Following the death of Clodomir in battle, Childebert and Chlotar have his sons murdered and divide his kingdom between them.

c.530–37 The Franks conquer Thuringia, Bavaria and Provence.

534 The **war in Burgundy** comes to an end when Gundomar, the king, is finally put to flight and the Franks take possession.

c.540 **St Benedict of Nursia** draws up the Benedictine Rule for his monastery at Monte Cassino in southern Italy. Its growing influence in northern and western Europe over the next three centuries will make the **Benedictines** the dominant monastic order of the early Middle Ages.

543 The kingdom is stricken by one of the periodic visitations of **plague** that recur throughout the century, most devastatingly in 559, 599 and again in 605.

> ❝ Idleness is the enemy of the soul. And therefore, at fixed times, the brothers ought to be occupied in manual labour; and again, at fixed times, in sacred reading . . . There shall certainly be appointed one or two elders, who shall go round the monastery at the hours in which the brothers are engaged in reading, and see to it that no troublesome brother chance to be found who is open to idleness and trifling, and is not intent on his reading; being not only of no use to himself, but also stirring up others. ❞
>
> Rule of St Benedict, 'Concerning the Daily Manual Labour',
> trans. Ernest F. Henderson

Brunhild and the royal feud

Brunhild (534–613), the queen of Austrasia, emerges from the violent turmoil of the 6th century as one of the most commanding figures in Merovingian history. Beautiful, learned and implacable, she spent much of her life at the centre of the political stage. After the murder of her sister by **Fredegund**, Brunhild's demand for revenge brought her husband **Sigebert** into conflict with his brother Chilperic. Sigebert's initial victories came to an end with his assassination, again at the instigation of Fredegund.

Treading a delicate line between hostile Neustria on the one hand and power-hungry Austrasian magnates on the other, Brunhild maintained the kingship for her son **Childebert II**, partly through an alliance with Guntram, king of Burgundy. By the time Childebert died in 595, he was king of both Austrasia and Burgundy, which passed to his two sons under the regency of their grandmother. For a time Brunhild ran both kingdoms while continuing with some success to prosecute the war against Neustria, now ruled by Fredegund and Chilperic's son **Chlotar II**. But in classic Merovingian style Childebert's two sons then turned on each other, leaving the previously defeated Chlotar to step in and claim the prize. With her grandsons dead, Brunhild made a last attempt to save the situation by having her great-grandson **Sigebert II** proclaimed king of Burgundy and Austrasia, but she had run out of support. Handed over to Chlotar, the old woman was tortured for three days before being tied naked to the tail of a horse and dragged to her death.

555–58 By a mixture of brutality and longevity **Chlotar** manages to gain control of all the territory formerly divided between himself and his brothers, thereby restoring the unity of the Frankish kingdom.

561 On the death of Chlotar the kingdom is once again divided. It is shared between his four remaining sons (a fifth has been put to death by him the previous year for persistent rebellion): **Sigebert**, **Chilperic**, **Charibert** and **Guntram**.

567 The death of Charibert results in a repartitioning of the country that produces the three kingdoms of **Austrasia**, **Neustria** and **Burgundy**, ruled respectively by Sigebert, Chilperic and Guntram.

c.567 Chilperic and Sigebert marry **Galswintha** and **Brunhild**, both daughters of the king of the Visigoths.

568 Galswintha is murdered on the orders of Chilperic and his concubine **Fredegund**. This and Chilperic's rapid remarriage to Fredegund lead to war with Sigebert. The mutual hatred of Fredegund and Brunhild runs through the royal feud that sets Neustria against Austrasia for the next forty years.

569 The **Lombards**, having established themselves in Italy the previous year, make the first of a series of incursions into Gaul.

c.570 The Irish monk **St Columba** lands in Brittany.

575–94 **Gregory of Tours** writes his *History of the Franks*.

Gregory of Tours

Born into an aristocratic Gallo-Roman family in the Auvergne, **Gregory** (c.538–94) numbered several prelates among his immediate relations and ancestors. He himself was appointed **bishop of Tours** in 573, a position of considerable power that involved him in several of the disputes which troubled the Merovingian royal family in the later years of the century. Above all, however, he is remembered as the author of the **Historiae Francorum** (*History of the Franks*), which he started writing in 575. Its Christian bias sometimes overlays historical fact with moral parable, but it is none the less a crucial source for the history of the 6th century. Gregory's narrative conveys with impressive starkness the brutal texture of life at the time. No document better reveals the sheer savagery that underlies the bleak record of murder, torture and betrayal of which Merovingian political history is largely composed.

> One day, returning from the hunt at dusk, when Chilperic was dismounting from his horse and had one hand on a slave's shoulder, a certain man came and stabbed him with a dagger under the armpit, then with another blow pierced his belly. A tide of blood issued at once from his mouth and the open wounds and put his wicked soul to flight.
>
> Gregory of Tours, *History of the Franks*, trans. Ernest Brehaut

575 **Sigebert**, having defeated Chilperic at the **battle of Vitry**, is murdered by agents of Fredegund. He is succeeded as king of Austrasia by his son **Childebert II**.

584 **Chilperic** is murdered. He is succeeded as king of Neustria by his 4-month-old son **Chlotar II**.

587 The **treaty of Andelot** (brokered by Gregory of Tours) restores peace among the Franks. Guntram, king of Burgundy, and Childebert II of Austrasia both agree that if either of them dies without a male heir, the other will inherit his kingdom.

592 Guntram dies without an heir and is succeeded by Childebert II.

595 On the death of Childebert II, his two sons **Theodoric II** and **Theodebert II** inherit Burgundy and Austrasia respectively, while their grandmother Brunhild remains a dominant force behind the thrones. Almost immediately they are faced by a Neustrian challenge from **Chlotar II** and his mother Fredegund.

597 Fredegund dies.

c.599 Theodebert throws off Brunhild's regency and banishes her from Austrasia.

600 In the continuing war with Theodebert II and Theodoric II, Chlotar II is defeated at **Dormelles**. The two brothers go on to win further victories, but, having gained possession of most of Chlotar's kingdom, they then turn on each other.

612 Theodebert is defeated by Theodoric and handed over to his grandmother Brunhild, who has him disposed of.

613 On the death of Theodoric, Brunhild tries to have his 12-year-old son **Sigebert II** proclaimed king of Burgundy and Austrasia, but the Austrasian magnates, headed by Pepin of Landen and Arnulf of Metz, reject this move and deliver both Brunhild and Sigebert to **Chlotar II** for execution. With their death, Chlotar is left undisputed ruler of the Franks and appoints a **mayor of the palace** to be in charge of each of the three kingdoms.

614 Chlotar convenes an assembly of the nobility. The **Edict of Paris** ratifies the system of administration by mayors of the palace, which in effect recognizes the beginnings of a shift of power from the sovereign to the nobles. **Pepin of Landen** is appointed mayor of the palace in Austrasia. **Arnulf** is made bishop of Metz and entrusted with the education of Chlotar's son **Dagobert**. The marriage of Pepin's daughter and Arnulf's son will be the origin of the Carolingian dynasty.

623 Chlotar names Dagobert king of the Austrasians, under the tutelage of Pepin and Arnulf.

629–39 Chlotar II dies, leaving Dagobert to succeed him. The Neustrian aristocracy choose Dagobert's half-brother **Charibert**, but in the course of the next year Dagobert gains acceptance first in Burgundy, to which he gives considerable autonomy, and then in Neustria by creating a separate kingdom for Charibert in **Aquitaine** (which he repossesses three years later on Charibert's death). Dagobert establishes his court in the Neustrian capital of **Paris** rather than in Austrasia. During his reign he campaigns successfully against the Frisians and later against the Gascons and Bretons.

In the middle ages this bronze chair was known as Dagobert's throne. It is now thought to date from the late-8th to early-9th century

c.635 The monks of **St-Denis** are given the right to hold a fair as a means of raising revenue. Martyred in the second half of the 3rd century, St Denis is acquiring a popular following that owes much to the Benedictine monks of the abbey of St-Denis, founded by Dagobert just north of Paris.

> There was nothing left for the monarch to do but to be content with his name of King, his flowing hair, and long beard, to sit on his throne and play the ruler, to give ear to the ambassadors that came from all quarters, and to dismiss them, as if on his own responsibility, in words that were, in fact, suggested to him, or even imposed upon him... When he had to go abroad, he used to ride in a cart, drawn by a yoke of oxen driven, peasant-fashion, by a Ploughman.

Einhard, *The Life of Charlemagne*, trans. Samuel Epes Turner

639 On the death of Dagobert the kingdom is again divided. His son **Sigebert III** inherits Austrasia, his other son, **Clovis II**, Neustria and Burgundy. This is the start of the so-called 'rois fainéants', the last of the Merovingian kings, whose power passes into the hands of the mayors of the palace.

640 Pepin, Austrasia's mayor of the palace, dies. Sigebert III is defeated in his campaign against duke **Radulf of Thuringia**, who has refused to recognise him.

641 **Eloi** is made **bishop of Noyon**. An accomplished goldsmith in his youth, he has risen to become a trusted adviser of both Chlotar II and Dagobert. Renowned for his piety, he abandons the court on the death of Dagobert and turns to a spiritual life. After his death in 660 he is soon hailed as a saint and becomes the centre of a popular cult in medieval France.

656 On the death of Sigebert III, Pepin's son **Grimoald**, who is mayor of the palace of Austrasia, exiles Sigebert's son **Dagobert II** to Ireland, and puts his own son **Childebert the Adopted** on the throne.

657 Clovis II dies and is succeeded as king of Neustria and Burgundy by his eldest son **Chlotar III**.

c.658 Ebroin becomes mayor of the palace of Neustria.

662 Unreconciled to the usurpation of power by Grimoald and Childebert the Adopted, a faction of the Austrasian nobility hand them over to the Neustrians, who execute them. Chlotar III's brother becomes king as **Childeric II**, with Wulfoald as his mayor of the palace.

c.670 Gold coins cease to be used as currency. **Parchment** replaces papyrus for official documents.

673 On the death of Chlotar III, Ebroin puts his (Chlotar's) brother **Theodoric III** on the throne of Neustria and Burgundy, but the magnates of Burgundy call in the Austrasians, and Theodoric's brother Childeric II drives him out, assuming sole sovereignty of the three kingdoms.

675 Childeric II is murdered by the magnates of Neustria, enabling Ebroin to regain power and reinstall Theodoric III as king of Neustria and Burgundy.

677 An inconclusive war between Neustria and Austrasia leads to a treaty defining their respective frontiers.

679 Ebroin revives the conflict between Neustria and Austrasia, defeating the Austrasians near Laon. In the same year, however, Wulfoald is replaced as Austrasia's mayor of the palace by the more formidable **Pepin II of Herstal**.

c.680 The assassination of Ebroin, for which Pepin is probably responsible, cripples Neustrian power.

c.679–80 The **Abbey of Moissac** is founded.

686 When the Neustrian mayor of the palace dies, he is succeeded by his son-in-law **Berchar**, whose unpopularity with the magnates opens the way to a challenge from **Pepin of Herstal**.

687 Pepin defeats Berchar at the **battle of Tertry**. He can now concentrate in his own hands the role of mayor of the

The spread of monasticism

There had been **monastic communities** in Gaul since the second half of the 4th century, but it was **St Benedict of Nursia** (c.480–547) who established what was to become the prevailing character of monastic life in medieval Europe. Sometime after 534 he drew up the rules for the community of Monte Cassino in Italy, stressing the importance of both study and manual work, and imposing vows of poverty, chastity and obedience. In the first half of the 7th century, as monasticism gained ground, his influence spread into Gaul.

The importance of the monasteries was not lost on the Carolingians, who provided generous endowments for them. Here as elsewhere, the Carolingian emperors were keen to promote uniformity, and at the **Council of Aix-la-Chapelle** in 817 the rule of St Benedict was imposed on monasteries throughout the empire. The **Benedictine movement** reached its zenith with the **abbey of Cluny**, founded in 909, which became vastly wealthy and a centre of both spiritual and temporal power. With power came corruption. It was the need for a hard, reforming edge to monasticism that led to the founding of the more austere **Cistercian** order at the end of the 11th century. From the 13th century the rise of the mendicant orders, particularly the **Dominicans** and **Franciscans**, marked the waning of the great age of the monasteries.

Sculpture of *The Visitation* at the abbey church of Moissac

palace for the three kingdoms, allowing Theodoric III to act as the figurehead king. Pepin establishes **Norbert**, count of Paris, as his representative in Neustria and Burgundy; he also marries his son to Berchar's widow, putting him in charge of the Burgundian army.

690–95 Pepin campaigns against the **Frisians**, who concede defeat in 695.

709–12 Pepin campaigns against the **Alamanni**.

711 Having defeated the Byzantine empire in North Africa, the **Muslim Arabs** invade Spain, bringing to an end the kingdom of the Visigoths. From Spain, the Arabs will later launch incursions into southern France.

714 December: On the death of Pepin of Herstal, his widow Plectrude imprisons Pepin's illegitimate son **Charles** (later known as **Martel**, the Hammer) in an attempt to secure power for her grandsons.

715 The Neustrians rise against Plectrude and defeat her forces near **Compiègne**.

716 Charles Martel, who has escaped from prison and raised an army, defeats the Neustrians at **Amblève**.

717 Charles Martel wins another victory over the Neustrians at **Vincy**. The death of Plectrude later in the year leaves him master of Austrasia.

719 Charles Martel conclusively defeats the Neustrians to gain control of the kingdom

Arabs (sometimes referred to as Saracens) penetrate the south of France, occupying Narbonne.

720–38 Charles Martel leads a series of expeditions against the **Saxons**, gradually forcing them into submission.

720–21 Charles Martel recognises **Chilperic II** as king of the Franks.

Charles Martel and the Carolingian dynasty

By the late 7th century the Merovingian kings were becoming little more than figureheads, their power eclipsed by that of the mayor of the palace. **Charles Martel** (688–741), the illegitimate son of one of these mayors, **Pepin of Herstal**, took the process to its natural conclusion. Imprisoned by Pepin's widow **Plectrude**, Charles managed to escape, raise an army and eventually impose himself on the enfeebled Merovingian crown as mayor of the palace to Chilperic II and Theodoric IV. Over the next twenty years his restless military campaigns forged a stronger and more unified Frankish kingdom. In the north he defeated the Germans; in the south, having answered a call from the duke of Aquitaine for help against Arab incursions from Spain, he defeated the Arab forces at Poitiers in 732 and then, still ostensibly combating the Arab threat, went on to bring the southern part of France under Frankish control.

While Charles did not hesitate to confiscate church lands as rewards for his vassals, he was also aware of Christianity's value as a unifying force: missionary efforts among the conquered Germans and Frisians received his full support. When he died in 741, the throne had been vacant for four years, left so by Charles in the knowledge that the Merovingians' day was over. He had paved the way for his sons **Carloman I** and **Pepin the Short** to found the new Carolingian dynasty.

721 Chilperic II dies and is succeeded by **Theodoric IV**

732 Having defeated Eudes d'Aquitaine at Bordeaux, the Arabs sweep on to Poitiers. On 25 October Charles Martel defeats them in a celebrated battle at Moussais, near **Poitiers**, and is hailed as the saviour of Christendom.

736–39 Charles Martel conducts successful campaigns in Provence and the southwest.

737 Theodoric IV dies. Charles Martel, confident of the power base he has now built up, does not need to replace him.

741 Death of Charles Martel (22 October). Having crushed a revolt against their succession, his two sons, **Pepin III the Short** and **Carloman**, divide the kingdom.

742 **Plague** rages through the kingdom and then dies away until its resurgence in the 14th century.

743 Carloman and Pepin establish Chilperic II's son, **Childeric III**, on the throne. A monk from St-Bertin, he has a purely ceremonial role.

743–46 Pepin and Carloman campaign in Aquitaine and Germany.

743–44 Zealous to reform the Frankish Church, Pepin and Carloman call a series of **ecclesiastical councils** at Cologne, Estinnes and Soissons under the direction of **Bishop Boniface**, who sets out to reinforce clerical authority and ensure a more disciplined and virtuous priesthood.

744 Pepin institutes **markets** in those episcopal cities that do not already have them.

747 Carloman retires to Rome before becoming a monk at Monte Cassino. This leaves Pepin sole mayor of the palace.

750 After a strong hint from Pepin himself, the pope decrees that Pepin, who wields the power, should wear the crown.

751 Childeric III, the last Merovingian king, is deposed and packed off to the abbey of St-Bertin, where he dies in 755. In November Pepin is **elected king** by the assembly of magnates at **Soissons**. His subsequent anointment by the Frankish bishops introduces a religious element that heralds a change in the nature of kingship. As in the days of the Old Testament, this is a king chosen by God. A new dynasty is in place.

752–68 For the duration of his reign Pepin leads a series of campaigns designed to extend and secure the boundaries of his kingdom, notably against the Arabs in the south and the

Saxons in the north. A few months before his death in 768 he achieves the subjugation of **Aquitaine**.

Charlemagne

Born in either 742 or 747, **Charlemagne** was associated with the kingship in 754, when he and his brother were crowned at the same time as their father **Pepin the Short**, a measure designed to ensure the succession. On the death of his brother in 771, Charlemagne lost no time in overriding the claims of his nephew and establishing himself as sole king. By the end of the century, after a string of campaigns that took him into Germany, Italy and Spain, he was the most powerful sovereign in Europe, in control of territory that stretched east to the Tyrol and as far south as Rome.

The palace he built at **Aix-la-Chapelle** in the 790s was already the nerve-centre of an empire, and when **Leo III** called for help in restoring his papacy, Charlemagne, with an appropriate show of reluctance, seized the opportunity for an **imperial crown**. On 23 December, 800, Leo was reinstalled as pope at St Peter's in Rome; two days later, on Christmas Day, he duly returned the compliment by crowning Charlemagne emperor. For the first time since 476 there was again a Roman empire in the west.

Religious, deeply serious, fanatically methodical, Charlemagne left his stamp on every aspect of the empire, from the regulation of monastic life to the weight of the currency and the handwriting of official scribes. For a brief moment Europe enjoyed both political stability and cultural renaissance. **Alcuin**'s literary and educational revival was a part of this, as were the exquisite altars, reliquaries and book-covers created by anonymous metal-workers. The cultural legacy was more enduring than the political stability. Even if the Vikings had not already been turning their ships towards France, the practice of dividing the empire among the emperor's heirs would have been enough to put an end to any hopes of lasting domestic peace. Charlemagne's empire disintegrated, but in creating it he had earned his sobriquet, **Carolus Magnus** – Charles the Great.

754 Pepin consolidates his dynastic aspirations when **Pope Stephen II** crowns him, along with his two sons Charles (later known as **Charlemagne**) and **Carloman**, at St-Denis. In return, Pepin strengthens the links between the Carolingian monarchy and the papacy by defending the pope against the Lombards and re-establishing him (754–56) in possession of what become the Papal States.

755 Pepin restores the **royal monopoly** of the currency.

756 Pepin imposes payment of **tithes** to the clergy throughout the kingdom.

768 Following his death, Pepin is buried at St-Denis and the kingdom is divided between his two sons. An uprising the following year in Aquitaine is put down by Charlemagne.

771 On the death of Carloman, Charlemagne takes possession of his territories and rules as sole king. Carloman's wife and son take refuge with the Lombards. For the rest of the century, Charlemagne, like his father, undertakes a relentless series of military campaigns. His aim is to create a **unified empire** by stamping out regional autonomy, subjugating the Saxons and establishing marches to protect his more vulnerable frontiers.

773–74 Charlemagne responds to a convenient appeal for help from the pope and crosses the Alps to lay siege to the Lombard king **Desiderius** in Pavia. After the capitulation of Desiderius, Charlemagne takes the title **king of the Lombards**.

778 Charlemagne crosses into Spain to fight the **Arab Muslims** but is halted at Saragossa. His retreat is remembered for the episode narrated in the *Chanson de Roland* (song of Roland): the massacre of the army's rearguard and the death of Roland, its commander, ambushed by Basques in the gorge at **Roncesvalles** on 15 August.

c.780 Charlemagne's monetary reforms establish the **silver denier** as the unit of currency.

781 Charlemagne gives Aquitaine the status of a kingdom, proclaiming his son **Louis** its king, while another son **Pepin** is named king of the Lombards. They are crowned by the pope in Rome.

782 The **Saxons**, having apparently submitted to Frankish rule and accepted Christianity some six years earlier, rise against Charlemagne. Faced with what seems a mixture of treachery and apostasy, Charlemagne embarks on a cruel war of repression which lasts intermittently until 804. At **Verden** 4500 Saxon prisoners are beheaded in a single day, an act of slaughter that shocks even Charlemagne's contemporaries.

786 Charlemagne demands an **oath of loyalty** from all free men in the kingdom, renewing the requirement in 792 and again in 802.

789 Charlemagne issues his capitulary **Admonitio generalis** governing the conduct of civil and ecclesiastical life. In its concern for the moral welfare of the realm, it suggests a new concept of the king's role.

791 Charlemagne leads the first of a series of expeditions against the **Avars**, a Steppe people who are causing unrest in the Danube basin.

794 Charlemagne begins construction of the palace at **Aix-la-Chapelle** (present-day Aachen) that will become his permanent residence and the hub of the empire.

799 Charlemagne institutes a policy of **mass deportation** of Saxons, replacing them with Franks.

The **Vikings** make their first appearance, raiding the Vendée.

A Frankish expedition to **Brittany** fails to crush its independence.

From Norsemen to Normans

From the end of the 8th century the **Vikings** descended on France, ravaging the coast and sailing up the estuaries of the Loire and the Seine. Able to negotiate the rivers in their long boats, they struck deep into Frankish territory, bringing misery and death to local inhabitants. In 845 they got far enough to besiege Paris, returning again in the winter of 885–86. Since their interest was plunder, the rich monasteries were often a prime target, but for the same reason the Vikings could usually be bought off by a sufficiently large bribe.

The transformation from plundering Norsemen to more or less respectable **Normans** was set in motion in 911 by the treaty of St-Clair-sur-Epte.

BIBLIOTHEQUE NATIONALE DE FRANCE

The Viking chieftain **Rollo** accepted a huge grant of territory around Rouen, Lisieux and Evreux from King Charles the Simple in exchange for converting to Christianity and recognising the Frankish king as his lord. By adept political manoeuvring in 924, Rollo extended this territory to include Le Mans and Bayeux. The basis of Normandy had taken shape.

Vikings en route to France, from the *Life of St Aubin*

> Charles was large and strong, and of lofty stature, though not disproportionately tall; the upper part of his head was round, his eyes very large and animated, nose a little long, hair fair, and face laughing and merry. He used to wear the national, that is to say, the Frank, dress – next his skin a linen shirt and linen breeches, and above these a tunic fringed with silk; while hose fastened by bands covered his lower limbs, and shoes his feet, and he protected his shoulders and chest in winter by a close-fitting coat of otter or marten skins. Over all he flung a blue cloak, and he always had a sword girt about him, usually one with a gold or silver hilt and belt.

Einhard, *The Life of Charlemagne*, trans. Samuel Epes Turner

800 **Pope Leo III**, deposed by a group of Roman nobles, is restored to power by Charlemagne, whom he crowns **emperor** on 25 December.

800–06 Charlemagne undertakes sweeping administrative reforms, issuing a series of **capitularies** (collections of ordinances) including decrees on the general administration of the empire, the military obligations of free citizens and the evils of usury and speculation. Among other measures, he formalises the system of **missi dominici** – imperial officers sent out in twos, one layman and one prelate, to oversee local administration across the empire.

804 Death of **Alcuin**. A cleric from York, Alcuin has been one of Charlemagne's closest advisers and a leading figure in the Carolingian renaissance. As abbot of **St-Martin de Tours**, he has promoted the use among his monks in the scriptorium of the Carolingian minuscule, a clear form of writing that introduces spaces between words.

811 The death of Charlemagne's eldest son Charles, following the death in the previous year of his second son Pepin, leaves Louis sole heir to the empire.

813 Charlemagne reinforces Louis' position by having him crowned emperor.

814 Death of Charlemagne (28 January). He is succeeded by his son **Louis I le Pieux** (the Pious).

816 In October Louis' coronation at **Reims** by Pope Stephen IV reaffirms the religious sanction of the Carolingian dynasty.

817 In an effort to maintain the integrity of the empire, Louis' **Ordinatio imperii** appoints **Lothair** his successor. His other two sons must be satisfied with Aquitaine (Pepin) and Bavaria (Louis the German).

819 Following the death of his first wife **Irmingarde** in 818, Louis marries **Judith**, a princess of the Alamanni.

823 A son, **Charles**, is born to Louis and Judith.

829 Louis' determination to provide an inheritance for Charles (known as the Bald) leads to the catastrophic unravelling of previous arrangements. A new division of the empire, announced at the **assembly of Worms**, faces widespread opposition.

830–43 An uprising against Louis, led by Lothair and supported by many of the clergy and nobility, begins thirteen years of **civil war**. Louis is twice deposed and reinstated; Lothair, Pepin, Louis the German and Charles make and break alliances with one another as they jockey for a larger stake in the inheritance; efforts to find a peaceful solution repeatedly founder. Meanwhile, the **Viking raids** grow more threatening and the **Saracens** penetrate as far as Provence.

833 In June Lothair and his brothers depose Louis at the so-called **Champ du mensonge** (Field of the Lie) in Alsace.

834 In a realignment of the brothers, Lothair is defeated and Louis reinstalled on the throne.

838 On the death of Pepin, Louis assigns Aquitaine to Charles the Bald rather than to Pepin's son Pepin II.

839 In a final effort to resolve the inheritance, Louis divides the empire between Lothair and Charles, with his other son, **Louis the German**, retaining only Bavaria.

840 Death of Louis le Pieux. **Lothair** moves to take over the empire.

841 Louis the German and Charles the Bald unite to defeat Lothair at the **battle of Fontenoy-en-Puisaye** (25 June).

THE TREATY OF VERDUN, 843

0   200 km

N

Magdeburg

Aix-la-Chapelle

Soissons

Mainz

Paris

Verdun

FRANCIA ORIENTALIS
(EAST FRANCIA)

Metz

FRANCIA OCCIDENTALIS
(WEST FRANCIA)

Lyon

Milan

FRANCIA MEDIA
(MIDDLE FRANCIA)

Ravenna

Toulouse

Pamplona

Burgos

Barcelona

Rome

The treaty of Verdun

The bloody rivalry for Louis le Pieux's inheritance led finally to the defeat of **Lothair** by **Charles the Bald** and **Louis the German** at the battle of Fontenoy-en-Puisaye in 841. Forced to negotiate, Lothair agreed to an equal division of the empire based on recommendations that would be made by 120 advisers, forty chosen by each of the brothers. The resulting **treaty of Verdun**, which created the three kingdoms of Francia Orientalis, Francia Media and Francia Occidentalis (East, Middle and West Francia), took a large step towards mapping the outlines of modern Europe. When everything had been weighed and considered – potential revenues, numbers of bishoprics, location of royal palaces and so on – it was decided that Lothair should retain the title of emperor and get the central kingdom, Louis should have **East Francia**, which became the basis of Germany, and Charles the Bald **West Francia**, comprising the area between the rivers Escaut, Meuse, Saône and Rhône that became the basis of France.

842 Louis and Charles renew their alliance with solemn oaths taken at Strasbourg on 14 February. After a successful campaign, they force Lothair to a preliminary peace agreement in the summer. The **Oaths of Strasbourg** are the first official texts to be written in the **French language**.

843 In August the surviving contenders for Charlemagne's empire reach an agreement under the **treaty of Verdun**. In November, at the assembly of **Coulaines**, Charles pays his debt to the magnates whose far from unwavering support has enabled him to gain power in West Francia: he will rule with their help, and the security of the Church's possessions will be guaranteed.

844 **Pepin II**, who feels himself cheated of his inheritance by his uncle Charles the Bald, rebels against Charles for control of Aquitaine. In the following year Charles recognizes Pepin as prince of Aquitaine in exchange for Pepin's acceptance of Charles's suzerainty.

845 The Vikings lay siege to Paris and are persuaded to retire only by a substantial bribe from Charles.

Encouraged by the break-up of the Carolingian empire, **Duke Nominoë** of Brittany asserts Breton independence, taking over the area around Rennes and Nantes and defeating Charles at the **battle of Ballon** (22 November).

848 Charles the Bald is elected king of Aquitaine by the magnates, but conflict with Pepin II continues for another sixteen years until the latter's death.

851 Under the **treaty of Angers**, Charles recognizes the right of Nominoë's son Erispoë to the title of king and confirms him in possession of the counties of Retz, Nantes and Rennes.

853 The abbey of St-Martin de Tours is burned by the **Vikings**.

855 On the death of Lothair (29 September), his kingdom is divided between his three sons: Louis II gets Italy and the title of emperor; Lothair II, Lotharingia; Charles, Provence.

856 The Vikings begin major invasions along the Seine, the Loire and the Gironde.

858 The Benedictine **abbey of Vézelay** is founded by **Girart de Vienne**. Later, as the repository of the putative remains of Mary Magdalene, it will become an important place of pilgrimage.

858–59 West Francia is invaded by Louis the German, with the support of the magnates (notably Robert the Strong), but the intervention of **Hincmar**, archbishop of Reims, enables Charles the Bald to defeat Louis and retain his throne.

863 Death of Lothair's son Charles. His kingdom of Provence is divided between his brothers **Lothair II** and **Louis II**.

869 Death of Lothair II. Charles the Bald seizes the opportunity to march into Lotharingia and have himself crowned king at Metz in September.

870 Under the **treaty of Meersen**, Charles the Bald and Louis the German divide up Lotharingia.

875 Following the death of Louis II in April, Charles the Bald is crowned emperor by Pope John VIII in Rome (25 December). In spite of this elevation, Charles is an increasingly weak figure, holding power only at the will of the magnates, the pope and the prelates.

876 On the death of Louis the German, his kingdom is shared between his three sons, **Louis le Jeune** (the Young), **Charles le Gros** (the Fat) and **Carloman**. Charles the Bald tries to take advantage of the situation by occupying Aix-la-Chapelle and Cologne but is forced to withdraw after being defeated by Louis the Young at **Andernach**.

877 The pope asks Charles for help against Arab incursions in southern Italy. At the **assembly of Quierzy** in June, prior to his departure for Italy, Charles entrusts the regency to his son **Louis le Bègue** (the Stammerer) and a council of high-ranking clergy and nobles. In a further concession to the magnates, he recognizes the principle of hereditary office. After an abortive campaign in Italy, he dies on the way home. Louis II the Stammerer is crowned king at Compiègne on 8 December.

> **❝** The dregs of the Carlovingian race no longer exhibited any symptoms of virtue or power, and the ridiculous epithets of the bald, the stammerer, the fat, and the simple, distinguished the tame and uniform features of a crowd of kings alike deserving of oblivion. **❞**
>
> Edward Gibbon, *The Decline and Fall of the Roman Empire* (1766–88)

878 At the **Council of Troyes** in August-September Pope John VIII requests help from the Carolingians, but the monarchy is too weak to respond. In November Louis the Stammerer and Louis the Young meet at **Fouron** to reaffirm the provisions of the treaty of Meersen and guarantee their respective successions.

879 Louis the Stammerer is succeeded by his two sons **Louis III** and **Carloman**, who divide the kingdom. In October, **Boso**, brother-in-law of Charles the Bald, has himself proclaimed king of Provence.

881 Charles the Fat, son of Louis the German, is crowned emperor in Rome on 12 February. In August Louis III defeats the Vikings at **Saucourt-en-Vimeu**.

882 The death of Louis the Young in January leaves **Charles the Fat** sole king of the **East Franks**. The death of Louis III in August leaves Carloman sole king of the **West Franks**.

884 In November the Vikings reach Paris. On the death of Carloman in December, Charles (later **Charles III le Simple**), the 4-year-old posthumous son of Louis the Stammerer, becomes sole heir to the throne, but the nobles opt for Charles the Fat, who receives their oaths of loyalty in June at Ponthieu.

885–86 Besieged by the Vikings, Paris is defended by **Count Eudes** (Odo, son of the Neustrian noble Robert the Strong). In contrast to Eudes, Charles the Fat proves largely ineffectual, managing in the end merely to buy off the Vikings, who turn to ravage Burgundy.

887 Charles the Fat's loss of credit in the west is matched by the erosion of his power in the east. In December, a month before his death, he is deposed.

888 Following the death of Charles the Fat in January, **Eudes**, the hero of the Viking siege, is elected king by the Frankish magnates and crowned at Compiègne (29 February). A Robertian rather than a Carolingian, he quickly strengthens his hold on power by defeating the Vikings in June at **Montfaucon-en-Argonne**.

890 **Louis**, son of Boso, is crowned king of Provence (6 June). At about this time the Muslim Arabs establish themselves in the region.

893 On 28 February **Charles III le Simple** (the Simple) is crowned king of the Franks at Reims, leading to a struggle for power with Eudes, whose popularity has waned after a number of reverses at the hands of the Vikings.

897 After four years of conflict, Eudes agrees to recognize Charles the Simple as his successor.

898 On 1 January Charles III the Simple becomes king of the Franks on the death of Eudes. Already the power of the Carolingian kings is largely dispersed among the magnates, and the next half century sees a progressive devolution of the kingdom into semi-autonomous territories.

909 The **abbey of Cluny** is founded by Guillaume le Pieux (the Pious), duke of Aquitaine, as a centre of Benedictine reform at a time of growing monastic laxity.

911 The Frankish armies defeat the Vikings at Chartres in July. In the wake of this victory, Charles the Simple agrees the treaty of **St-Clair-sur-Epte** with the Viking chieftain Rollo. Following the death of Louis the Child, Lotharingia (Lorraine) accepts the sovereignty of Charles the Simple.

918 **Richard le Justicier**, who has gradually gained control of the region of Burgundy, takes the title **duc de Bourgogne**, effectively marking the foundation of the duchy of Burgundy.

920–22 Charles the Simple makes the mistake of slighting the Neustrian magnates. Headed by Robert, younger son of Robert the Strong, they raise a rebellion that drives him out of the kingdom.

922 **Robert I** is elected king of the Franks in place of Charles the Simple and crowned at Reims (30 June). In September Richard duc de Bourgogne is succeeded by his son **Raoul**.

923 Robert I is killed during an indecisive engagement with Charles the Simple at Soissons (15 June). In the following month the magnates elect **Raoul de Bourgogne** king of France. Charles the Simple is held prisoner until his death in 929.

925 **Henry I of Germany** (Henry the Fowler) occupies Lorraine and reabsorbs it into his kingdom.

936 King Raoul is succeeded by Charles the Simple's son, **Louis IV** (crowned at Laon on 18 June). Louis owes his throne to the support of **Hugues le Grand**, who expects an appropriately docile sovereign.

937 In an attempt to break free from the control of Hugues le Grand, Louis leaves Paris and establishes himself at Laon.

Hugues le Grand: the kingmaker

For the last twenty years of his life **Hugues le Grand** (c.893–956), son of King Robert I, was the most powerful man in the kingdom. As **dux Francorum** (leader of the Franks) – a title bestowed on him by Louis IV – he came next after the king in precedence, and in power well before. With important territories between the Seine and the Loire, and high prestige among the magnates, he could have claimed the kingship in either 936 or 954, but he preferred the role of king-maker, retaining for himself the power behind the throne. His relationship with successive monarchs was turbulent, but at a time when the Carolingian dynasty was in decline, he alone had the authority to impose his political will. As the father of **Hugues Capet**, first of the Capetian kings, he was also father of the new dynasty that was to shape France's future.

939 Louis accepts the sovereignty of Lorraine, offered to him by rebels against the Holy Roman Emperor **Otto I**.

939–41 Hugues le Grand leads an uprising against Louis, besieging Reims and Laon. Louis mounts a vigorous defence, but support for the rebels from Otto I, angered by Louis' interference in Lorraine, proves decisive.

942 In November Louis makes peace with Otto I.

945–46 Taken captive by **Viking rebels**, Louis is handed over to Hugues le Grand. After keeping him prisoner for a year, Hugues yields to pressure to release him, but conflict between the two continues.

950 Excommunicated by French and German bishops as well as by the pope, Hugues finally makes peace with Louis.

954 After the death of Louis IV on 10 September, Hugues le Grand declines the kingship, opting instead to act as regent for Louis' son **Lothair**, who is crowned at Reims on 12 November.

956 Hugues le Grand dies (16 June) having recently received, at his own insistence, the duchies of Burgundy and Aquitaine. After his death the regency passes to Lothair's uncle, **Bruno**, archbishop of Cologne.

969 The death of Bruno leaves Lothair free to distance himself from the Germanic connections of his youth.

978 Lothair lays claim to Lotharingia and marches into Metz and Aix-la-Chapelle. The German emperor **Otto II** then regroups his forces and launches a devastating counter-attack that brings him to the gates of Paris, where he is halted by **Hugues Capet**, son of Hugues le Grand.

979 In June Lothair associates his son **Louis** with the kingship and has him crowned at Compiègne.

980 In July Lothair reaches a peace agreement with Otto II.

985 Reluctant to abandon his territorial ambitions, Lothair again enters Lorraine and takes possession of **Verdun**.

986 Lothair is succeeded by his son **Louis V le Fainéant** (Do-Nothing).

987 Following the death of Louis V in May, the magnates elect **Hugues Capet** king of the Franks in preference to the last surviving Carolingian claimant, Charles de Lorraine.

3
The Capetians

987–1328

The **Capetian period** sees the start of France's emergence as a more or less unified political entity. When **Hugues Capet** was crowned king of the Franks, his realm amounted to an area round Paris roughly corresponding to the Île de France, and that was all. Not even Paris itself acknowledged his sovereignty. Until the late 12th century, France remained what it had become with the break-up of the Carolingian empire – a collection of largely independent territories under the control of rulers who defended the integrity of their fiefs by a mixture of violence, diplomacy and marital alliances. In the south and west, important parts of what later became France were under the sway of either Spain or England. The Capetian monarch was distinguished from the barons who surrounded him by little more than the intangible authority that came from his anointment as sovereign. To maintain the succession and hang onto hereditary lands was itself an achievement. Only with **Philippe Auguste** did the dynasty begin to make real territorial gains. In the century and a half between his accession and the death of the last Capetian king, royal power was gradually extended across a large part of the country. And France under the Capetians had been quietly prospering: as forest and marshland were cleared, villages multiplied; in the countryside, agriculture grew more efficient with the adoption of the heavy plough; urban trade fostered the growth of a new merchant class; the population was rising towards 13 million.

But prosperity did not mean tranquillity. The conquest of England by **Guillaume de Normandie** (William of Normandy) in 1066 had far-reaching consequences. By linking the English throne to extensive territories in France, it opened the way to future disputes over sovereignty, laying the foundations of four hundred years of conflict. From the middle of the 12th century, the main threat was the mighty **Angevin empire** controlled by England's **Plantagenet** kings. It was this, as Philippe Auguste realized, that the Capetians would have to dismantle if they were truly to become kings of France. In the treacherous waters of medieval realpolitik, they were aided by two critical factors. First, they managed with admirable consistency to produce a male heir. Second, in spite of periodic quarrels, they stayed on reasonable terms with their bishops, if not always with the pope. For much of this time the Church was struggling with calls for reform, first from Popes **Leo IX** and **Gregory VII**, and later from the new orders of **Dominican** and **Franciscan** friars, but it continued to wield immense power, both spiritually and temporally. Its growing political influence could be decisive, and more often than not this was exercised on behalf of the Capetians.

Culturally, Capetian rule was marked by a surge of intellectual and artistic energy, reflected in the works of medieval literature created by writers like **Béroul**, **Marie de France**, **Chrétien de Troyes** and **Guillaume de Lorris**, and also in the range of philosophical enquiry that brought men such as **Pierre Abélard**, **Thomas Aquinas** and **Duns Scotus** to teach at the **University of Paris**. In the north of France, while Crusaders went to plant their banner in the Holy Land, western Christendom set about its defining statement of ecclesiastical power and spiritual aspiration with the building of the great medieval **cathedrals**. It was left to the south, where **Cathar heresy** flourished in the towns and villages of the **Languedoc**, to develop a brief interlude of courtly civilization inspired by the poetry and music of the **trouba-**

dours. By the end of the 13th century this was gone, along with the independence of the southern states that had sustained it. France was becoming a nation.

987 On 3 July **Hugues Capet** is elected king of west Francia, establishing the start of the **Capetian dynasty**. To secure the succession, his eldest son **Robert** is crowned in the same year – a practice that will be continued by subsequent Capetian kings (see 1223).

c.989 The **Peace of God** (Paix de Dieu) movement starts in Aquitaine. Inspired by the Church, it is intended to limit the violence of the warrior and landowning classes. The practice of holding peace councils will continue into the 11th century, giving rise to the **Truce of God** (Trêve de Dieu), which seeks to proscribe military activity at particular times of the week and year. Ironically, these peace movements, by giving the Church authority in matters of warfare, pave the way for the **Crusades**.

> Dearest brothers in the Lord, these are the conditions which you must observe during the time of the peace which is commonly called the truce of God, and which begins with sunset on Wednesday and lasts until sunrise on Monday:
> 1. During those four days and five nights no man or woman shall assault, wound, or slay another, or attack, seize, or destroy a castle, burg, or villa, by craft or by violence.
> 2. If anyone violates this peace and disobeys these commands of ours, he shall be exiled for thirty years as a penance, and before he leaves the bishopric he shall make compensation for the injury which he committed. Otherwise he shall be excommunicated by the Lord God and excluded from all Christian fellowship.
>
> *Truce of God* – Bishopric of Terouanne (1063)

996 On 24 October, following the death of Hugues Capet, **Robert II le Pieux** (the Pious) succeeds as sole king.

c.1000 The porch and belfry of **St-Germain-des-Prés** in Paris are built.

1002 Robert begins the **conquest of Burgundy**. Over the next three years the duchy is brought under Capetian control.

1016 **Foulques Nerra**, comte d'Anjou, begins the conquest of Touraine. During the next quarter of a century, he will establish the basis of **Angevin** power. A classic example of the feudal warlord, Foulques Nerra goes on to make himself master of Maine, Vendôme and Gâtinais, while avoiding outright confrontation with the Capetians.

1020–21 The sculptures carved on the lintel of **St-Genis-des-Fontaines** mark the first dated example of **Romanesque** architectural sculpture.

1022 Robert has three canons burnt at Orléans. This is the first official execution of **heretics** in western Europe.

1023–24 **Bishop Hildebert** begins construction of the abbey church of **Mont-St-Michel**.

1025 After the death of Robert's eldest son, his second son, **Henri**, is crowned at Reims.

1031 On 20 July, following the death of Robert II, **Henri I** succeeds as sole king.

1032–34 A revolt by the king's younger brother, **Robert**, ends with his submission in exchange for the **duchy of Burgundy**.

c.1033 The monk **Helgaud de Fleury** writes his *Life of Robert the Pious*. By recording the king's supposed ability to cure blindness and disease, he emphasises the distinctive sacramental powers invested in the Capetian monarchy.

c.1046 Death of **Raoul Glaber**, the monk whose *Historiae* (Histories) provide a valuable source of information about the events of the time.

1047 With the help of Henri I, **Guillaume II, duc de Normandie** (later William the Conqueror), puts down a rising of Norman barons and thereafter tries to establish a system of central control by restricting the building of castles.

1049 **Leo IX** is elected pope and initiates a programme of Church reform for which neither the king nor the northern bishops show much enthusiasm. The **Council of Reims** reinforces papal supremacy by excommunicating a number of noblemen whose marriages are illegitimate and by sacking some of the more blatantly unsuitable bishops.

Hugues (later canonized) becomes **abbot of Cluny** and rules it until his death in 1109. This is the period during which the great monastery is at its zenith, owning vast territories and wielding political and spiritual influence that extends across Europe.

1060 On 4 August Henri I dies. He is succeeded by his son **Philippe I**, under the guardianship of Philippe's uncle, **Count Baudouin V** of Flanders.

1064 During a visit to Normandy, **Harold Godwinson**, the future king of England, swears an oath of fealty to Guillaume de Normandie, which Guillaume will later use in support of his claim to the English throne.

1066 **Guillaume de Normandie** (William the Conqueror) defeats **Harold of England** at the battle of Hastings on 14 October and is crowned king of England. Guillaume's conquest brings greatly increased power and prestige, but his extended territories render him vulnerable to the attacks of rival French princes, whom he spends much of the next twenty years holding at bay.

In this scene from the Bayeux tapestry, Harold Godwinson swears fealty to Guillaume de Normandie (William the Conqueror)

1070 The town of **Le Mans** petitions unsuccessfully for rights of self-government. Similar moves by other towns will lead to the creation of communes independent of the local nobility.

c.1075 The **Bayeux tapestry** is woven, probably by English women in Canterbury. A celebration of the Norman conquest, it has the additional purpose of presenting a narrative that legitimates William's claim to the English throne.

1086 **Guillaume IX**, comte de Poitou, becomes **duke of Aquitaine**, which he rules until his death in 1127. The first known troubadour, he is, by his own account, 'one of the greatest noblemen in the world as well as one of the greatest deceivers of noblewomen'.

c.1088 Work begins on the third abbey church of **Cluny**. After its completion in c.1130, it will remain the largest church in western Christendom until the late Renaissance.

1092 Philippe I discards his wife and marries **Bertrade de Montfort** of Anjou. Since she is already wife of the count of Anjou, their marriage is regarded as bigamous, which leads to conflict with the Church.

Troubadours

Lyric poets who flourished in the southern half of France during the 12th and early 13th centuries, the **troubadours** had a significance that was both social and literary. As the poets of courtly love, they exercised a civilizing influence on the rude aristocracy of the time; as supremely skilled creators of verse forms (the word troubadour, like its northern counterpart, **trouvère**, is derived from the word for finder or inventor), they shaped the direction of a crucial strand of European literature. Writing in the **langue d'oc** of southern France, the troubadours elaborated a code which reversed the accepted hierarchy and set the lady on a pedestal, with the lovesick lord as her humble vassal who must sue for mercy.

Musicians and performers as well as poets, the troubadours have left us some 2500 of their songs. Apart from Guillaume d'Aquitaine, others whose names have come down to us include **Jaufré Rudel**, poet of the *amor de lonh* (distant love), and **Arnaut Daniel**, the master of complex verse forms whom Dante meets in Purgatory and whose words later find their way into T. S. Eliot's *The Waste Land*. The society for which they wrote was rich, sophisticated and pleasure-loving. Nothing could have been more remote from the northern barons who swept into the Languedoc with fire and sword to rid the land of heresy. By the middle of the 13th century, the era of the troubadours was more or less at an end, their world consumed by zealotry and the lust for plunder.

1094 Philippe I is **excommunicated** by Pope Urban II for his marital irregularities.

1095 At the **Council of Clermont** Urban II preaches the **First Crusade** to recover the Holy Land from Islamic control. In an indulgence granted to crusaders by the Council of Clermont, the pope declares: 'Whoever for devotion alone, not to gain honour or money, goes to Jerusalem to liberate the Church of God can substitute this journey for all penance.'

The Crusades

From the outset France took a leading part in the Crusades, which form a leitmotif to three centuries of her history. A mixture of pilgrimage and holy war, they were underpinned by a growing sense of the need to channel the violence of the warrior class. This was a theme taken up at the Council of Clermont in 1095 by Pope Urban II, who used the occasion to preach the **First Crusade**. His call to arms was greeted with fervour. In the wake of the knights marched a rag-tag army of paupers, led by **Peter the Hermit**, most of whom were duly massacred by the Turks.

After much hardship and a good deal of brutality, the Crusaders finally entered **Jerusalem** in 1099, sealing their victory with the indiscriminate slaughter of Jews and Muslims. The Crusaders then divided the Holy Land into four Christian states: Edessa, Antioch, Tripoli and the kingdom of Jerusalem. This was the high point of crusading fortunes. Across the next two hundred years , there were to be seven more Crusades, but none of them achieved more than partial success. After the disastrous **Second Crusade**, which ended in humiliation, the **Third**, led by **Philippe Auguste** (see p.69) and **Richard Coeur de Lion**, managed at least to restore Christian access to Jerusalem, by then under the control of **Saladin**. The **Fourth Crusade**, which never reached the Holy Land, was chiefly notable for the barbarous sack of **Constantinople**. By way of prelude to the **Fifth Crusade**, some 30,000 children tramped to Marseille intent on a crusade of their own. Some of them found their way down to Italy, others got caught up in the campaign against the Cathars, many were briskly shipped on to Africa by enterprising slave-traders. And so ended the **'Children's Crusade'**.

In the last phase of the movement, **St Louis** (see p.81) was an enthusiastic but largely unsuccessful Crusader, vainly hoping to make progress by targeting the Muslim power-base of Egypt. When it was all over, there was little to show: the Holy Land remained a part of the Muslim world. True, the traffic between west and east had produced a number of economic and cultural benefits, but the cost in human suffering had been immense.

1096–99 France participates in the First Crusade, providing the largest of the crusading armies, headed by comte **Raimond de Toulouse**.

1098 **Robert de Molesme** founds the monastery of **Cîteaux**, and with it the **Cistercian order**, committed to following a stricter version of the Benedictine rule.

1099 Jerusalem is captured by Crusaders. **Godefroy de Bouillon** becomes king of Jerusalem, to be succeeded the following year by his half-brother, **Baudouin**.

c.1100 Composition of the *Chanson de Roland*.

1108 Philippe I dies on 29 July. **Louis VI le Gros** (the fat) becomes king and is crowned at Orléans on 3 August. Over the next thirty years he strives to assert his authority against a troublesome aristocracy. Among those who initially refuse him homage are the dukes of **Aquitaine**, **Burgundy** and **Normandy**.

1109 Hostilities break out between Louis VI and **Henry I** of England over the possession of Normandy. They continue fitfully until a peace agreement is reached in 1120, following the defeat of Louis at the **battle of Brémule** (1119).

> ❝ Says Oliver: 'Pagans in force abound,
> While of us Franks but very few I count;
> Comrade Rollanz, your horn I pray you sound!
> If Charles hear, he'll turn his armies round.'
> Answers Rollanz: 'A fool I should be found;
> In France the Douce would perish my renown.
> With Durendal I'll lay on thick and stout,
> In blood the blade, to its golden hilt, I'll drown.
> Felon pagans to th' pass shall not come down;
> I pledge you now, to death they all are bound.' ❞

From *La Chanson de Roland*, trans. Charles Scott Moncrieff (1919)

1112 In an attempt to set up an independent commune, the townspeople of **Laon** rise against the authority of their bishop and murder him. The rebellion is subsequently crushed by Louis.

1115 The Benedictine monk **Bernard** (1090/91–1153) is appointed to establish a Cistercian monastery at **Clairvaux**. As Bernard of Clairvaux (canonised in 1174), he will become one of the spiritual leaders of 12th-century Christendom. His claim that he 'deems as dung whatever shines with beauty, enchants the ear, delights through fragrance, flatters the taste or pleases the touch', gives a measure of the ascetic cast of his faith.

La Chanson de Roland

The greatest surviving *chanson de geste* (epic poem in Old French), the ***Chanson de Roland*** can be seen as the starting point of French literature. Based on a minor incident in the campaigns of Charlemagne, it tells of the death of **Roland**, ambushed with the rearguard of the Christian army in the gorge of **Roncesvalles**. After seven years of warfare, the poet explains, Charlemagne has conquered all of Spain but Saragossa, whose king is offering terms. At Roland's suggestion, his father-in-law **Ganelon** is given the dangerous job of treating with the Saracen king. Resenting what he takes to be Roland's malice, Ganelon conspires with the Saracens. As the Frankish army marches back into France, the ambush is sprung. With heroic obstinacy, Roland refuses to sound his horn for help until it is too late. The battle is glorious but the odds overwhelming. By the time Charlemagne gets back to the gorge, he can do no more than avenge the heroes' deaths.

Recounted in about 4000 lines of decasyllabic verse, the *Chanson de Roland* was probably composed by the Norman poet **Turold**, whose name appears in the final line of the poem. Though the action is set in 778, the poem's atmosphere is imbued with the religious passions of the First Crusade. Dignified in rhythm and sober in language, it exercised a huge influence over later French poetry.

A young Roland with attendants and a bishop. From an early manuscript of *La Chanson de Roland*

c.1119 The order of the **Knights Templar** (see p.85) is founded by French knights in the Holy Land to protect pilgrims and defend Jerusalem.

1122 Pierre le Vénérable is elected **abbot of Cluny**. In the same year, **Suger** (1081–1151) is elected **abbot of St-Denis** and rules it until his death. He acts as a close adviser to Louis VI, whose life he later writes.

> **❝** Neither stone nor wood hid the bare earth, which served for a floor. Windows scarcely wider than a man's head admitted a feeble light. In this room the monks took their frugal meals of herbs and water. Immediately above the refectory was the sleeping apartment. It was reached by a ladder, and was, in truth, a sort of loft. Here were the monks' beds, which were peculiar. They were made in the form of boxes, or bins, of wooden planks, long and wide enough for a man to lie down in. A small space, hewn out with an axe, allowed room for the sleeper to get in or out. The inside was strewn with chaff, or dried leaves, which, with the woodwork, seem to have been the only covering permitted. **❞**
>
> Contemporary description of conditions at the monastery of Clairvaux

1128 **Matilda**, daughter of Henry I of England, marries **Geoffroy Plantagenêt**, comte d'Anjou. After Henry's death she fails in her attempt to win the throne of England but does secure the right of succession for her son, who will become **Henry II** of England, the first of the **Plantagenet** kings.

c.1130–60 Building of the cathedral of **Sens**.

1137 **Aliénor** (Eleanor of Aquitaine) inherits Aquitaine on the death of Guillaume X. She is married to the future **Louis VII** on 22 July, ten days before he succeeds to the throne on the death of Louis VI.

1144 Consecration of the enlarged **church of St-Denis**. Abbot Suger's architectural additions represent a significant move away from Romanesque towards the creation of what later becomes the **Gothic style**.

Pierre Abélard: philosopher and theologian

The son of a Breton knight, **Pierre Abélard** (1079–1142) was one of the central figures in the intellectual life of 12th-century Europe. A brilliant student of philosophy, he was also a dazzling teacher – not least in the eyes of the young **Héloise**, for whom he was engaged as tutor by her uncle **Fulbert**, canon of Notre-Dame cathedral. Their legendary love affair resulted in a secret marriage and the birth of a son whom they named, somewhat unusually, Astrolabe. With impressive savagery, Canon Fulbert revenged himself by having Abélard castrated. In 1119 both Héloise and her former lover entered the monastic life, she to a nunnery at Argenteuil, he to St-Denis.

If Abelard's popular fame rests primarily on the doomed love affair, the mark he left on Europe's intellectual life belongs to this later period. A superb dialectician, he crystallized his approach in *Sic et Non* (c.1122), which sets out to examine some of the apparent inconsistencies in Christian teaching. Inevitably, his attitudes brought him into conflict with the orthodoxies of the time, represented most forcefully by the Cistercian **Bernard of Clairvaux**. In 1121 the Council of Soissons convicted him of heresy for his views on the Trinity, expressed in his *Theologia*, and ordered him to burn the offending treatise. Later, his subversive teaching to the students who flocked to him on the Mont-Ste-Geneviève outside Paris led to further condemnation, this time by the **Council of Sens** in 1140. Again, his main accuser was Bernard of Clairvaux, whose fulminations are perhaps the best tribute to Abélard's lucid commitment to a theology shaped by intellect rather than authority: 'Scrutiniser of Majesty and fabricator of Heresy, he deems himself able by human reason to comprehend God altogether… Thus the human intellect usurps everything to itself, leaving nothing to Faith; it wants to go too high in enquiries which are beyond its power.'

Apart from his philosophical writings and the autobiographical *Historia Calamitatum* (c.1136), Abélard also wrote poems, letters and hymns. For the last months of his life, he enjoyed the protection of **Pierre le Vénérable** at the abbey of Cluny. His remains, alongside those of Héloise, are now entombed at the Père Lachaise cemetery in Paris.

> Precisely because it evoked the mystical archetype of the political order of the French monarchy, the style of St-Denis was adopted for all the Cathedrals of France and became the monumental expression of the Capetian idea of kingship.
>
> Otto von Simson, *The Gothic Cathedral* (1956)

1146 Following the loss of **Edessa** to the Saracens, Bernard of Clairvaux preaches the **Second Crusade** on Easter Sunday at Vézelay.

1147 Louis VII and Aliénor depart for the Second Crusade, leaving Abbot Suger as **regent of France**.

1151 Death of Abbot Suger.

c.1151 At about this time **Pierre Lombard**'s *Quatre Livres des sentences* (Four books of sentences) collects the teachings of the medieval Church in a form that will be used as a standard textbook for the next three centuries.

1152 The marriage of Louis VII and Aliénor d'Aquitaine is annulled. Aliénor marries **Henri Plantagenêt** (1133–89) in the same year, thereby bringing a vast area of France (roughly one third) into the possession of the future Henry II of England. Nominally the king of France's vassal, Henry is now a formidable rival. From this point the Capetian strategy, ultimately successful, is to chip away at the Angevin empire until it is dismembered. The hostilities, which continue intermittently until the end of the 13th century, are sometimes referred to as the first Hundred Years' War.

1153 Death of St Bernard.

1154 Louis VII marries a second time, to **Constance de Castille**. In December, on the death of King **Stephen** (Étienne de Blois), **Henri Plantagenêt** succeeds to the English throne as **Henry II**.

Aliénor d'Aquitaine (1122–1204)

Eldest daughter of the duc d'Aquitaine, the 15-year-old **Aliénor** should have been an ideal match for the future **Louis VII**. She was beautiful, clever, high-spirited, and she had a large part of south-west France as her dowry. The couple were distantly related, but this caused Louis no serious qualms until it became clear that the marriage was a failure and that she was unlikely to bear him a son. Despite the pope's reassurances, Louis' scruples grew stronger. In 1152 Aliénor gave birth to a second daughter, perhaps fathered by her uncle **Raimond de Poitiers**, who was rumoured to have had an affair with her in Antioch during the Second Crusade. A divorce was arranged on grounds of consanguinity. Within two months Aliénor was married again, to Henry Plantagenet. She provided him with four sons, two of whom, **Richard** and **John**, were future kings of England. In later years, when relations with Henry had cooled, she established herself at Poitiers, where she presided over a brilliant court. By siding with her sons, now estranged from their father, she earned Henry's lasting displeasure. He imprisoned her at Chinon until his death, when she emerged again to resume her political role, acting as Richard's regent during the **Third Crusade**. In her seventies she was still tough enough to make the journey to Spain to bring back her granddaughter, **Blanche de Castille**, for her marriage to the future Louis VIII. A patron of the arts, notably through her contribution to Abbot Suger's rebuilding of St-Denis, Aliénor was a woman of strongly independent spirit whose career is all the more striking in the context of a medieval world that tended to view her sex with deep mistrust.

1159 Henry II asserts his wife Aliénor's claim to **Toulouse** but is halted by Louis VII, who defends the town in person.

1160 After the death of Constance, Louis marries a third time, to **Adèle de Champagne**.

c.1160 *Floire et Blancheflor* is composed – the earliest rendering in verse of the celebrated legend that later appeared

The Cathar heresy

The **Cathar heresy** (unreliably derived from the Greek katharos = pure) is an important footnote to both the religious and the political history of France. Based on the **Manichaean** belief in two eternally warring principles of Good and Evil, it originated in the Balkans and found its way into the Midi during the 12th century, where it was taken under the protection of the powerful counts of **Toulouse**. The Cathars developed a religious organization that alarmed the Catholic establishment not only by its outright rejection of Roman Catholic dogma but also by its creation of an alternative ecclesiastical hierarchy based on the distinction between the elite, or **Perfects**, and the common adherents, known as **Believers**. The Perfects, who achieved their status by receiving the Cathar sacrament of **consolamentum** – a form of spiritual baptism – embraced an ascetic code that rejected meat-eating and forbade sexual intercourse. (Fortunately for the continuance of the sect, the Believers were not expected to meet such demanding standards until they received the consolamentum just before death. On the contrary, since the material world as a whole was regarded as evil, Catharism tended to play down the moral distinctions between one kind of involvement with it and another.) The poverty and simplicity of

in English as *Flores and Blancheflour*. The next twenty years see a flowering of medieval literature. It is during this period that **Chrétien de Troyes** composes his *Lancelot and Yvain*, **Béroul** his *Tristan*, and **Marie de France**, the earliest known French woman poet, her *Lais*.

1163 **Maurice de Sully**, bishop of Paris, initiates the construction of the cathedral of **Notre-Dame**, completed in the mid-13th century.

1165 Birth of the future **Philippe II Auguste** to Louis VII and Adèle de Champagne.

the Perfects were in stark contrast to the sometimes ostentatious wealth of the Roman Catholic Church, and their popularity soon drew hostile attention from the Catholic hierarchy.

In 1208 **Pope Innocent III** preached the **Albigensian Crusade**, so-called because Albi in southern France was a Cathar centre. This was the cue for a brutal assault by the northern barons under the leadership of **Simon de Montfort** which led finally to the eradication of the heresy. In 1244 the Cathars made a last stand in the fortress of **Montségur**, near the Pyrenees, where some two hundred of them were captured and burned at the stake. This was not quite the end of Catharism. In 1278 in Verona 178 Cathars were likewise committed to the flames, and it was not until 1321 that the last Cathar bishop was captured in Tuscany.

For France, the consequences of the Albigensian Crusade went far beyond the suppression of religious heresy. The Provençal civilisation of the south was intimately bound up with Catharism, and it suffered the same fate. Along with it went the power of the southern princes. The crushing of the Cathars was a significant step towards the unification of north and south under Capetian control.

1166 The **duchy of Brittany** is seized by Henry II, precipitating renewed warfare between England and France.

1167 A **Cathar Synod** is held at **St-Félix-de-Caraman**, one of a number of heretical assemblies in southern France that mark the spread of Catharism during the mid-12th century.

1170 **Thomas Becket**, whose stand against the authority of Henry II has been supported by Louis VII with the aim of undermining Plantagenet power, is murdered in **Canterbury Cathedral**.

c.1173 Peter Waldo, a merchant from Lyon, founds the **Waldensian sect**, which espouses an orthodox Catholicism but dismays the clergy by its public preaching (often critical of the contemporary church), its commitment to a vernacular Bible and its embarrassingly Christian poverty. In 1184 it is declared heretical.

1179 Philippe II Auguste (Philip Augustus) is crowned at Reims on 1 November, some months before his ailing father dies.

1180 On 15 February Philippe Auguste orders the arrest of all **Jews** in the kingdom. In April he marries **Isabelle de Hainaut**, niece of the count of Flanders, who brings him the county of Artois as part of her dowry. On 18 September Louis VII dies, leaving Philippe Auguste sole king. For the first five years of his reign, Philippe faces a coalition of rebellious nobles, including Flanders, Burgundy and Champagne.

1184 Pope Alexander III launches the **Inquisition** with the papal bull **Ad abolendam**. Set up as a tribunal to combat heresy, the Inquisition will be made a permanent Catholic institution by Pope Gregory IX in 1231.

1185 Philippe Auguste's domestic conflicts are brought to an end by the **treaty of Boves**, which confirms him in possession of Artois, Vermandois and the city of Amiens, and leaves him free to turn his attention to the Plantagenets.

c.1186 Philippe Auguste orders the streets of Paris to be paved.

1187 The capture of Jerusalem by the Muslim leader **Saladin** (Salah ad-Din) prompts preparations for the **Third Crusade**.

1188 Philippe Auguste resumes hostilities against Henry II of England, exploiting the animosity between Henry and his sons. The eldest, Richard, sides with the French king, doing homage to him at **Bonmoulins** in November.

Philippe II Auguste

After two centuries of relatively undistinguished monarchs, the Capetians finally produced in **Philippe Auguste** (1165–1223) a king who would leave his mark on the history of France. In the course of his reign – from 1180 to 1223 – he vastly increased Capetian lands, enhanced the city of Paris and established the beginnings of an efficient state bureaucracy. Intelligent and unrelenting, he set out to destroy the Angevin empire ruled by the Plantagenet kings of England. Having forced Henry II to accept the loss of Maine, Touraine and Anjou by winning the allegiance of his eldest son Richard, Philippe then made it his aim to chisel away the foundation of Richard's power. As long as Richard was alive, the French king's ambitions were held in check, but his younger brother King John proved a feebler adversary. The fate of the Angevin empire was effectively sealed on 27 July, 1214 when an anti-Capetian alliance was routed by Philippe at the **battle of Bouvines**, south of Tournai. There was no great slaughter, but the resulting **treaty of Chinon** left Philippe in possession of most of the French territory formerly controlled by England.

For Parisians Philippe was the king who paved their streets and girded the city with a massive wall, parts of which can still be seen in the excavations on view in the Louvre. As Capetian possessions increased, so also did the need to administer them, and Philippe, quick to learn from the example of Normandy, oversaw the beginnings of a professional system of management that would prise the kingdom away from its feudal origins. At the start of his reign the Capetian kings were scarcely more than territorial overlords of an area of northern France; by the time he died, they were on their way to being true rulers of France.

1189 Under the treaty of **Azay-le-Rideau**, Henry II, faced with the prospect of fighting his own heir to protect his possessions, does homage to Philippe Auguste (4 July) and renounces his claim to the Auvergne. He dies two days later, succeeded by his son, **Richard I Coeur de Lion**.

Houses of God

It is hard for us now to grasp the staggering impact of **Gothic cathedrals** on the medieval imagination. In towns where most of the inhabitants lived among a clutter of narrow streets and gloomy hovels the sheer scale of these magnificent buildings, flooded with light from their stained-glass windows, must have been awe-inspiring. And this, of course, was exactly the intention. In their height and light and grandeur they were a testament to the glory of God – and of his Church.

By adapting the principles of Roman architecture, the builders of the 10th and 11th centuries had created structures that answered the practical needs of a modern church, providing ambulatories and chapels under stone vaulting that gave a degree of protection against fire. It was the weight of these stone vaults that required the massive walls and piers characteristic of the period. Windows, which would weaken the structure, had to be kept to a minimum. Much of the decorative energy of **Romanesque** architecture was channelled into the remarkable relief sculptures that are a feature of French churches such as those at Moissac, Vézelay and Autun. But from the early 12th century, architects began to develop new ways of distributing weight. The pointed arch replaced the round arch of the Romanesque; the ribbed vault and the flying buttress made their appearance. Graceful windows, filled with stained glass, could now be opened in the walls. These were the innovations that came together in Abbot Suger's plans for **St-Denis**. His church was to herald a new style of architecture that over the next century reached its zenith in the construction of the great French Gothic cathedrals – Notre-Dame, Reims, Amiens, Chartres, Strasbourg and the rest – that would stand through time as one of the supreme achievements of the European Middle Ages.

1189–90 On the right bank of the Seine, Philippe Auguste constructs an **encircling wall** some 2800 metres long. Work on the palace of the **Louvre** begins at the same time. These projects reflect Paris's huge growth in population and importance during the first two centuries of Capetian

The west front of Reims Cathedral was begun in 1252 but the towers were not completed until 1475

rule. Henceforth, it is the undisputed capital of the kingdom, and within a century it will be the largest city in western Christendom.

1190 From about this date, salaried officials (**baillis**, or, in the Midi, **seneschals**) are assigned fixed places of residence in the provinces, where they function as royal representatives. This is part of a general growth in administrative sophistication, reflected also in the formation of what becomes the *Parlement*, acting as the monarch's final court of appeal.

1191 Having set out the previous year, Philippe joins the **Third Crusade** (1189–92) as joint leader with Richard I of England. A few months after arriving in Palestine, Philippe pleads illness as an excuse for returning to France, where, in spite of undertakings given to Richard, he immediately sets about undermining the English king's power.

1193 Philippe Auguste marries and almost at once repudiates **Ingeborg of Denmark** – for reasons never satisfactorily explained. While Philippe makes inroads into Plantagenet territories, Richard Coeur de Lion, on his way back from the Holy Land, is imprisoned by **Leopold**, duke of Austria, before being handed on to **Henry VI**, the new Holy Roman emperor.

1194 Ransomed from imprisonment by his mother Aliénor d'Aquitaine, Richard recovers much of the land seized by Philippe Auguste, defeating the French king at the **battle of Fréteval** on 3 July.

Following a fire which all but destroys the existing cathedral, work starts on rebuilding **Notre-Dame de Chartres**.

1196 Philippe Auguste marries **Agnès de Méran**.

1198 Philippe provokes a troublesome conflict with the papacy by refusing Pope Innocent III's demand that he reinstate Ingeborg of Denmark as his queen. This will only be fully resolved when he recalls her in 1213. On 28 September Philippe is defeated by Richard Coeur de Lion at the **battle of Courcelles**.

1199 The death of Richard Coeur de Lion leaves his brother **John** (Lackland) asserting a weak title to the throne of England and facing a revolt among his French possessions. France is placed under **interdict** by Pope Innocent III.

1200 On 22 May, under the **treaty of Le Goulet**, Philippe Auguste recognizes John's title to the English crown in exchange for John's acknowledgement of the king of France as his lord.

The granting of special privileges to its teachers and students marks the founding of the **University of Paris**, which is followed a few years later by the universities of **Montpellier** (1220) and **Toulouse** (1229).

The *Magnus liber organi*, one of the earliest collections of liturgical polyphony, is written around this time.

1202 Following King John's failure to compensate Hugues de Lusignan for stealing his fiancée, **Isabelle d'Angoulême**, the court of Philippe Auguste orders the confiscation of John's French lands.

1202–04 France participates in the **Fourth Crusade**, which culminates in the **sack of Constantinople**.

1202–06 Philippe gains control of most of John's French possessions, including Normandy, Maine, Touraine, Anjou, Poitou, Brittany and the Auvergne.

1204 The **Château-Gaillard**, built by Richard I to defend Rouen, falls to Philippe Auguste after an eight-month siege.

1206 **St Dominic** (Domingo de Guzmán), founder of the **Dominican Order** of friars, begins preaching in southern France. Over the next ten years the Dominican presence in the south steadily increases in an effort to combat the Cathar heresy. The Dominicans will play a key role in the Inquisition.

1207 Having returned **Poitou** to King John a few months before under the **treaty of Thouars**, Philippe once again invades it, regaining most of the area in the following year.

1208 Pope Innocent III preaches the **Albigensian Crusade** against the Cathars.

1209 At the head of the crusade, Simon de Montfort attacks Raimond VI, comte de Toulouse, for protecting the Cathars. In July he sacks **Béziers**.

c.1210 Work begins on **Reims Cathedral**

c.1210 Geoffroy de Villehardouin writes his *Histoire de la conquête de Constantinople* – important both as an eyewitness account of the Fourth Crusade and as one of the earliest prose works of French history.

1211–28 The abbey of **Mont-St-Michel** is rebuilt following a fire in 1203.

1213 Simon de Montfort's victory over the count of Toulouse and the supporting force of Peter II of Aragon at the **battle of Muret** (12 September) marks an important

> ❝ Between the moment when the rector deflowered me and that moment where he gave me to my husband, one day, I do not remember when, I was at the door on the Baille de Montaillou with my mother Fabrissa. The rector was walking up towards the château and he rested a short while with us and we talked jokingly of the sin of lechery. And then he said that to have relations with a woman, as long as it was pleasing to her, was not a sin. He said also that one woman was as good as another and that the sin was the same with one or with another. This said, he continued at once to the château of Montaillou. ❞
>
> Testimony to the Inquisition by a widow suspected of Catharism,
> trans. by Nancy P. Stork

TRIP/B.GADSBY

In Carcassonne widespread tolerance of Catharism ended in 1209 when Simon de Montfort conquered the city

stage in the subjection of southern France to Capetian rule.

1214 **King John** lands at La Rochelle in February to head an anti-Capetian coalition consisting of the Holy Roman emperor **Otto IV**, the **count of Flanders**, and the **count of Boulogne**. John himself is defeated by Louis, son of the French king, at **La Roche-aux-Moines** on 2 July; the other members of the alliance are crushed by Philippe Auguste on 27 July at the **battle of Bouvines**. This decisive battle, which effectively brings the Angevin empire to an end and guarantees Capetian supremacy in France, becomes the focus of a nascent sense of national pride. The **treaty of Chinon** (18 September) forces John to acknowledge Capetian gains.

1215 **Robert de Courçon**, the papal legate, gives the **University of Paris** its first statutes, covering both the academic and social conduct of university life. Among other provisions, they forbid the teaching of Aristotle's *Metaphysics*.

Simon de Montfort becomes **count of Toulouse** when the fourth Lateran Council assigns him the lands of Raimond VI, who is judged to have shielded heretics.

1216 Philippe's eldest son, **Louis**, invades England in support of his wife Blanche de Castille's claim to the throne. He is repulsed at Lincoln the following year.

The **Dominican order** receives formal approval from Pope Honorius III.

1217 The Dominicans establish themselves in Paris.

1218 Simon de Montfort dies while besieging Toulouse, which has been reoccupied by Raimond VI.

1218–21 The **Fifth Crusade** leads to a negotiated reoccupation of part of Jerusalem. During the winter of 1218–19, the Crusaders lay siege to **Damietta** in Egypt. As so often, they are more at risk from disease than from Saracen swords.

1219 Some ten years after the founding of their order by St Francis of Assisi, **Franciscan friars** establish themselves in Paris.

1223 On 14 July Philippe Auguste dies, leaving the Capetians in control of a greatly enlarged kingdom. **Louis VIII** succeeds to the throne and is crowned at Reims on 6 August, the first Capetian since Hugues Capet not to be crowned in his father's lifetime.

1225 Louis VIII and Blanche de Castille endow the king's younger sons with territories to provide for their maintenance. Artois is given to Robert, Anjou and Maine to Charles, Poitou to Alphonse. The aim of this system of **appanage** is to minimize dangerous family conflict, but in practice it creates, alternative centres of power which will later destabilize the kingdom.

1226 Louis VIII leads an expedition against the Cathars, capturing **Avignon** and forcing the Languedoc into submission. On his return from the south, he dies of dysentery (8 November). **Louis IX**, 'St Louis', succeeds to the throne and is crowned at Reims on 29 November. From 1226 to 1234, during his minority, his mother Blanche acts as regent.

> **❝** We ate no fish in the camp all Lent, save mudeels; and the eels, being greedy fish, used to feed on the dead bodies. And from this misfortune, together with the unhealthiness of the country, where there never falls a drop of rain, we were stricken with the 'camp-sickness', which was such that the flesh of our limbs all shrivelled up, and the skin of our legs became all blotched with black, mouldy patches, like an old jack-boot, and proud flesh came upon the gums of those of us who had the sickness, and none escaped from this sickness save through the jaws of death. **❞**
>
> From *The Memoirs of the Lord of Joinville*, trans. Ethel Wedgwood

1227–28 Blanche successfully resists a coalition of rebellious princes.

1229 In April Blanche imposes a peace on Raimond de Toulouse which greatly weakens the power of the southern princes. Under the **treaty of Paris**, the whole of the Languedoc will in a generation pass into Capetian hands.

c.1230–40 **Guillaume de Lorris** composes the first part of the *Roman de la Rose*, an allegorical romance that offers an influential exposition of the doctrine of courtly love. This doctrine is contested in the second part of the poem, written some forty years later by **Jean de Meung**.

1233 The Inquisition is established in the Languedoc under the direction of the Dominicans.

1234 Louis IX attains his majority and marries **Marguerite de Provence**.

1240 Louis buys the **Crown of Thorns**, said to have been worn by Christ at the Crucifixion, from the emperor of Constantinople.

1241–47 The English philosopher and scientist **Roger Bacon** teaches at the University of Paris.

1242 In another outbreak of hostilities between France and England, Louis IX defeats the English king **Henry III** and an alliance of the nobility of southern and western France at **Taillebourg** and **Saintes**.

1244–48 The **Sainte-Chapelle** is built to house the Crown of Thorns.

1244 On 20 March the capture of **Montségur** marks the final defeat of the Cathars.

1245 The Dominican **Albertus Magnus** starts teaching at Paris. His influence will be important in promoting an interest in the writings of the Greek philosophers, particularly Aristotle. Among his students at the convent of St-Jacques is the

Italian **Thomas Aquinas** (c.1225–74), whose *Summa theolo-giae*, written in the 1260s, will make him the Roman Catholic Church's greatest western philosopher and theologian.

1248 Louis leads the **Seventh Crusade** to the Holy Land, taking his family with him and leaving Blanche de Castille as regent.

1249 **Damietta** in Egypt is captured by the Crusaders. On the death of Raimond VII in the same year, the county of Toulouse is inherited by **Alphonse de Poitiers**, the king's brother.

1250 After initial successes, Louis and his plague-stricken army, retreating from **Mansurah**, are captured by Muslim forces. On payment of a heavy ransom, Louis is released and rejoins his wife in **Acre**. For the next four years he remains in the Holy Land, attempting to strengthen the Christian fortifications and forge strategic alliances.

In France work begins on the construction of **Strasbourg Cathedral**.

1252 Death of Blanche de Castille.

1252–59 **Thomas Aquinas** returns to Paris to study for the degree of master of theology, and from 1256 to 1259 teaches at the university.

1254 As part of an attempt to overhaul the machinery of state, Louis issues a decree forbidding ministers of justice to accept bribes.

The supreme law-court, which had previously moved around with the king, becomes fixed in Paris as the **Parlement de Paris**.

1257 **Robert de Sorbon** founds the college in Paris that will later become the Sorbonne.

1258 Under the **treaty of Corbeil**, signed on 11 May, **James I of Aragon** renounces his claim to territories in

Blanche de Castille

Granddaughter of Henry II of England and Aliénor d'Aquitaine, **Blanche de Castille** (1188–1252) learnt at an early age what it meant to be part of a political dynasty. When she was eleven, her uncle, King John of England, arranged for her to be married to **Louis of France**, son of King Philippe Auguste, an event which took place the following year. In 1216, when John died, she claimed the throne of England, supported by her husband who mounted an invasion on her behalf. The attempt was unsuccessful, but in 1223 Louis inherited the French throne as Louis VIII. His brief reign ended three years later, leaving Blanche to act as **regent** for their 12-year-old son, the future **St Louis**. Realising that any delay would increase the danger from potential rivals, Blanche managed, within three weeks of his father's death, to have Louis IX crowned at Reims cathedral. Once she had neutralised the threat from rebel lords by a mixture of military action and diplomacy, she turned her attention to the heretics in the south, forcing Raimond VII de Toulouse to accept the **treaty of Paris** (1229), which laid the foundations of Capetian supremacy in the south. Even when Louis came of age, Blanche, domineering and pious, continued to exercise wide-ranging personal and political influence – to a degree that Louis' wife, **Marguerite de Provence**, found hard to tolerate. When Louis embarked on the **Seventh Crusade** in 1248, Marguerite preferred to accompany him rather than stay with Blanche, who was again made regent. In spite of illness, Blanche went on governing through her last four years and presided over council meetings until a few months before her death.

Blanche of Castille

southern France and Louis IX renounces his claim to **Catalonia** (also known as the Franco-Spanish March).

The treaty of Paris, signed on 28 May, between Louis IX and Henry III of England, brings to a temporary end many years of hostility between the two nations. Henry renounces his claim to territories in the west of France, Louis hands over territories in Limousin, Quercy and Périgord.

1265–68 Charles d'Anjou, Louis IX's brother, conquers Naples and Sicily, of which he has been declared king by the pope.

1266 Louis IX introduces the silver **livre tournois**, which thereafter becomes the basis of French currency, eroding the status of currencies issued by other rulers.

1269–72 Thomas Aquinas teaches at Paris for a second period.

1270 Having embarked on the **Eighth Crusade**, Louis lands in Tunisia. Initial victories are again followed by a visitation of the plague.

On 25 August Louis dies and his son **Philippe III le Hardi** (the Bold, b.1245) becomes king and is crowned at Reims a year later.

1271 Philippe III inherits the county of Toulouse following the deaths in the previous year of both his uncle Alphonse and Alphonse's wife Jeanne de Toulouse.

1274 The translation into French of a Latin chronicle from the earlier part of the century marks the start of the *Grandes Chroniques de France*, the official history of France up to the mid-15th century.

1282 On 30 March a mass uprising, known as the **Sicilian Vespers**, is set off by an incident at evensong in a church outside Palermo. The French are ousted from the island and Charles d'Anjou replaced by **Peter III**, king of Aragon. This initiates a long conflict between the French and the Aragonese for control of Sicily.

Louis IX (Saint Louis)

Across a gulf of more than seven centuries it is hard to disentangle the life of **Louis IX** (1214–70) from the work of the hagiographers who laid claim to him within a few years of his death. The second son of Louis VIII and Blanche de Castille, he succeeded to the throne at the age of 12 and, thanks largely to the skill and determination of his mother, managed to retain the crown against rebellious barons at home and the predatory king of England abroad. A man of extreme piety, he responded to the loss of **Jerusalem** in 1244 by leading the **Seventh Crusade**. Its ill success did not prevent his setting off again in 1270 on the **Eighth Crusade**, which proved fatal to him.

A more lasting achievement was the programme of **administrative reform** that Louis initiated between these two Crusades. As well as ensuring that provincial administration was subject to scrutiny by the king's officers, he made strenuous efforts to bequeath France a system of justice that was free of bribery. The fact that Louis was often called on to arbitrate disputes that had arisen outside France suggests that his reputation for dispensing **impartial justice** was more than a creation of his biographers. His record of intolerance towards Jews, Muslims and Cathars earns him no credit today, but in his judicial and monetary reforms, in his concern for the welfare of his subjects, and in the diplomatic and military success with which he defended his territory, he stands out as one of France's greatest medieval kings. He was canonized 27 years after his death.

1283 **Philippe de Beaumanoir** completes his *Livre des coutumes et usages du Beauvaisis*, which records the legal customs of the Beauvaisis region. Since French law at the time is based primarily on custom rather than written statute, compilations of this kind are of considerable significance.

1284 The marriage of Philippe's son, the future Philippe IV, to **Jeanne de Navarre** brings the territories of Navarre, Champagne and Brie under Capetian control.

In the continuing conflict with the Aragonese, Philippe III

leads a French army across the Pyrenees against Peter III.

1285 After an inglorious campaign Philippe, defeated, dies of fever. He is succeeded by **Philippe IV le Bel** (the Fair), who withdraws from the conflict.

1291 The **loss of Acre** on 28 May signals the end of a western Christian presence in the Holy Land.

1294 **Philippe IV** opens a ten-year period of hostilities with England, competing with **Edward I** for control of Aquitaine. Edward is supported by the Flemings, who, though subjects of the French king, depend primarily on England for their vital supply of wool.

1295 The financial strains of war and the costs of an expanding administration lead the king into the first of a series of unpopular revaluations of the coinage, prompting a **monetary crisis** that deepens over the next ten years.

1296 Philippe comes into conflict with **Pope Boniface VIII** over taxes imposed on the clergy in support of the French war effort.

1297 Boniface VIII **canonizes** Louis IX, partly under pressure from the French king, Louis' grandson.

Flemish merchants in France are arrested. Philippe IV captures **Lille**.

1299 The **treaty of Montreuil-sur-mer** proposes marital alliances between the royal houses of France and England.

1301 Boniface VIII again comes into conflict with Philippe after the French king arrests one of his bishops as a traitor. Boniface suspends Philippe's right to tax ecclesiastics.

1302 In April Philippe convenes an assembly of clergy, nobility and town representatives that anticipates the formation of the **états généraux** (Estates General). In what is the first of a series of assemblies designed to boost support for such potentially divisive measures as his taxation of the clergy, Philippe asserts his supremacy over the pope in matters temporal. This provokes Boniface VIII to issue his bull **Unam sanctam** in November, which reaffirms in uncompromising terms the supreme power of the pope. Philippe is threatened with excommunication.

In the so-called **Bruges Matins**, on 18 May, the soldiers of the occupying French garrison are massacred by rebellious Flemings. Philippe sends a French army, led by **Robert d'Artois**, to restore order and exact revenge. On 11 July a largely untrained Flemish infantry militia inflicts a devastating defeat on this army at **Courtrai**. The engagement becomes known as the **Battle of the Golden Spurs**, since many of the dead French knights were equipped with the golden spurs won in tournaments. Among those killed is **Pierre Flote**, one of the king's closest counsellors. Along with **Guillaume de Nogaret** and **Enguerrand de Marigny**, he has had an important influence on Philippe's policies.

1303 A treaty between France and England returns Aquitaine to Edward I and reaffirms the marriage proposals contained in the **treaty of Montreuil**, notably that Philippe's daughter Isabelle should marry the future Edward II of England. This results in some years of peace between the two kingdoms but will later provide a pretext for Edward III, son of Edward II and Isabella, to claim the throne of France.

In his increasingly bitter conflict with **Boniface VIII**, the French king charges the pope with heresy and immorality. In September Guillaume de Nogaret, Philippe's minister, seizes the pope at **Agnani**, but before the ageing pontiff can be brought to the council to answer Philippe's charges, he dies of shock.

1304 On 18 August Philippe defeats the Flemish at the **battle of Mons-en-Pévèle**.

1304-07 The Franciscan philosopher and theologian **Duns Scotus** (c.1266–1308) teaches at Paris. His controversial defence of the doctrine of the **Immaculate Conception**, which raises accusations of heresy, leads to a hasty departure for Cologne in 1307.

1305 Philippe forces a humiliating peace agreement on **Flanders**, under which the Capetians annex Lille, Douai and Béthune. Resentment at his terms will bring about a resumption of hostilities in 1312.

A Frenchman from the Bordeaux region, Bertrand de Got, is elected **Pope Clement V**.

1306 In financial straits, Philippe expels all **Jews** from France and expropriates their goods. As in the past, the hounding of Jews is a temporary expedient; within a decade they will be allowed to return in exchange for paying increased taxes.

1307 On 13 October Philippe moves against the **Knights Templar**, arresting those in France and confiscating their goods. The charges against them are heresy and immorality, but the wealth they have amassed as international financiers makes them a particularly attractive target.

1308 Philippe's daughter, **Isabelle de France**, marries **Edward II** of England.

1309 Clement V establishes the papal curia at **Avignon**, where it remains until 1377.

Joinville completes his *Vie de Saint Louis*, which provides a vivid picture of his relationship with the king and their participation in the Seventh Crusade.

1310 Marguerite Porète, a Beguine from Hainaut and author of the *Miroir des simples âmes*, is burned at the stake for heresy, becoming the first person to be executed in Paris on the findings of the Inquisition.

1312 A papal bull issued by Clement V suppresses the order of the Knights Templar.

1314 On 19 March the grand master of the Templars, **Jacques de Molay**, is burned at the stake after retracting a confession made under torture.

The end of Philippe's reign is overshadowed by scandal when two of his daughters-in-law are accused of adultery, and the third of complicity. Philippe himself, a moralist to the last, presides over the trial, torture and execution of the two knights accused with them.

On 29 November Philippe IV dies and is succeeded by his eldest son, **Louis X**.

1315 Louis X's wife **Marguerite de Bourgogne** is strangled in prison, having been convicted of adultery shortly before the death of Philippe IV. In July Louis marries **Clémence**, daughter of Charles I of Hungary.

Under pressure from nobles provoked by Philippe IV's fiscal extortions, Louis agrees a charter confirming their former rights and immunities.

1316 On 5 June Louis X dies. His brother Philippe is appointed regent for the unborn child of his pregnant widow. The child, **Jean I**, dies five days after his birth in September and Philippe declares himself king, as **Philippe V**.

1322 On 3 January Philippe V is succeeded by his brother, **Charles IV le Bel** (crowned 11 February).

1323 A rebellion is raised in Flanders that smoulders on for the next five years.

Trouble breaks out between England and France over territorial rights in Aquitaine, the so-called **'war of St-Sardos'**.

1328 On 1 February Charles IV dies without a male heir. **Edward III** of England, grandson of Philippe IV, claims the French throne, but the bishops and nobility declare for Philippe IV's nephew, **Philippe VI de Valois**, who is crowned at Reims on 29 May. The consideration given to the fact that Philippe is 'natif du royaume' (a native of the kingdom) reflects Capetian success in fostering an embryonic sense of national identity.

4
The Valois

1328–1589

When the first of the **Valois** monarchs was crowned in 1328, France was a fragmented medieval kingdom on the threshhold of a long, fruitless war that threatened its very existence as an independent state. By the time the last Valois monarch died in 1589, it had become, in spite of difficulties and divisions, a Renaissance power whose cultural and political influence was felt across Europe.

Fighting was the business of the Valois kings, and the history of the dynasty presents above all a spectacle of recurring warfare. The **Hundred Years War** was a bleak struggle for survival fought on French soil and followed in the second half of the 15th century by a series of domestic campaigns to reestablish the authority of the French Crown. Within a few years, the scene of battle had moved to Italy. Like many sovereigns before and since, **Charles VIII** preferred adventures abroad to problems at home. The **Italian Wars** provided an intoxicating outlet for royal vanity and military zeal, but they also drained the exchequer and inaugurated the centuries-long quarrel with the **Habsburg** rulers of the Holy Roman Empire. Finally, there were the **Wars of Religion** that overshadowed the closing years of the Valois dynasty. The **Reformation** launched by Martin Luther in 1517 had altered the political as well as the religious landscape of Europe; and France, subject to influences from both north and south, was particularly vulnerable to the tensions that arose. More bitterly divided between **Protestant** and **Catholic** than any other country in Europe, it was to suffer internal conflict that long outlasted the initial round of wars.

Amid this turmoil, the old order was changing. The Hundred Years War and the ravages of the **Black Death** accelerated the erosion of feudal labour practices, while military reorganisation undermined the feudal basis of warfare. The complexities of governing a more centralized kingdom, allied to the widespread sale of offices, encouraged the growth of an administrative class. To meet the cost of expensive wars, the system of taxation had to be revised. Outside Paris, the founding of new universities and the spread of regional *parlements* fostered the development of provincial cities. Artistic influences from Italy furnished the seeds of a cultural renaissance. All these were aspects of France's emerging identity in a Europe that was now poised to enter the modern age.

The Early Valois
1328–1461

Gibbon's melancholy verdict that history is 'little more than a register of the crimes, follies, and misfortunes of mankind' could serve as an epigraph for the period of the **Hundred Years War** (1337–1453). The war itself, sustained by English claims to the French throne and large areas of French territory, was a vicious, futile seesaw that went first in England's favour then France's, before repeating the cycle across another half century. For the hapless population, the interludes of peace, when marauding bands of unemployed soldiers terrorized the countryside at will, were scarcely preferable to the long years of warfare.

The English were only part of the problem. On the death of **Charles V**, who had managed to claw back much of his kingdom from enemy hands, the country was left with the 12-year-old **Charles VI** as its sovereign. For the next 50 years France was a theatre for the competing rivalries of the boy's relations, whose hunger for power led in the end to the bloody civil war between **Armagnacs** and **Burgundians**, the two parties representing the **duc d'Orléans** and the **duc de Bourgogne**. French fortunes were at an ominously low ebb in 1429 when the unlikely figure of **Jeanne d'Arc** (Joan of Arc) came on the scene and the tide began to turn. Within a quarter of a century English power in France had been broken for good.

Almost as horrifying as the war itself was the backdrop of social disintegration against which it was played out. Since 1315, the worsening climate had spread periodic **famine** through the land. Hunger was followed by plague. Starting in the south at the end of 1347, the **Black Death** spread like a fatal stain across the countries of Europe, leaving empty villages in its wake. Meanwhile, the costs of incessant warfare imposed a relentless burden of taxation on the stricken peasantry. The fierce eruptions of popular rebellion against these conditions were suppressed with matching ferocity. France lurched on towards the hope of better times.

Not surprisingly, it was a period more barren of cultural landmarks than any other in the last thousand years of France's history. The great age of cathedral building was over, the world of the troubadours had vanished long ago. Only at the sumptuous **court of Burgundy** was there an artistic flourishing to bear comparison with what was happening in Italy. It is perhaps appropriate that the greatest poet of this murderous age should be **François Villon**, himself a thief and murderer, who left behind a poetry that still flashes with haunting images of a world on the edge of darkness.

1328 Philippe VI de Valois is crowned at Reims (29 May).

On 23 August Philippe crushes Flemish rebels at the **battle of Cassel**. After his disputed accession to the throne, this victory is hailed as a judgement of God, sealing his legitimacy and reinforcing the support of the barons who have given him the crown.

1329 On 6 June **Edward III** of England does homage to Philippe for **Guyenne** (the name used for the area of Aquitaine under English control), whose revenues the French king has been withholding.

1334 Work begins on the construction of the **Palais des Papes** at Avignon.

1337 In the wake of worsening relations with Edward III of England, Philippe VI confiscates Guyenne (24 May).

On 7 October Edward III repudiates his homage to Philippe VI and claims the throne of France, signalling the start of the **Hundred Years War**.

1340 In February, following a revolt against the **count of Flanders**, the Flemish recognise Edward III as king of France.

The French fleet is destroyed by the English at **Sluys**, near Bruges (24 June).

1341 The extension of the **gabelle** (salt tax) to the whole kingdom heralds a steady increase in the tax burden on French subjects.

1346 In July Edward III lands in France. The French army is routed at the **battle of Crécy** (26 August). Among those killed is the French king's brother, **Charles d'Alençon**.

1347 After a year-long siege, **Calais** surrenders to the Eng-

Knights fighting at the battle of Crecy from the *Grandes Chroniques de France*

lish on 4 August. To avert the threat of a general massacre, six of the richest citizens – remembered as the **Burghers of Calais** – offer themselves (in what may have been a stage-managed public spectacle) as sacrificial victims to Edward III; they are spared at the intercession of Queen Philippa. Edward fortifies and garrisons Calais, establishing it as an English outpost for the next two centuries. By now both countries are feeling the economic effects of prolonged warfare, and in September Philippe VI and Edward III agree a **truce**. Renewed in 1351, it lasts for the next eight years.

> **❝** It is almost impossible to credit the mortality throughout the whole country. Travellers, merchants, pilgrims and others who have passed through it declare that they have found cattle wandering without herdsmen in the fields, towns and waste-lands; that they have seen barns and wine-cellars standing wide open, houses empty and few people to be found anywhere... **❞**
>
> Gilles Li Muisis, quoted by Philip Ziegler, *The Black Death* (1969)

In December the **Black Death** first appears in France, probably brought by a Genoese galley that has touched at Marseille.

1348 The Black Death spreads northwards. Within a year it kills something like a third of the population of France.

1349 In spite of **Clement VI**'s threat to excommunicate Christians who mistreat Jews, **pogroms** become increasingly frequent as part of a hysterical reaction to worsening economic conditions and the appalling consequences of the plague. In February, 900 Jews are burnt to death in **Strasbourg**.

The province of Dauphiné is bought by the French Crown, and the king's grandson Charles takes the title of **Dauphin**. Thereafter, it becomes a traditional appanage of the king of France's eldest son.

Processions of flagellants, who hope by their penitence to expiate the sins that have brought the plague upon Christendom, make their appearance in northeastern France. A source of alarm to the authorities in both their unruliness and their religious heterodoxy, they are condemned by a papal bull on 20 October. Philippe VI prevents them from getting beyond Troyes.

1350 On 22 August Philippe VI dies, leaving a country that

> Each scourge was a kind of stick from which three tails with large knots hung down. Through the knots were thrust iron spikes as sharp as needles which projected about the length of a grain of wheat or sometimes a little more. With such scourges they lashed themselves on their naked bodies so that they became swollen and blue, the blood ran down to the ground and bespattered the walls of the churches in which they scourged themselves. Occasionally they drove the spikes so deep into the flesh that they could only be pulled out by a second wrench.
>
> Henry of Herford, quoted by Philip Ziegler, *The Black Death* (1969)

in the space of a decade has seen its growing prosperity drained by warfare, plague and a heavily devalued currency. His son, **Jean II le Bon**, is crowned king on 26 September.

1355 The war with England is revived in the autumn, when the **Black Prince**, son of Edward III, lands in France and begins campaigning in the southwest.

1356 The Black Prince, relying again on the bowmen who had brought victory at Crécy, utterly defeats the French army at the **battle of Poitiers** (19 September). The French king is taken prisoner, leaving the dauphin Charles in command.

> Now, sirs, though we be but a small company, let us not be abashed therefor; for the victory lieth not in the multitude of people, but whereas God will send it. If it fortune that the day be ours, we shall be the most honoured people of all the world; and if we die in our right quarrel, I have the king my father and brethren, and also ye have good friends and kinsmen; these shall revenge us.
>
> The Black Prince, addressing his forces before the battle of Poitiers, from Froissart, *Chronicles*, trans. Lord Berners (1523–25)

Etienne Marcel's uprising

A prosperous clothier and provost of the Paris merchants, **Etienne Marcel** came to prominence in the early months of 1358 as the leader of a reformist movement against the royal house. The traumatic defeat of the French army at **Poitiers** (1356), only ten years after Crécy, had left the nation in crisis: socially, there was widespread disillusionment with an incompetent and self-serving aristocracy; financially, there was despair at the crippling ransom demanded for the captured king; politically, there was a vacuum created by the sovereign's absence. All three elements contributed to Marcel's uprising. The intention was to remove corrupt royal officials and bring the administration, especially with regard to tax revenues, under the supervision of the **états généraux** (Estates General). But the situation spun out of control with the murder of two of the dauphin's counsellors. Marcel was no longer talking about reform, he was at the head of a city in revolution. It was a difficult position to maintain: he lacked support outside Paris, particularly after the suppression of the **Jacquerie**, and even within Paris his popularity quickly evaporated when he opened the gates to the turbulent army of mercenaries led by his dubious ally, **Charles le Mauvais**, king of Navarre. At the end of July, six months after the insurrection had started, Marcel was assassinated, leaving the way clear for the dauphin to return to the city.

1358 The first **treaty of London** is drawn up in January. Still reeling from the defeat at Poitiers, the French agree to a **ransom** of four million gold écus for their king and a peace settlement which leaves the English Crown in possession of almost a third of France in exchange for abandoning its claims to the French throne.

In Paris, an uprising led by **Etienne Marcel** forces the dauphin to flee the city. Lasting from February to July, this insurrection coincides in its later stages with a peasants' revolt known as the **Jacquerie** (Jacques being a generic term for French peasants) that sweeps the countryside around **Compiègne**. Supported by many of the better-off, who feel threatened by rising taxation, the revolt is ruthlessly crushed by **Charles le Mauvais** (the Bad), king of Navarre. In August, the dauphin re-enters Paris and announces a general amnesty.

1359 Having delayed signing the first treaty of London, Edward proposes a **revised treaty**, which demands even greater territorial concessions from the French. Its rejection leads to a resumption of hostilities.

1360 In October, after an unspectacular spring campaign, Edward III ends up agreeing to a diluted version of the first treaty of London. Under the **treaty of Calais** he gets full sovereignty over **Aquitaine**, but his other territorial gains are reduced, and the ransom for Jean II is fixed at three million écus.

1364 Unable to raise his ransom, **Jean II** returns to England according to the terms of his parole and dies in comfortable captivity on 8 April. He is succeeded by the dauphin, now **Charles V** (crowned 19 May), who at once faces conflict with his brother-in-law, the king of Navarre, an ally of the English. The royal army, led by **Bertrand du Guesclin**, defeats Charles le Mauvais at **Cocherel**. Over the next fifteen years, Charles V, having learnt from the experience of Crécy and Poitiers, avoids large pitched battles, but French forces under du Guesclin continue to harass the English, eroding their hold on French territory.

1368 After a costly expedition to Spain the previous year to restore the unreliably pro-English Pedro the Cruel to the throne of Castile, the Black Prince tries to repair his finances by imposing a **hearth tax** on Aquitaine.

1369 When a rash of petitions against the new tax are laid before the king of France, the Black Prince is ordered to appear before the king's court, the *Parlement* of Paris. His refusal prompts the confiscation of Aquitaine and a new round of hostilities that bring gains to the French.

Philippe le Hardi (the Bold), having been granted the duchy of Burgundy in 1363 by his father Jean le Bon, marries **Marguerite de Male**, daughter and heiress of the count of Flanders. For the next hundred years the court of Burgundy will be one of the richest and most splendid in Europe.

1370 Work begins on building the **Bastille**, a massive fortress to defend Paris.

1370–77 A number of Aristotle's works are translated into French by **Nicole Oresme**.

1372–73 Du Guesclin, now **Constable of France**, reconquers Maine, Poitou, Anjou and Angoumois.

c.1373 **Jean Froissart** (c.1337–c.1410) composes the first book of the *Chroniques*. His work provides valuable, though not always reliable, details of the period, coloured by an overriding concern with the ideal of chivalry.

1375 For a decade and a half, English raids, the so-called *chevauchées*, will have a ruinous effect on French rural life, already under pressure from poor harvests.

1376 Death of the Black Prince.

1377 **Guillaume de Machaut** dies in Reims. A celebrated lyric poet and musician, who has influenced Geoffrey Chaucer, Machaut is the composer of the first polyphonic setting of the complete Ordinary of the Mass.

1378 **Pope Gregory XI** dies in Rome, a few months after transferring the papacy back there from Avignon. Popular pressure leads to the election of an Italian pope, who takes the name **Urban VI**, but a majority of the cardinals later repudiate their decision and elect another cardinal, **Robert of Geneva**, who takes the name **Clement VII**.

After an unsuccessful attempt to dislodge Urban, Clement returns to Avignon. This marks the start of the **Great Schism**, which splits the countries of western Christendom, some giving obedience to Urban, others to Clement.

The duchy of Burgundy

From the early 5th century the Burgondes, a Scandinavian people who had established themselves in the northern Alps on the borders of the Roman empire, began pushing westward until they controlled an area that stretched from the Seine basin to Provence. Conquered by the Franks in 534, Burgundy remained for three centuries a possession of the Merovingian and Carolingian kings. After the **treaty of Verdun** (843), much of it passed to what later became Germany, but by 918 the Carolingian noble **Richard le Justicier** had acquired enough territory between the Loire and the Saône to establish himself as the first duke of the new **duchy of Burgundy**. From this basis the Capetian dukes built up a formidable domain, whose fortunes were greatly increased by advantageous marriage settlements.

With its capital at **Dijon**, Burgundy was extensive, economically prosperous and relatively well administered, while the abbeys of Cluny and Cîteaux gave it a central importance to western Christendom. By the end of the 14th century the dukes of Burgundy were able to maintain a court which far outdid that of the king of France, providing a refuge for art and culture in a war-torn age. The sculptures of **Claus Sluter** and the paintings of **Rogier van der Weyden** and **Jan van Eyck** are outstanding examples of the early Flemish art that was created under the patronage of the Burgundian court. But the wealth and power of Burgundy were a direct challenge to the authority of the French Crown, which Louis XI was determined to meet. The death of **Charles le Téméraire** at Nancy put an end to Burgundy's golden age, and five years later the **treaty of Arras** (1482) brought the duchy permanently back into the possession of the French king.

1380 On 13 July Bertrand du Guesclin dies while campaigning against the bands of unemployed soldiers known as *routiers*.

Charles V dies (16 September). By this time, the English hold on France has been reduced to five cities: Calais, Cherbourg, Brest, Bordeaux and Bayonne.

The throne passes to the 12-year-old **Charles VI le Fou** (the Mad) who is crowned on 4 November. For eight years the country will be ruled by his uncles: **Louis d'Anjou** (d.1384), **Jean de Berry** and **Philippe de Bourgogne**, with Philippe in the ascendant.

The Hundred Years War continues in sporadic campaigning, but for much of the next quarter of a century both France and England are more concerned with internal problems.

1382 A fortnight of civil unrest in Paris begins on 1 March when the *maillotins* attack tax officials with lead mallets taken from the Hôtel de Ville. Other uprisings against high taxation affect Rouen and towns in the Languedoc.

1384 On the death of the comte de Flandres, Philippe de Bourgogne inherits the counties of Flanders and Artois.

1385 Charles VI marries **Isabelle of Bavaria** (17 July).

1388 On 3 November Charles dismisses his uncles and takes the reins of government himself, recalling many of his father's former advisers.

1392 Charles goes mad, intermittently imagining himself to be made of glass. Meanwhile, the kingdom is fought over by his brother, **Louis d'Orléans**, and his uncle, the duc de Bourgogne, who act as co-regents along with the duc de Berry.

1393 On 28 June at the so-called **'bal des ardents'** a carelessly held torch sets alight the fancy-dress costume of one of the king's attendants. Four are killed in the resulting blaze, and the king barely escapes. There are rumours that the incident, which exacerbates the king's madness, was a murder attempt by his brother.

1394 A new decree expels the **Jews** from the kingdom.

1397 The English abandon **Brest**.

1404 Philippe le Hardi is succeeded as duc de Bourgogne by his son, **Jean sans Peur** (the Fearless), presaging increased friction between the houses of Orléans and Burgundy.

1405 **Christine de Pisan**'s feminist allegory *La Cité des dames* indicts a misogynistic culture and sets out to celebrate the capacities and moral qualities of women.

1407 On 23 November the assassination of the **duc d'Orléans** (on the orders of Jean sans Peur) sparks a fierce war between Armagnacs (the party of the Orléans family) and Burgundians.

1409 The Burgundians gain the upper hand and maintain a controlling influence until 1413.

The **University of Aix-en-Provence** is founded.

1410–16 **Pol** and **Hennequin de Limbourg** work on *Les très riches heures du duc de Berry*, one of the finest examples of book illumination and a masterpiece of the International Gothic style.

1413 Following a failed popular rebellion in support of fiscal and administrative reform, instigated by the **duc de Bourgogne** and led by the butcher **Simon Caboche**, the Burgundians flee Paris. The dauphin invites back the Armagnacs, who establish a supremacy that lasts until 1418.

Henry V, newly crowned king of England, asserts a claim to the throne of France.

1415 Henry V lands in France and, after taking **Harfleur**, inflicts an overwhelming defeat on the French at the **battle of Agincourt** (25 October).

The battle of Agincourt

In August 1415 **Henry V** landed in Normandy at the head of around 11,000 men to claim the French throne. Within a month half of them were dead. Some had fallen at the capture of **Harfleur**, but most were victims of disease. Unwilling to return home without a further show of force, Henry was determined to march his remaining troops north to Calais. When the French army came upon them at **Agincourt** (present-day Azincourt), they were tired, hungry and soaked by persistent rain. The odds were staggering: a French force of between 20,000 and 30,000 against something under 6000. But the French knights, encased in 70lb or more of practically impenetrable armour, were about to discover that they belonged to a bygone age. When battle was joined on the morning of 25 October, the nimbler English soldiers, mostly bowmen who could also wield swords and axes, hacked the cumbersome French forces to death. Around 6000 Frenchmen fell; of the English, fewer than 500. Among the dead were the flower of French chivalry, some of them killed in combat, others suffocated under piles of armour-clad bodies, not a few murdered on Henry's orders after they had been taken prisoner – "all those noblemen of France were killed in cold blood and cut in pieces, heads and faces, which was a fearful sight to see" (*Chronique de Jean le Fèvre de St Rémy*). Agincourt had opened a path to the French Crown and written the epitaph of medieval knightly warfare.

1416 Jean sans Peur, duc de Bourgogne, recognises **Henry V** as rightful king of France.

1417 An English army lands at **Trouville** to undertake the conquest of Normandy.

On 11 November the Great Schism ends with the election of **Pope Martin V** at the **Council of Constance**.

1418 In May the Burgundians enter Paris, massacre the Armagnacs and regain control of the government, which they retain until 1435. The dauphin withdraws to **Bourges**.

In July the English lay siege to **Rouen**. Five months later some 12,000 'useless mouths' (mainly old men, women and children) are expelled from the city. When Henry refuses them passage through the English lines, they die of cold and starvation on the ground between the besieged and the besiegers.

1419 After the fall of Rouen in January, the English go on to conquer the rest of **Normandy**.

On 10 September the first steps towards an agreement between the dauphin and the Burgundians come to an abrupt end when one of the knights at the peace conference assassinates Jean sans Peur. The Burgundians at once move to ally themselves more closely with the English.

In December, the dauphin retreats south of the Loire, leaving the English and the Burgundians in control of most of northern France.

1420 Under the **treaty of Troyes**, Charles VI is compelled to disinherit the dauphin and marry his daughter **Catherine** to Henry V of England, who is recognised as heir to the French throne. Henry is within sight of his goal, but the dauphin still represents an alternative focus of allegiance.

1421 The dauphin's troops defeat the English at the **battle of Baugé** (22 March).

1422 Henry V of England dies on 31 August. His son by Catherine, less than a year old, succeeds him as **Henry VI**. Following the death of Charles VI, on 21 October, Henry is proclaimed king of England and France, with the **duke of Bedford** acting as his regent in France. Meanwhile, the former dauphin has also proclaimed himself king of France, as **Charles VII**.

1423 On 30 July the royal army, with a strong contingent of Scottish allies, is defeated by Anglo-Burgundian forces at **Cravant**.

Jeanne d'Arc, maid of Orléans

Born into a prosperous peasant family in Domrémy on the borders of Lorraine, **Jeanne d'Arc** (c.1412–31) became persuaded when she was scarcely out of childhood that it was her mission to save France. Guided by voices she attributed to St Michael, St Catherine and St Margaret, she managed against all the odds to make contact with the French king and win him over. That a 17-year-old girl from a humble background should have been able, in the space of weeks, to put herself at the heart of the royal army, idolized by the soldiers and deferred to by their commanders, is one of the mysteries of history. What is undeniable is that her presence helped transform the military and political situation. Not only was she instrumental in lifting the **siege of Orléans**, she also urged on the irresolute dauphin to his long-deferred coronation at Reims.

When she was captured some months later at **Compiègne**, the newly made king, with regal aplomb, left her to her fate; he was by that time more concerned to negotiate with the Burgundians than to fight them. The physical and moral courage that shine through Jeanne's life were all she had to sustain her in the face of a court determined to prove that God was not on her side – and therefore not on the king's. Still in her teens, she was burnt at the stake for heresy on 30 May, 1431, while a Dominican held a cross high above the flames for her to look upon. A quarter of a century later, in 1456, her sentence was revoked and the **maid of Orléans**, la Pucelle as she was known to the French, was rehabilitated. Canonized by Pope Benedict XV on 16 May, 1920, Jeanne d'Arc had already been the subject of poems, operas and novels by figures as diverse as Voltaire, Schiller, Verdi and Péguy. Twentieth-century representations of her range from plays by George Bernard Shaw and Jean Anouilh to the films of – among others – Carl Dreyer, Robert Bresson, Roberto Rossellini and Jacques Rivette.

Paul Dubois' equestrian statue of Jeanne d'Arc made for the city of Reims

1424 On 17 August the dauphin's **Franco-Scottish** army is again defeated by the English, at **Verneuil**.

1428 Advancing south, the English and Burgundian armies lay siege to **Orléans** in October.

1429 The peasant girl **Jeanne d'Arc** (Joan of Arc), inspired by the conviction that she can save France, meets Charles VII at Chinon. On 8 May the siege of Orléans is raised, and French troops, with Jeanne d'Arc at their head, go on to defeat the English at the **battle of Patay** (18 June). Charles VII, hitherto mockingly dubbed the 'king of Bourges', can now be crowned at Reims on 17 July, giving an important boost to his authority.

1430 Jeanne d'Arc is taken prisoner at **Compiègne** and sold by **Jean de Luxembourg** to the English.

1431 Jeanne d'Arc is imprisoned and interrogated. After confessing her errors, she then retracts and is burnt at the stake as a relapsed heretic on 30 May.

In December Charles negotiates a truce with the **duc de Bourgogne**.

On 16 December Henry VI of England is **crowned** king of France in Paris.

1435 On 21 September the **treaty of Arras** brings Burgundy into alliance with Charles VII in exchange for territorial and personal concessions to Philippe. The way to Paris is open, but after a century of war the landscape of northern France is a scene of desolation.

Jan van Eyck paints *The Virgin of Chancellor Rolin* (now in the Louvre) for Nicolas Rolin, Chancellor of Burgundy.

1436 Royal troops capture Paris (13 April).

1437 Charles VII enters Paris (12 November).

1438 The **Pragmatic Sanction of Bourges** gives the French king greater control over the financial and judicial affairs of the Church.

1439 On 2 November a decree establishes the basis for a standing army, to be paid for out of a direct tax, the *taille*.

Henceforth, the raising of troops will be a royal prerogative. This is a direct threat to the private armies that maintain the power of regional princes and leads to rebellion the following year, but the reforms provide France with a military organization that over the next three years enables Charles to make important territorial gains in the Île de France and Aquitaine.

1440 Between February and July a revolt against Charles VII – known as the **Praguerie** by analogy with contemporary unrest in Bohemia – is successfully checked, but periodic eruptions of discontent among the princes continue for some years.

On 26 October **Gilles de Rais**, who had fought alongside Jeanne d'Arc, is executed as a sorcerer, having been tried for a number of offences, including the murder of children.

1443 **Toulouse** is granted a regional *parlement* (a high court of law). This is part of a development which over the next century takes in various cities, including Bordeaux, Grenoble, Dijon, Aix and Rouen, gradually extending a common legal and administrative framework across different parts of the realm and at the same time eroding the power of local princes in favour of independent urban communities.

1444 A **treaty** concluded at Tours between the French and the English brings a period of peace.

1448 The French retake **Le Mans**.

1449 The French retake **Rouen**.

1450 An English army lands at **Cherbourg** on 15 March and links up with surviving troops from the siege of Rouen to make a force of some 5000 men. They meet the French at the **battle of Formigny** (15 April) where the English forces are all but wiped out. In the course of the summer the French regain control of Normandy.

Agnès Sorel, mistress of Charles VII, dies. For the past six years her influence on his choice of ministers has been great – and greatly resented. Rumours abound that she has been poisoned on the orders of the dauphin, the future Louis XI.

1453 The **Ottoman Turks** take Constantinople.

French forces win the last battle of the Hundred Years War at **Castillon** (17 July). After their victory they sweep on to take **Bordeaux** on 19 October. **Calais** alone remains in the hands of the English.

1455–56 A re-examination of the trial of Jeanne d'Arc leads to her rehabilitation. The original trial and sentence are declared invalid.

1461 Death of **Charles VII** (22 July).

The Later Valois
1461–1589

With the Hundred Years War at an end, the economy of France began to recover and its population to increase. The political history of the next century and a half can be resumed in terms of three more or less consecutive chapters: the **postwar consolidation** of the French Crown, the **Italian Wars**, and the **Wars of Religion**.

The long struggle against England had shifted the balance of power away from the monarchy towards the regional nobles on whom the king had depended for political and military support. The business of subordinating them to royal authority was in part a question of re-emphasizing the mystique of sovereignty, and this the Valois kings did with a will; but it was also, decisively, a question of asserting military supremacy. The death of **Charles le Téméraire** in 1477, and with it the defeat of Burgundy's aspirations, was the climax of a broader strategy, skilfully executed by **Charles VII** and **Louis XI**, that had gone a long way towards establishing the territorial boundaries of modern France. (The most important exception was Brittany, which became part of France in 1532.)

By the end of the 15th century France was at war again. In pursuit of his claim to the kingdom of Naples, **Charles VIII** invaded Italy in 1494, beginning another extended period of warfare that ended only in 1559 when France surrendered its territorial gains in Italy under the **treaty of Cateau-Cambrésis**. This, however, was a war on foreign soil, hugely expensive but with few of the devastating side-effects that the Hundred Years War had brought in its train. Indeed, by keeping the more violent elements beyond French borders, it left the country free to go about its economic business in relative peace.

But another source of internal strife was already on the horizon. Religious differences, temporarily suppressed by the **Council of Constance**, had been thrust back into prominence by **Martin Luther** in 1517. Between 1562 and 1598 they broke out in a series of religious wars that saw the Catholic forces, headed by the **Guise family**, pitted against the **Huguenots**. Inevitably, these were political as well as religious conflicts, focused ultimately on the allegiance of the king himself. No one better reflects this than the figure of **Henri de Navarre**, who was brought up a Huguenot, converted to Catholicism, then back to Protestantism, before reconverting to Catholicism in order to secure the throne as **Henri IV** – at which point he brought matters to some sort of conclusion by imposing a degree of religious toleration through the **Edict of Nantes**.

Throughout this period, France had been putting down the roots of a national culture. In 1470, twenty years after

Johannes Gutenberg introduced the use of movable type to Europe, the first print shop opened in France. It was the start of a process that was to turn the country into one of the great publishing centres of 16th-century Europe. As print gained ground, so also did the language of the north, the *langue d'oïl*, leaving the southern *langue d'oc* to become increasingly the language of an oral tradition. The writings of **François Rabelais** and the poets of the Pléiade testify to the literary vitality of the language during this period, but also to the enriching effects of Renaissance influences encouraged by François I, whose enthusiasm for the art and ideas of Italy led to the development of the School of Fontainebleau. By the time of Henri IV's accession, France was preparing to claim its place as the dominant cultural force in Europe.

1461 Charles VI is succeeded by **Louis XI** (crowned 15 August), who is determined to rein in the power of the feudal lords. His main strategy will be directed towards neutralising the threat represented by Burgundy.

1465 The *Ligue du Bien public* (League of the Public Weal) groups a number of rebellious princes around the king's brother, the **duc de Berry**. Concerned to protect their privileges against Louis XI's assertion of royal power, they invoke the public good, demanding reform. After some indecisive military engagements, Louis reaches a negotiated settlement with them, handing back to the **duc de Bourgogne** the towns of the Somme purchased from him two years earlier.

1467 **Charles le Téméraire** (the Bold) inherits Burgundy on the death of Philippe le Bon. A less moderate figure than his father, he loses no time in pursuing plans for a separate Burgundian state between France and Germany.

1468 In October Louis XI and Charles le Téméraire meet at **Péronne** to work out an agreement, but a revolt in **Liège**, which Charles suspects Louis of supporting, sours the atmosphere. After holding the French king a virtual prisoner, Charles imposes his own terms for a treaty and obliges Louis to join the punitive expedition against Liège.

1469 The first **printing press** in Paris is installed at the Sorbonne.

1472 Following a period of sporadic hostilities with the French king, Charles le Téméraire besieges **Beauvais**. The 18-year-old Jeanne Laisné (known as **Jeanne Hachette** from her practice of fighting with a small axe) wins a place in French folk history when she rallies the inhabitants by wresting a flag from the enemy standard bearer. The failure of the siege marks an important point in the decline of Charles le Téméraire's fortunes.

1475 **Edward IV** of England lands with an army at Calais to claim the French throne but is bought off by Louis XI under the terms of the **treaty of Picquigny** (29 August).

Charles le Téméraire invades **Lorraine** but in the following year is defeated by the **Swiss Confederation** at the battles of Grandson and Morat.

1477 On 4 January Charles le Téméraire dies before the walls of **Nancy**, fighting to retake it from **René II** of Lorraine. His death brings to an end the great age of the duchy of Burgundy.

Marie de Bourgogne, daughter of Charles le Téméraire, marries **Maximilian of Austria** (28 August). This has the effect of bringing the vast Burgundian possessions into the orbit of the Habsburgs, creating a challenge to French power that will dominate France's foreign policy for the next three centuries.

1479 Louis XI's attempts to recover Burgundian territory from Maximilian are checked by the defeat of a French army at the **battle of Guinegate**.

1480–81 The French Crown acquires **Anjou**, **Maine** and **Provence** following the death of King René d'Anjou.

1482 The **treaty of Arras** (23 December) between Louis XI and Maximilian of Austria leaves France in possession of Burgundy and Picardy.

1483 Louis XI is succeeded by the 13-year-old **Charles VIII** (30 August).

1484 Charles VIII is crowned at Reims (30 May). For the next seven years his sister **Anne de Beaujeu** and her husband act as regents.

1484–91 Attempts by Breton nobles, in alliance with **Louis d'Orléans**, to maintain Brittany's independence from the French Crown end in defeat at the battle of **St-Aubin-du-Cormier** (1488) and invasion by royal forces. Charles forces **Anne, duchesse de Bretagne**, to annul her recent marriage by proxy to Maximilian of Austria and marry him instead. The marriage takes place in December 1491, and she is crowned queen of France at St-Denis two months later.

1489 **Philippe de Commynes** begins his *Mémoires*, which will deal in reflective, somewhat pessimistic terms with the reign of Louis XI and the Italian expedition of Charles VIII.

1492 Charles VIII signs the **treaty of Etaples** with **Henry VII** of England. Like his treaties the following year with the emperor of Austria and the rulers of Spain, this is designed to clear the way for his Italian campaign.

1494 Death of King **Ferdinand I of Naples** (25 January). Charles VIII asserts his title to the throne, inherited from the Angevins, thus initiating the series of **Italian Wars** which drag on, at huge cost and with little gain, for the next fifty years.

1495 Having crossed into Italy the previous year, Charles VIII enters Naples in triumph (22 February). However, a coalition of Italian states has been forming to oppose him. At the **battle of Fornovo** (6 July) Charles achieves a slender victory which enables him to get back to the Alps, but by the end of the year most of his territorial gains have evaporated.

1498 Charles VIII dies (7 April). He is succeeded by his cousin, the 36-year-old son of the poet Charles d'Orléans, who becomes **Louis XII** (crowned at Reims on 27 May).

1499 In order to retain Brittany, Louis marries Anne de Bretagne, Charles's widow, having first arranged for his marriage to **Jeanne de France** to be annulled. The Italian Wars enter a new phase with Louis' pursuit of his claim to the **duchy of Milan**.

1500 French forces occupy **Lombardy**, where they will remain for most of the next twenty years. Louis XII agrees a treaty with **Ferdinand of Aragon** which is intended to divide the spoils of Italy between France and Spain.

1503 After further conflict, the French are finally driven out of Naples. Southern Italy becomes the Spanish sphere of operation, the northern half is left to the French.

1505 Louis XII revises the arrangement for his daughter **Claude** to marry the Habsburg **Charles of Austria** (the future emperor Charles V) and has her betrothed to **François d'Angoulême**, heir presumptive to the French throne.

1508 The **Tour St-Jacques**, still a landmark in present-day Paris, is built for the church of St-Jacques-de- la-Boucherie.

1511 Alarmed at increasing French power in Italy following Louis' successful campaigns against Genoa (1507) and Venice (1509), **Pope Julius II** forms the **Holy League**, which unites the papacy, Spain, Venice, Switzerland and England against France.

François I: Renaissance prince

Jean Clouet's famous portrait of **François I** (1494–1547) shows us the image of a Renaissance prince – which is exactly what he was, both in his strengths and his weaknesses. He was a vain and profligate monarch who dragged France through a series of unsuccessful and ruinously expensive wars, but he was also a chivalrous, intelligent and humane ruler who did much to lay the foundations of France's great intellectual and cultural heritage. Brought up with his sister **Marguerite de Valois** by their widowed mother, he succeeded to the throne at the age of 20 in 1515. For the first four years everything went according to plan: military success in Italy, a concordat with the pope, a stream of Italian artists and scholars travelling north to enhance the brilliance of the French court. His reign looked set to be a golden age. But in 1519 the king of Spain was elected **Charles V**, Holy Roman emperor. With territories that now all but encircled France, Charles, a cold, devious and ambitious man, could not but be François' enemy. Personally and politically, they were opposites, and for the rest of the French king's life they worked to destroy each other. Captured after the **battle of Pavia** in 1525, François never fully recovered from his subsequent imprisonment in Madrid. Diminished in his own eyes, and troubled by illness, he grew more erratic in his behaviour and less effective in his opposition to the calculating emperor.

Politically, it is hard not to see his reign as a failure, but François' talents did not all go to waste. An admirer of **Erasmus**, he tried, initially at least, to hold at bay the religious intolerance of the times; he founded the port of **Le Havre**, and supported **Jacques Cartier**'s voyages to Canada; he was responsible for both the **Collège de France** and what became the **Bibliothèque Nationale**. Above all, he was a man in whom the French people can still see those qualities on which they most pride themselves: wit, elegance, cultivation, intellectual curiosity, sexual magnetism, *savoir vivre* – in a word, style. The France in which Rabelais and Ronsard could write, Goujon could sculpt and Clouet could paint was in part the France created by François I.

In Paris, the great humanist scholar **Erasmus** prepares his *Praise of Folly* for the press.

1512 In spite of victories against the League, the French hold on Italy is weakened.

1513 Lodovico Sforza, supported by the Swiss, returns to Milan.

1515 Death of Louis XII (1 January). His son-in-law, François d'Angoulême, succeeds as **François I**, crowned at Reims on 25 January. François' taste for Italian culture provides a conduit for Renaissance art and ideas but also acts as a spur to further military adventures in Italy, which begin with his defeat of an Italian army of Swiss mercenaries at the **battle of Marignano** (14 September), paving the way for the French reoccupation of Milan. It is on this occasion that the **Chevalier Bayard**, celebrated by the French as the knight '*sans peur et sans reproche*' (without fear and without reproach), is chosen to arm François I for the battle.

1516 Under the **Concordat of Bologna**, following François I's victory, the pope is obliged to confirm the king's rights over the French Church, notably in the appointment of bishops, the levying of taxes on the clergy and the limiting of Rome's jurisdiction in legal matters. On 29 November, François agrees a treaty of **'Perpetual Peace'** with the Swiss, who continue to provide mercenaries for the French Crown until the fall of Louis XVI in 1792.

1517 Martin Luther draws up his **'Ninety-five Theses'**, which quickly generate a groundswell of support that challenges papal authority and destroys the unity of Christendom. **The Reformation** has begun.

1519 The Habsburg **Charles V**, king of Spain since 1516, is elected Holy Roman Emperor. His territories now threaten France with encirclement.

In May, **Leonardo da Vinci** dies at Cloux near Amboise, where he has spent the last two years of his life, dignified by the title 'first painter, architect and mechanic of the King'.

1520 François I meets **Henry VIII** of England on the **Field of the Cloth of Gold**, near Calais. The setting is magnificent, but François fails to secure the desired alliance against Charles V.

1521 Hostilities break out between France and Charles V.

1522 The French are driven from Milan.

1523 At home, François faces a rebellion from the powerful **Charles de Bourbon**, who sides with Charles V and flees the country.

The château of Azay-le-Rideau built for the Treasurer of France in 1523

TRIP/A.TOVY

In an attempt to streamline the collection of taxes and increase his own control of them, François establishes a **central treasury** (the *Trésor de l'épargne*) for the receipt of all royal income, both 'ordinary' revenues from his own domains and 'extraordinary' revenues from taxation throughout the kingdom.

1524 Charles de Bourbon returns to invade Provence at the head of an imperial army but is repulsed at Marseille.

François leads French forces into Italy, retakes Milan and lays siege to **Pavia**.

Lutherans are persecuted in Paris and Lyon, the two centres of printing in France, where translations and adaptations of Luther's writings are now being published.

1525 At the **battle of Pavia** some 28,000 French troops, with François I at their head, are routed by the Habsburg army. François himself is captured and sent to **Madrid** as a prisoner. In a letter to his mother he writes, 'Nothing remains to me but my honour and my life.'

1526 The **treaty of Madrid** (14 January) imposes humiliating peace terms. Among the French territories that François agrees to surrender are those in Italy, Flanders and Artois. Once back in France, he refuses to ratify the treaty.

1527 After Protestant mercenaries employed by Charles V sack **Rome**, François again declares war and invades Italy.

1528 François begins extensive alterations to the palaces of the **Louvre** and **Fontainebleau**.

1529 The **treaty of Cambrai**, brokered by the mother of François and the aunt of Charles (and accordingly known as the 'Paix des Dames'), moderates the terms of the treaty of Madrid.

1530 François founds what will become the **Collège de**

The School of Fontainebleau

One of the happier consequences of François I's desire to enhance the prestige of the French monarchy was his importation of Italian artists to decorate the palace at **Fontainebleau**. François had campaigned in Italy and seen the magnificent state in which Renaissance princes such as the Sforzas lived; he wanted the same for France, or more specifically, for himself. In 1528 he began transforming the old medieval castle at Fontainebleau, and a couple of years later brought **Rosso Fiorentino** from Italy to help with the work. Rosso was joined in 1532 by **Primaticcio**, and together they elaborated a decorative style that modified **Italian Mannerism** to produce a distinctively French version which was widely influential in northern Europe. Later, **Niccolò dell'Abbate** also came up from Italy to work on the palace.

Among other Italian artists whom François I lured to Fontainebleau, the most famous was **Benvenuto Cellini**, who spent five years there from 1540 to 1545 and created for the king the superb golden saltcellar which has passed to the Kunsthistorisches Museum in Vienna, as well as the bronze relief, the *Nymph of Fontainebleau*, now in the Louvre. Cellini's autobiography makes it clear that François was no mere figurehead in all this; he took an active and detailed interest in what was being done. For the French king, disappointed in his hopes of military victory over the Habsburg empire, the palace created by these artists under his patronage was a statement of France's cultural supremacy in northern Europe.

France. Established as a centre for the study of ancient languages, it quickly attracts the hostility of the university but survives thanks to royal patronage.

1532 Brittany becomes part of France.

1533 The **duc d'Orléans**, the future Henri II, marries **Catherine de Médicis**, though for most of their marriage she plays a subordinate role to his mistress **Diane de**

Poitiers, whose support for the staunchly Catholic **Guise family** has a significant influence on Henri's policy.

1534–36 On two expeditions **Jacques Cartier** explores the **St Lawrence River** as far as present-day Montréal, establishing a French foothold in Canada. He fails, however, to bring back the riches that François I desperately needs for the prosecution of his wars.

1534 On 17 and 18 October the **'Affair of the Placards'** dramatically affects the religious climate in France. Anti-Catholic posters denouncing the Mass and the veneration of saints are posted around Paris, Orléans and Amboise, and even on the door of the king's chamber. In response, a massive procession is held, attended by the king himself and rounded off with the burning of half a dozen Protestant heretics. Hitherto, François has taken a relatively tolerant line on religious dissent, but from now on he adopts repressive measures that are a grim step towards the later Wars of Religion.

In the crypt of St-Denis, on Montmartre, the Spaniard **Ignatius Loyola** and six students from the University of Paris take the vows that mark the beginnings of the **Society of Jesus**. The Jesuits will become a leading force in the Catholic Counter-Reformation.

1535 Hostilities between François I and Charles V are resumed when the death of **Francesco Sforza** without a male heir leaves the succession to the duchy of Milan undecided.

1539 The **ordinance of Villers-Cotterêts** makes French, in place of Latin or regional dialects, the language of all legal and official documents.

1541 **John Calvin**'s *Institutes* are published in French. Their influence as a statement of Protestant principles gives Calvin (1509–64) an importance second only to Luther's in the history of the Reformation. His central belief that individuals are predestined to salvation or damnation has remained the basis of a major division in Protestant thought.

François Rabelais

Priest, scholar, doctor and author of some of the most extraordinary books in French literature, **François Rabelais** (c.1494–1553) is one of a handful of writers whose names have passed into the language – to use the term 'Rabelaisian' is to evoke an unmistakable cluster of attributes. Son of a wealthy lawyer in Touraine, Rabelais became a Franciscan novice before transferring to the Benedictines and then leaving the order to study medicine in **Montpellier**. It was while working as a doctor for the Hôtel-Dieu in Lyon that he published *Pantagruel* (1532), followed two years later by *Gargantua* (1534). The adventures of his giants, written in colourful, exuberant language that sets medieval learning against the challenge of the new humanism, and leavens both with flights of scatological humour, were an immediate success. But he was living in intolerant times; it took more than the thin veil of an anagrammatic pseudonym (Alcofribas Nasier) to protect a writer who broached serious topics with such a dangerous mixture of scholarship and frivolity. Repeatedly his books were condemned by the Sorbonne, but Rabelais had the gift of attracting powerful friends. Under the patronage of a series of prelates and aristocrats, he continued to travel and practise medicine, publishing his *Tiers Livre* (third book of Pantagruel's adventures) in 1546 and the *Quart Livre* in 1548. With the dispensation of the pope, he was received back into the Benedictines and lived as a secular priest. He was buried in St-Paul-des-Champs, Paris.

Jacques Cartier returns to Québec, but his expedition again alienates the native **Iroquois** and fails to produce material gains. France withdraws from overseas exploration for half a century.

1542 **Benvenuto Cellini** creates his *Nymph of Fontainebleau* for the portal of the palace.

1543 François forms what is, for a Christian king, an unprecedented alliance with the **Ottoman Turks** against Charles V.

1545 In December the opening of the **Council of Trent** signals the start of the Catholic **Counter-Reformation**. Over the next eighteen years, it takes an increasingly harsh line on Protestantism while seeking to reform Catholic institutions from within.

1547 François I is succeeded by his son as **Henri II** (crowned at Reims on 26 July).

1548 The *Confrères de la Passion* buy part of the old Hôtel de Bourgogne, where they build a theatre. Since the *Parlement* has forbidden the representation of the mystery of the Passion, or other sacred subjects, they begin performing secular plays there, turning it into Paris's **first theatre**.

1549 **Joachim du Bellay**'s *Défense et illustration de la langue française* provides a manifesto for the new poetic school of Ronsard and marks an important stage in the recognition

Title page of an early edition of *Pantagruel*, with a portrait of Rabalais on the left

of French as a language of learned and polite discourse.

Pierre Lescot, responsible the previous year for the **Fontaine des Innocents** in Paris, is given the job of finishing the Louvre.

1551 The **Edict of Chateaubriant** reinforces repressive measures against heresy, imposing the death penalty for Lutheran beliefs.

1552 After concluding a treaty with the **German Protestant princes**, Henri II renews hostilities against the Holy Roman Empire, occupying the three bishoprics of Metz, Toul and Verdun in Lorraine. An attempt by Charles V to recapture Metz later in the year is thwarted by the brilliant defence of **François de Guise**.

1555 In Lyon, the physician and astrologer **Nostradamus** (1503–66) publishes *Vraies centuries et prophéties*, his first book of prophecies. In the wake of its success he is taken up by Catherine de Médicis.

1556 The **treaty of Vaucelles** brings to an end the current phase of the ongoing struggle between France and the Holy Roman Empire.

> But to conclude, I say and maintain, that of all torcheculs, arsewisps, bumfodders, tail napkins, bung-hole cleansers, and wipe breeches, there is none in the world comparable to the neck of a goose, that is well downed, if you hold her neck betwixt your legs … And think not that the felicity of the heroes and demigods in the Elysian fields consisteth either in their Asphodel, Ambrosia or Nectar, as our old women here used to say; but in this, according to my judgement, that they wipe their arses with the neck of a goose, and such is the opinion of Master Duns Scotus too.

François Rabelais, *Gargantua*, Bk.I, trans. Sir Thomas Urquhart (1653)

The group of poets centred on **Ronsard** takes the name **Pléiade** (formerly used by a group of Hellenist poets) after the constellation of seven stars. Their aim is to find new poetic forms and to create a literature in the French language. Along with Ronsard himself, the original seven are du Bellay, Jodelle, Baïf, Pontus de Tyard, Belleau and Peletier (or, according to some, Dorat).

1557 France intervenes in Italy to support **Pope Paul IV** against **Philip II** of Spain, who is allied with the English.

Catherine de Médicis

Born in Florence, the daughter of the duke of Urbino and a Bourbon princess, **Catherine de Médicis** (1519–89) became the wife of one French king and the mother of three others. Her marriage to the future **Henri II** in 1533 took her to the court of François I, where she displayed social and intellectual gifts that won the king's approval. Though her influence on Henri II was eclipsed by that of **Diane de Poitiers**, she bore him ten children and briefly acted as regent for him in 1552. His accidental death thrust her into lasting political prominence as regent for her sons **François II** and **Charles IX**. Throughout the 1560s she played a moderating role in the religious conflicts of the time, but her attempts at reconciliation were undermined by the fanaticism and ambition of the Guise family. Her role in the **massacre of St Bartholomew** (see p.124) is uncertain. It seems likely, however, that after the failed attempt on Admiral de Coligny's life, with the Crown apparently at risk from a Protestant backlash, she assented to the initial murders that set the massacre in train. The last years of her life were spent in trying to guide the policies of her son Henri III and to preserve the independence of the Crown both from the hostility of the **Catholic League** and from its poisoned embrace. By the time she died, the enduring but unjust image of a wicked Italian ogress had already been well established by the Huguenot pamphleteers.

1558 The **duc de Guise** recaptures Calais from the English.

A limited form of **public lighting** – a lantern at each street-corner – comes to Paris.

The Huguenots

The French Protestants probably acquired the name **Huguenots** from the German word *Eidgenossen* meaning confederates, used in the 1520s of the faction that supported an independent Geneva. In France it was first applied by Catholics as a pejorative term at the time of the Amboise conspiracy, before later being adopted by the Protestants themselves. Although the Huguenots attracted little official hostility at the start, the **Affair of the Placards** in 1534 left François I with the conviction that this new allegiance was politically as well as theologically subversive, a view supported by the practice within Huguenot communities of setting up separate administrative structures to maintain their independence. The ensuing persecution flared into the religious wars of the later 16th century.

Calvinist in its essentials, **French Protestantism** had by this time attracted something like ten percent of the population, mostly from the educated classes. The **Edict of Nantes** (1598) ushered in a period of relative calm, but the religious intolerance of Louis XIV, no doubt intensified by the dangerous precedent of the Puritan revolution in England, led to further persecutions. The **revocation** of the Edict of Nantes in 1685 was the cue for a mass exodus of Huguenots, many of them valuable craftsmen and entrepreneurs, to neighbouring Protestant countries. It took the Revolution to restore French Protestants to full enjoyment of their civil rights, and over the past two centuries the political sympathies of Protestants in France have tended to remain with the left. In French society today, where between two and three percent of the population are still Protestant, the religious tensions of the past have given way to newer sources of domestic conflict.

1559 The **treaty of Cateau-Cambrésis** (3 April) brings the Italian Wars to an end. Demoralized by recent defeats in the field, financially exhausted, and facing internal religious conflict, France finally agrees to a peace that allows it to retain Calais, along with control of the three bishoprics of Metz, Toul and Verdun. In exchange, it renounces territorial ambitions in Italy and Savoy.

On 10 July Henri II is killed in a jousting accident and succeeded by the sickly **François II**.

1560 In March extreme Protestants try to capture François II in order to remove him from the influence of the Guise family. The **Amboise conspiracy**, as it comes to be known, is hopelessly bungled, and the repression that follows hardens the lines of opposition that will lead to the Wars of Religion.

On 5 December François II is succeeded by his brother **Charles IX**. Their mother Catherine de Médicis, widow of Henri II and regent for François II, continues her regency, exercising a political influence that will be one of the defining features of the next three decades. The period is characterized by increasing competition for power among the nobility, centred on the families of **Guise**, **Montmorency** and **Bourbon**.

1562 On 1 March **François de Guise** sends in troops to massacre Huguenots worshipping at **Vassy**. Together with the Amboise conspiracy, this puts an end to the fragile attempts to find a compromise, inspired by the Chancellor, **Michel de l'Hôpital**, which had led to the Conference of Poissy the previous year. Conflict between Catholic and Protestant forces is now inevitable. The **Wars of Religion** that follow are usually divided into eight separate episodes: 1562–63; 1567–68; 1569–70;1573–74; 1576; 1577; 1579–80; 1585–98. Their violence is a reflection of the depth of division within the country, balanced between the Catholic dominance in the south of Europe and the

The St Bartholomew's Day Massacre

The origins of the massacre of **St Bartholomew's Day** lie in the religious and political controversies that had been brewing in France since the Reformation. The **Affair of the Placards** in 1534 had emphasized a faultline in French society. Against a background of deepening religious intolerance, the political rivalries of the time acquired a new intensity, manifested in the religious wars that started in 1562. For some years **Catherine de Médicis** had adopted the role of mediator, but by 1572 she viewed with increasing mistrust the influence of the Huguenot **Gaspard de Coligny**, Admiral of France, over her son **Charles IX**. The Catholic Guise family, who blamed Coligny for the assassination of the duc de Guise nine years earlier, were quick to offer a solution. A botched attempt to murder Coligny on 22 August provoked a whirlwind of outrage and rumour, creating an atmosphere heavy with the threat of violence from both sides.

How much of what followed was planned – by the Guise family, by Catherine de Médicis, by the king himself – and how much was simply due to the momentum of events, is still disputed. At the least, it seems likely that the assassination of a number of prominent Huguenots was authorised by the king. But once the murders started, there was too much hatred in the air to bring them quickly to an end. Sometime before dawn on 24 August, the bells of **St-Germain-l'Auxerrois** rang out and the frenzy of killing began. Coligny's corpse was flung from a window, decapitated, emasculated and later dragged to the gibbet at Montfaucon; the duc de Guise rode through the streets urging on the slaughter. Some 3000 Huguenots were killed in Paris alone, many of their bodies hurled into the Seine. Within days the massacres had spread to the provinces: Rouen, Lyon, Orléans, Bourges, Bordeaux. Overall, as many as 11,000 Huguenots probably met their deaths. In Spain, which had feared a war with France promoted by the Huguenot faction, there was rejoicing; in Rome, Pope Gregory XIII had a medal struck to celebrate the event. But for France it meant another quarter of a century of civil strife.

Protestant dominance in the north. The new religion has a powerful hold among sections of the aristocracy, but not enough to overturn the Catholic allegiance of important courtiers and institutions.

1563 **François de Guise** is assassinated on 24 February by a Huguenot, suspected by Catholics of being an agent of the **Admiral de Coligny**. The **Edict of Amboise** guarantees the Huguenots freedom of conscience and fosters an interval of comparative peace. Charles IX and Catherine de Médicis travel round the kingdom, partly in an attempt to promote reconciliation.

1564 The date of the start of the year is fixed as 1 January rather than Easter. **Philibert Delorme** begins building the palace of the **Tuileries** for Catherine de Médicis.

1569 The **third war of Religion** begins badly for the Protestants with defeats at **Jarnac** (13 March) and **Moncontour** (3 October). Admiral de Coligny becomes head of the Protestant army.

1570 Coligny's defeat of the Catholic army at **Arnay-le-Duc** leads to the **peace of St-Germain**, which puts a temporary stop to the Wars of Religion, providing for limited freedom of worship and four Protestant strongholds.

1572 The murder of **Admiral de Coligny** on **St Bartholomew's Day** sets off the massacre of thousands of Protestants in Paris and the provinces.

1574 On 30 May Charles IX is succeeded by his brother, **Henri III**.

1576 Having prudently converted to Roman Catholicism in the wake of the St Bartholomew Massacre, **Henri de Navarre** abjures his Catholicism and takes command of the Protestant army. The **peace of Monsieur**, which guarantees a measure of religious freedom to the Huguenots, is followed by the formation of an embryonic **Catholic League**, led by the Guise brothers.

1577 In an attempt to defuse the threat represented by the extremist Catholic League, Henri III himself assumes leadership of it. He also embarks on a series of social and administrative reforms set out in the *Grande Ordonnance de Blois* (1579).

1578 On 31 May Henri lays the first stone of the **Pont Neuf**, though work on it makes little progress until the time of Henri IV.

1580 The first two volumes of *Essais* are published by **Michel Eyquem de Montaigne** (1533–92). A dedicated student of his own nature, with a profoundly sceptical intelligence, Montaigne is largely responsible for the creation of the reflective essay as a literary form. After serving as mayor of Bordeaux from 1581 to 1583, he retires permanently to his family estate.

1582 The introduction of the **Gregorian Calendar** imposes a jump from 9 to 20 December.

1584 The death of Henri III's brother, **the duc d'Alençon**, makes **Henri de Navarre** the heir apparent, prompting the formal establishment of the Catholic League. On 31 December, the **treaty of Joinville** between Philip II and the Guise guarantees Spanish support to the League.

1585 The banning of Protestantism by a royal edict of 18 July, in response to pressure from the League, triggers another stage in the Wars of Religion. Over the next three years a series of battles will leave neither side in a commanding position.

1588 After victory over a Huguenot army of German auxiliaries in November of the previous year, **Henri de Guise**, now acknowledged as a rival for Henri III's throne, comes to Paris against the king's orders. On 12 May (the **Day of the Barricades**) Henri III, besieged in the Louvre by a pro-Guise mob, abandons the city to the League and flees to **Tours**. In December, he has the Guise brothers, Henri and Louis, murdered at Blois, precipitating open rebellion in a number of French towns.

1588-89 Still in control of Paris, the League, headed now by Henri de Guise's son, the **duc de Mayenne**, institutes a reign of terror that anticipates the events of the Revolution. Henri III allies himself with Henri de Navarre and lays siege to the city.

1589 Death of Catherine de Médicis (5 January).

On 1 August Henri III is stabbed by **Jacques Clément**, a Dominican monk, and dies the following day. Henri de Navarre succeeds him as **Henri IV**, but the League declares his uncle king, as **Charles X**.

5
The Bourbons before the Revolution

1589–1789

F rance was a divided country. Half a century of intermittent **civil war** had weakened its economy and drained its resources. For the new dynasty, there was much to repair, both materially and spiritually. Aided by supremely able ministers, the early **Bourbon monarchs** set out to equip France with the military, cultural and administrative apparatus by which a modern state defines its reach. The army was overhauled and enlarged, the navy built up from almost nothing, the bureaucracy centralized, the arts and sciences supported by official patronage. Across the same period, territorial frontiers were expanded, explorers sent out, colonies planted. And at the centre of all these developments was the king himself, a figure more prominent, more powerful than ever before, whose own glory reflected the greatness of his nation.

Or so it seemed for most of the 17th century. But the relentless assertion of monarchical power led inevitably to repression at home and warfare abroad. Nothing that challenged the ideology of absolutism could be tolerated. The hounding of **Protestants** was motivated by more than a pious aversion to heresy: **Louis XIV** recognised with abhorrence that the whole basis of this new religion was a denial of ordained hierarchy. Intellectual dissent was equally suspect. There was no place in the politics of the *ancien régime* for the dangerous provocations of individual thought. Yet in spite of this – perhaps because of it – the centuries of Bourbon rule produced some of the most adventurous and subversive thinking in the history of Europe.

The rulers themselves were unable to profit from it. As the prestige of the monarchy began to decline in response to unsuccessful wars, unpopular royal liaisons, political stagnation and a worsening economy, the suppression of dissent became ever more difficult. In the end, an intolerant regime, in thrall to a deeply conservative alliance of clergy and nobility, simply could not answer the questions that were being asked by a probing intelligentsia, a thwarted bourgeoisie and a desperate peasantry. The world had moved on, and the institutions of government had failed to move with it. The age of France's greatest cultural flowering became the seedbed of **Revolution**.

Henri IV to the death of Mazarin 1589–1661

Faced with the legacy of a century of religious hatred, **Henri IV** had first to settle matters between Catholics and Protestants. Having neutralised Spain and swept up the remains of the Catholic League, he established, through the **Edict of Nantes**, the conditions for peaceful coexistence. It was from this basis that his chief minister **Sully** set out to rekindle the economy by embarking on a lavish building programme that included roads, canals, hospitals, urban spaces, and in one case (Henrichemont) a whole town. The regency of **Marie de Médicis**, dating from her son's accession to the throne as Louis XIII, marked a shift towards rapprochement with the Catholic countries of the south. Internally, this was reflected in a resurgence of religious tension: for the rest of the century Protestant privileges were steadily curtailed, though it was only with the personal rule of Louis XIV, after **Mazarin**'s death, that the pressure became general and severe. Until then, reasons of state prevailed. When France entered the bloody conflict of the **Thirty Years War** in 1635, it was political expediency rather than religious affinity that determined its allegiance.

The reason for this was simple: **Cardinal Richelieu** was making the decisions. France's history in the 17th century is shaped as much by a string of skilled and powerful ministers – Sully, Richelieu, Mazarin, **Colbert** – as by the kings they served. Richelieu and Mazarin in particular laid the foundations of an absolute monarchy. The **siege of La Rochelle** (1627–28) and the subsequent campaign in the **Cévennes** eliminated any threat from the Protestants, and the defeat of the rebellions known as the Frondes enabled Mazarin to ensure that henceforth neither nobles nor *Parlement* had a stong enough power-base to mount an effective challenge to the king. By the time Mazarin died in 1661, the way was clear for a new kind of monarchy.

Meanwhile, France had been uneasily aware that while it was absorbed by the religious wars of the 16th century, other European powers – Portugal, Spain, England, the Netherlands – had been creating lucrative empires overseas. Belatedly, French merchants and explorers set out to even the field. In Canada **Champlain** founded the colony of **Québec**. Elsewhere, France acquired valuable sugar-producing territories in the **Antilles**, while settlers around Cayenne formed the nucleus of **French Guiana**. At about the same time, French merchants established an important trading post in **Senegal**. When he came to power, Louis XIV had at least a fledgeling empire.

Culturally as well as socially, this was a period of consolidation. The rebuilding and embellishment of the capital, begun by Henri IV, was continued under Richelieu, whose patronage of the architect **Jacques Lemercier** gave Paris the **Palais–Royal** and the church of the **Sorbonne**. The founding of the *Académie française* in 1634 boosted the status of language and letters in a way that still conditions French culture. In painting and literature there is no lack of celebrated names – Philippe de Champaigne, Georges de La Tour, Pierre Corneille and Madeleine de Scudéry all lived and worked during this period – but perhaps more important than any one individual is a cultural shift in the tone of aristocratic society. At its heart is the birth of the **salon**. Mme de Rambouillet's *chambre bleue* was the beginning of a phenomenon that would exercise a major influence over French cultural life. Like Richelieu's *Académie française*, it fostered a new respect for matters of art and intellect that was to underpin the achievements of the next three centuries.

1589–93 A power struggle is played out between **Henri IV** and the forces of the **Catholic League**, supported by Philip II of Spain. Although Henri IV has notable victories over the Catholic forces at **Arques** (1589) and **Ivry** (1590), he is unable, in spite of a ruthless siege in 1590, to win Paris.

1593 Henri IV abjures Protestantism and reconverts to Catholicism.

1593–95 A revolt of the *croquants* – peasants in the Limousin and Périgord – is brutally suppressed. Like similar unrest in Normandy and Brittany, it comes as a response to continued high taxation, exacerbated by a series of harsh winters, harvest failures and plague.

1594 Since Reims is still in the hands of the League, Henri IV is crowned at Chartres (27 February). On 22 March he enters Paris, welcomed by the more moderate **bourgeois Catholics** who want above all to see a return to peace and stability.

In December the *Parlement* of Paris decrees the **expulsion of the Jesuits** after one of their pupils makes an attempt on the life of Henri IV.

1595 On 17 January, irked by Spain's support for lingering elements of the Catholic League, Henri declares war on **Philip II**. This has the welcome effect of shifting the political focus to an external conflict. Victory over the Spanish at **Fontaine-Française** (5 June) is followed by defeats in Picardy. Meanwhile, Henri's policy of combining pardon for prominent members of the League with substantial bribes for acquiescence in the new *status quo* reduces the level of internal discontent. In November he is reconciled with the leader of the Catholic League, the **duc de Mayenne**.

1596 Henri forms an alliance with **England** and the **United Provinces** against Spain. In the same year, **Sully** enters the *Conseil des Finances*.

1597 Massive state debts are liquidated by bankruptcy.

1598 On 13 April the **Edict of Nantes** provides for equal rights and, within certain constraints, freedom of worship for Protestants.

In May the **treaty of Vervins** brings the war with Spain to an end, securing France against further Spanish involvement in its internal affairs.

The future duc de Sully becomes superintendent of finances.

1599 Sully initiates an extensive **building programme** of roads, bridges and canals, designed, apart from modernizing the infrastructure, to revitalise the economy.

1600 On 11 August, tired of its duke's prevarications over a proposed exchange of territories, Henri declares war on **Savoy**.

On 5 October Henri marries **Marie de Médicis** by proxy, having secured an annulment of his marriage to **Marguerite de Valois**.

1601 Under the **treaty of Lyon** (17 January), Henri acquires territories in Savoy in exchange for French possessions in **Piedmont**. **Geneva** gains independence from Savoy and becomes a free city.

On 27 September the future **Louis XIII** is born at Fontainebleau.

1602 Henri establishes a team of **Flemish weavers** in the faubourg St-Marcel. Their workshops will later become the **Gobelins**.

In September Sully **devalues** the currency.

1603 Jesuits are permitted to return to France.

1604 Under the guidance of Sully, Henri allows government offices to become hereditary on payment of an annual sum, or *paulette*, equivalent to a sixtieth of what was originally paid for the office. This provides an important source of revenue for the Crown but will create problems for Henri's successors.

1605–12 Henri instigates the construction of the **place Royale** (now place des Vosges), which will be Paris's first great public square, a focus for public festivities and the hub of aristocratic life.

> ❝ The Pont Neuf [in its heyday] was not just a beautiful bridge; it was fairground, department store, employment exchange, picture-gallery and poor man's Harley Street. You could have a tooth out, go through the 'Situations Vacant', watch the tight-rope dancers, buy a Lancret or a Fragonard, join the army, pick up the new Marivaux or a first edition of *Manon Lescaut*, and arrange to go up in a balloon, watch a bull-fight, take fencing lessons and attend a surgical demonstration. ❞
>
> John Russell, *Paris* (1960)

NIK WHEELER/CORBIS

Completed in1607, the Pont Neuf spans the widest part of the river, and was the first Paris bridge to be built without houses attached to it

1607 In December Henri rides across the completed **Pont Neuf**.

1608 Samuel Champlain, explorer of the St Lawrence river, founds **Québec**.

St François de Sales publishes his *Introduction à la vie dévote*. Over the next three centuries, this popular work of devotion, which sets out to reconcile spiritual ideals with the business of everyday life, will go through some four hundred editions.

1610 On 14 May Henri IV, caught in a traffic jam in the rue de la Ferronerie in Paris, is assassinated by a rabid Catholic, **François Ravaillac**. The 8-year-old dauphin succeeds to the throne as **Louis XIII** (crowned at Reims on 17 October), with Marie de Médicis acting as regent.

1611 In January the resignation of Sully and others of Henri IV's ministers increases the influence of Marie de Medicis' favourite, **Concino Concini**, and his wife **Leonora Galigai**.

In May a **Protestant assembly** in Saumur expresses growing anxiety about the overtly pro-Catholic stance of Marie de Médicis and her advisers.

1612 In April a lavish celebration is held in the newly completed place Royale to mark the betrothal of Louis XIII to the eldest of the Spanish infantas and of **Elisabeth of France**, his sister, to **Philip**, heir to the Spanish throne. Both arrangements reflect the strategy of Marie de Médicis of linking France with other Catholic countries to oppose Protestantism.

1613 Concini is created **marshal of France**.

In Rouen arrangements are made to confine the poor in institutions. This is one of a series of moves during the 17th century to supervise and contain marginal and potentially disruptive groups. The mad, the sick, the poor, the homeless, the vagrant will all feel the pressures of increasing **social control**.

1614 The **prince de Condé** leads a revolt against the regency. The reliance of Marie de Médicis on Italian courtiers, headed by Concini, has alienated many of the nobility, who rally to Condé's standard. In spite of a temporary settlement, on the basis of Marie's agreement to call a meeting of the **Estates General** in October (the last before 1789), the uprising is renewed the following year.

1615 Champlain explores the region of the **Great Lakes** in Canada.

In August Marie de Médicis lays the first stone of the **palais du Luxembourg**.

In November Louis XIII marries the Spanish infanta, **Anne of Austria**, in Bordeaux.

1616 The future **Cardinal Richelieu** becomes secretary of state for foreign affairs.

1617 On 24 April Louis assumes the reins of power in dramatic style by having Concini murdered and Marie de Médicis exiled to the château de Blois. In a further move, he dismisses Richelieu and recalls former ministers of Henri IV. **Charles d'Albert de Luynes** is appointed constable of France. Leonora Galigai is burnt at the stake for witchcraft and *lèse majesté*.

1618 The **defenestration of Prague** (so called because three of the Holy Roman Emperor's Catholic administrators were thrown by Protestants from an upper window of Prague Castle) signals the start of the **Thirty Years War**.

1619 War breaks out between Louis and his mother after she escapes from Blois. **Richelieu** is brought back to resolve the crisis and brokers the **treaty of Angoulême** (30 April).

1620 In June a second war breaks out between Marie de Médicis and Louis. The defeat of Marie's forces in August is followed by the **treaty of Angers**.

In September and October Louis wages war against Protestant **Béarn**, successfully incorporating it into his kingdom.

On 25 December the Protestant deputies of **La Rochelle** decide to take up arms under the leadership of **Henri de Rohan** and his brother.

The Thirty Years War (1618–48)

This savage war was of crucial importance in defining the political map of 17th- and 18th-century Europe. It started as a rebellion of **Protestant Bohemians** against the rule of the Habsburg emperor **Ferdinand II** and gradually drew the rest of Europe into what had become a struggle between the Protestant princes of the north and the Holy Roman empire, aided by the Spanish Habsburgs. The German Protestants were all but defeated when first Denmark and then, with French support, Sweden entered the war against the Habsburgs.

It was only in 1635 that France herself took on a military role in alliance with the Protestant powers, including the Dutch who were fighting to eject Spain from the Spanish Netherlands. After a disastrous start, which brought Spanish forces to within reach of Paris, the French won a decisive **battle at Rocroi** (1643), paving the way for further victories that forced Ferdinand to negotiate. Under the **treaties of Westphalia** the Swiss cantons and the United Provinces of the Netherlands were recognized as independent, and France acquired territories in Alsace and Lorraine.

While the **Holy Roman empire** survived, its power had been seriously weakened, leaving a Europe composed mainly of sovereign states. Germany's independence from the empire had been dearly bought, since the clash of armies, mostly mercenaries who relied on pillage for their recompense, had taken place largely on its soil. France had emerged strengthened, but in so far as its gains provided the unspoken rationale for Louis XIV's military adventures later in the century, they were a doubtful blessing.

1621–22 Military operations against the Protestants are directed first by the **duc de Luynes** and then, after his death, by **Condé**, who massacres the inhabitants of **Nègrepelisse** in June 1622.

1622 On 5 September **Richelieu** is appointed Cardinal. He acts as intermediary in a rapprochement between Louis and his mother, who resumes her place on the Council.

The Hanging by Jacques Callot conveys some of the horror of the Thirty Years War which he witnessed first hand

The **peace of Montpellier** (18 October) reaffirms the provisions of the Edict of Nantes but reduces the number of Protestant strongholds to two, La Rochelle and Montauban.

1623 Louis XIII has a hunting lodge built at **Versailles**. This will become the site of his son's great palace.

1624 Richelieu's assumption of a place on the **High Council** marks the start of his role as chief adviser to Louis XIII.

Increased taxation to meet a growing economic crisis leads to peasant uprisings in **Périgord** and **Quercy** – another revolt of the *croquants*.

Louis commissions **Jacques Lemercier** to complete the *cour carrée* of the Louvre. It is from about this time that the literary salon of Mme de Rambouillet makes its mark.

The Salon

The gatherings arranged by **Mme de Rambouillet** (1588–1655) in her *chambre bleue* were the beginning of what was to become a central feature of French intellectual life for two and a half centuries. It was the **salon** that promoted the characteristically French mingling of the world of literature with that of social and political affairs. A civilizing influence on the manners of the aristocracy, it was also an institution that affirmed the status of literature in French society. If Richelieu, the duc de La Rochefoucauld and Mme de Sévigné were at home there, so too were sons of commoners like the writers Voiture and Corneille. That the salon should be a place presided over by women, where they could meet on terms of intellectual equality with men, was an important aspect of its tone and character. Under Louis XIV the royal determination to centre everything on Versailles sent the private salon into temporary eclipse, but during its heyday in the 18th century it was a shaping force within French society. Mme de Lambert, Mme de Tencin, Mme du Deffand, Mlle de Lespinasse, Mme de Geoffrin, Mme Necker and Mme Lavoisier were all women who received in their salons the social and intellectual elite of the age. Among these resorts of the aristocracy, many of the radical ideas of the **Enlightenment** were debated and refined.

1625 **Henrietta Maria**, daughter of Henri IV, marries **Charles I** of England by proxy in Paris.

Rubens completes his paintings for the east and west galleries of Marie de Médicis' palais du Luxembourg.

1626 In January a Royal Botanical Garden is created under the direction of **Jean Hébert**.

Duelling is banned (6 February). In spite of similar decrees in the past, there are now over three hundred and fifty encounters a year among the nobility.

On 31 July, in a bid to erode the power-base of the nobility, Louis orders the demolition of forts and strongholds that have no national strategic importance.

The **comte de Chalais** is executed for conspiracy, on Richelieu's orders (19 August).

Merchants from Rouen establish bases in **Senegal** and **Guiana**.

1627 In June the execution of two noblemen, Des Chapelles and Montmorency-Bouteville, for fighting a duel is further evidence of Richelieu's determination to check the rebellious tendencies of the aristocracy.

In September royal forces lay siege to **La Rochelle**. A Protestant stronghold with ties of sympathy to the English, it is both a military and a spiritual target in Louis' war against Protestantism. Having forbidden the evacuation of women and children, Richelieu directs the siege with cold efficiency, organising a blockade to starve the city into submission.

1628 On 28 October La Rochelle surrenders at the end of a siege that has killed three quarters of the inhabitants, reducing the population from 25,000 to fewer than 6000. Three days later, Louis and Richelieu enter the port in triumph.

> **“** For these reasons, we announce, declare, ordain, and will that all the strongholds, either towns or castles, which are in the interior of our realm or provinces of the same, not situated in places of importance either for frontier defence or other considerations of weight, shall be razed and demolished; even ancient walls shall be destroyed so far as it shall be deemed necessary for the wellbeing and repose of our subjects and the security of this state. **”**
>
> Edict of 1626 ordering the demolition of feudal castles

1629 In a quarrel over the succession to the **duchy of Mantua**, France intervenes against Spain, reflecting Richelieu's divergence from the policy of Marie de Médicis.

Royal forces campaign against Rohan in the Cévennes, taking the towns of **Privas** in May and **Alès** in June. The peace of Alès (28 June) again confirms the religious liberties decreed in the Edict of Nantes but abolishes the Protestant strongholds. Characteristically, Richelieu is more concerned with the political than with the religious threat.

On 21 November, Richelieu becomes **chief minister** and is created duke a week later.

1630 The **treaty of Ratisbon** (13 October) brings to a temporary end the hostilities between France and Spain over the Mantuan succession, but its terms are rejected by Richelieu. The situation is saved by the papal emissary **Giulio Mazarini** (Jules Mazarin), who arranges a last-minute truce at **Casale** (26 October). Richelieu's role in this conflict, apparently promoting war with a Catholic power, has alienated Marie de Médicis and the Catholic faction around her, the so-called *parti dévot*, who now seek his downfall.

On 11 November, the **Day of the Dupes**, Louis XIII is forced by his mother to choose between her and Richelieu. Thought to be on the point of dismissing Richelieu, he ends by supporting him. The Cardinal's adversaries, notably the Keeper of the Seals, **Michel de Marillac**, are arrested and imprisoned. Marie de Médicis leaves the court.

The **duc de Lévis-Ventadour** founds his *Compagnie du Saint-Sacrement*. Over the next three decades this religious society, with both clerical and lay members, exercises increasing influence as a Counter-Reformation focus for social piety and opposition to Protestantism. Its charitable works, often organised by women associates, are combined with a harsh moralism and a degree of secrecy that eventually leads to its suppression in the early 1660s.

1631 The king's brother, **Gaston d'Orléans**, breaks with Richelieu. In the summer, he joins forces in the Netherlands with Marie de Médicis, who has escaped from the château de Compiègne where she was sent to live.

In May **Théophraste Renaudot**, a doctor by profession and a protégé of Richelieu, launches France's first weekly newspaper, *La Gazette* (later *Gazette de France*), which presents a strictly official line on the news.

1632 Gaston d'Orléans supports a revolt led by the governor of the **Languedoc**, a Montmorency. After the rebels' defeat, Montmorency is beheaded and Gaston d'Orléans flees to Brussels.

1632–33 In a move to secure his northeastern frontier against the Holy Roman Empire, Louis establishes control over **Lorraine**.

1633 **Vincent de Paul** and **Louise de Marillac** found *les Filles de la Charité* (the Daughters of Charity) for the care of the poor who are sick, and for the instruction of girls. Along with similar missions founded by the *Compagnie du Saint-Sacrement*, of which Vincent de Paul is a member, this is one of a number of missionary enterprises in the first half of the century that manifest the Counter-Reformation spirit of active social piety mobilised to respond to the challenge of Protestantism. There is a strong female contribution to this charitable work.

1633–37 A series of **revolts** (often manipulated by the aristocracy), both in the cities and among the peasantry, express popular resistance to the increasing levels of **taxation** required by Richelieu's foreign policy.

1634 On 18 August **Urbain Grandier**, the curé of Loudun and suspected author of a pamphlet against Richelieu, is burnt at the stake for bewitching the town's Ursuline nuns. His fate (which will be the subject of Aldous Huxley's *The*

Devils of Loudun) has less to do with religion than with local politics and state manipulation of witchcraft hysteria.

1635 On 25 January Richelieu creates the *Académie française*. Culturally, the signs of France's growing confidence are all around. **Philippe de Champaigne** paints his celebrated portrait of Richelieu in this year, and **Claude**

Armand Jean du Plessis, duc de Richelieu

Born into the provincial nobility, **Richelieu** (1585–1642) studied at the Sorbonne before being appointed in 1607 to the bishopric of Luçon, a benefice held by his family. His rise to power was confirmed in 1624 by a seat on the **High Council**. Between 1624 and his death in 1642 Richelieu devoted his formidable abilities to consolidating the king's, and therefore France's, position. This identity of interests was central to Richelieu's development of the *raison d'état*, a theory of political action that subordinated all other considerations, moral, political and religious, to the interests of the state. Domestically, this meant suppression of any potential threat to the king's authority, whether from the Protestants he forced into submission or the nobles he brought to the scaffold. His own interests became by extension those of the state; to plot against him was to court an early death.

In foreign affairs, he was guided by the same light. The main external threat to France was the Habsburg empire, and the **Thirty Years War** was above all an opportunity to neutralise that threat. Richelieu's policy did check the Habsburgs and did produce territorial gains, but the fruits of war had a heavy economic price, reflected in the rural unrest that produced a succession of peasant revolts, each of them put down with ferocity. The figure of popular legend is the *éminence rouge* painted by Philippe de Champaigne, an icy tactician who pulls the strings of power with godlike detachment. But if Richelieu was callous in his pursuit of political ends, he was also the architect of France's greatness in the second half of the 17th century.

Cardinal Richelieu. Engraving after a painting by Philippe de Champaigne

Lorrain his *Rest on the Flight into Egypt*. At about the same time, **François Mansart** begins work on the château at Blois. In the theatre, **Pierre Corneille** is writing *Le Cid*, to be performed in 1636.

The founding of the *Compagnie française des îles d'Amérique* in February is followed later in the year by French conquests in **Guadeloupe** and **Martinique**. These are early steps in the creation of a 17th-century colonial empire, most of which will be lost in the course of wars with Britain in the following century.

After building a series of strategic alliances with the United Provinces, Sweden and a number of Italian states, Louis finally declares war on Spain (19 May), drawing France into the **Thirty Years War**. Richelieu's fear of Habsburg dominance has proved stronger than religious affinities. The conflict between his political pragmatism and the loyalties of the *parti dévot*, which favours an alliance with the Catholic powers against Protestantism, will remain a source of friction throughout the war.

1636 French involvement in the war begins badly. The capture of **Corbie** on 15 August brings the Spanish army from the Low Countries to within striking distance of Paris. The advance is checked but it emphasizes France's need for a vast increase in military resources, which involves a corresponding increase in both bureaucracy and taxation. In order to raise revenue, the sale of government offices becomes more widespread, swelling the ranks of the new *noblesse de la robe* (the nobility of the robe) and breeding discontent among the old *noblesse de l'épée* (the nobility of the sword).

1637 Anne of Austria, the king's wife and a leading opponent of Richelieu's policy, is discovered to have engaged in secret correspondence with Spain. Her confessor, the Jesuit

> The cardinal informed us that, with a view of establishing fixed rules for the language, he had arranged meetings of scholars whose decisions in these matters had met with his hearty approval, and that in order to put these decisions into execution and render the French language not only elegant but capable of treating all the arts and sciences, it would only be necessary to perpetuate these gatherings.
>
> From the letters patent establishing the *Académie française*

Caussin, is implicated. In spite of this scandal, Louis, detained at the Louvre by a night of bad weather in December, spends it with his wife, who conceives the future **Louis XIV**.

A *croquant* revolt, which has spread from Saintonge and Périgord to the southwest, is crushed.

René Descartes

Born in Touraine, **Descartes** (1596–1650) was educated by the Jesuits before taking a degree in law. In 1619 a dream convinced him to dedicate himself to philosophy. After some years of travel he settled in the **Netherlands**, where he was free of the distractions of Paris and sheltered from the intolerant winds of the Counter-Reformation. That his *Discours de la méthode* was written in French rather than Latin is evidence of Descartes' stated concern that anyone of sense, man or woman, should be able to read it. His goal was a complete **science of nature** that would start from a **scepticism** about all recognized sources of knowledge. Mistrustful of received authority, he took as his bedrock the fundamental intuition expressed in the phrase *Cogito ergo sum*, I think therefore I am. Among his most significant writings are the *Méditations métaphysiques* (1641) and his *Principia Philosophiae* (1644).

Aside from philosophy, Descartes made revolutionary discoveries in **mathematics** and also published work on physiology, optics and meteorology. In 1649 he dedicated his ethical treatise *Les Passions de l'âme* to **Queen Christina** of Sweden, who had invited him to her court. Weakened by the young queen's punishing regime (which included philosophical discussions at five in the morning), Descartes succumbed to pneumonia within a few months of his arrival. The scale of his achievement can be measured by his influence: until the mid-20th century, **Cartesian rationalism** and the empirical tradition that challenged it remained the two principal strands of modern European philosophy.

René Descartes publishes his *Discours de la méthode* at Leyden.

1638 The future Louis XIV is born at St-Germain-en-Laye (5 September).

Rouen merchants establish a trading post in **Senegal**. After a troubled start, it will become a centre for the French **slave trade** to America.

1639 The revolt of the '*nu-pieds*' against a rumoured imposition of the **salt tax** on areas previously exempt spreads through **Normandy**. Richelieu hires foreign mercenaries to crush it. In the following year, Chancellor **Séguier** takes up residence in Rouen to dispense exemplary justice to the rebels.

A royal decree of 26 November forbids **secret marriages** and reaffirms the requirement for parental consent.

1640 Louis overhauls the monetary system, introducing the **louis d'or** (gold louis).

Richelieu establishes the **Royal Printing House** in the Louvre.

Yielding to royal pressure, the painter **Nicolas Poussin** returns to Paris from Italy.

1641 Louis issues an **edict** (21 February) restricting the powers of the *Parlement* to intervene in affairs of state. Though the functions of the *parlements* around France are primarily judicial, with the Paris *Parlement* acting as the supreme court of law, the Paris magistrates have one important source of political power: their **right of remonstrance** enables them to prevent royal decrees from being registered. Louis' move to check this is part of an ongoing struggle that will be central to the years leading up to the Revolution.

1642 Louis' favourite, the **marquis de Cinq-Mars**, is beheaded on 12 September for his involvement in treasonable negotiations with Spain.

Death of Richelieu (4 December). His place in the Council of Ministers is taken by **Jules Mazarin**, appointed Cardinal the previous year.

1642–43 **Blaise Pascal** invents a form of calculator.

1643 **Michel Le Tellier** is made Secretary of State for War, a post he holds for over 40 years, during which time he

Blaise Pascal

Mathematician, scientist, philosopher and writer, **Pascal** (1623–62) displayed the kind of genius that can flourish only in a world undivided into specialisms. The son of a provincial magistrate, he showed a precocious talent for mathematics which resulted in the **calculator** that was to be the main basis of his celebrity during his lifetime. From 1651 to 1654 he divided his time between the Paris salons and a series of experiments into the nature of liquids and the density of air.

On the night of 23 November, 1654, Pascal underwent a mystical experience that was to change his life, prompting him to enter the monastery of **Port-Royal** in January of the following year. Thereafter he wrote only at the behest of the monastic authorities. His eighteen *Lettres provinciales* (1656–57), written in defence of the Jansenist **Antoine Arnauld**, who was under threat from the Sorbonne, are both a defence of Jansenism and a skilful dissection of some of the moral evasions of the Jesuits. The popularity of the work, burnt by the public executioner in 1660 on Louis XIV's orders, made it a powerful challenge to Counter-Reformation orthodoxy.

Pascal's *Apologie de la religion chrétienne* was never completed, but the fragments later published as his *Pensées* have remained his most lasting monument. It was in them that he formulated the argument for belief in God that has become known as **Pascal's wager**: if the sceptic gambles on believing in the existence of God and turns out to be wrong, nothing is lost; if, on the other hand, God does exist, the payoff is eternal life. Pascal's own faith had to endure a cruel illness that killed him on 19 August, 1662.

transforms the French army into the most formidable military force in Europe.

A royal decree of 16 April extends the powers of the police, the judiciary and the treasury.

Louis XIII dies at St-Germain-en-Laye (14 May), and is succeeded by **Louis XIV**, with Anne of Austria as regent. Mazarin is confirmed as chief minister.

On 19 May, in a remarkable display of military tactics and personal bravery, the duc d'Enghien, the future **Grand Condé**, defeats the Spanish forces that have attacked Rocroi, hoping to take advantage of Louis' death to march on Paris.

Molière (Jean-Baptiste Poquelin) founds the *Illustre Théâtre*.

1644 **Popular unrest** spreads through southern France.

At Marseille, **coffee** is imported from Turkey for the first time.

1645 **Jean-Baptiste Colbert** begins his rise to power as an assistant to Le Tellier. The prosecution of the war imposes an increasing burden of taxation, exacerbated by the poor harvests which lead to famine later in the decade.

Mazarin introduces **Italian opera** to Paris with a production of Luigi Rossi's *Orfeo* at the Palais-Royal.

1648 Simmering discontent at the rise in taxes and the erosion of civil liberties boils over into a confrontation between the *Parlement* and the monarchy. A particular source of disquiet is the wide-ranging power of the *'intendants'*. Since France's entry into the Thirty Years War, these centrally appointed administrators have played an increasingly intrusive role throughout the kingdom, taking over many of the powers of the provincial governors. In consequence they are much resented by local *parlements* and other forms of provincial administration. After a period of apparent compromise (26–28 August), Mazarin suddenly arrests **Broussel**, one of the leaders of the Paris *Parlement*, precipitating the two days of barricades that mark the beginning of the parliamentary Fronde. The term Fronde (*fronde* = sling or catapult – a weapon favoured by lawless Parisian children) refers specifically to the rebellions by *Parlement* and the nobility between 1648 and 1653.

On 24 October the **treaties of Westphalia** bring the Thirty Years War to an end with agreements that broadly strengthen the position of Sweden and France while weakening that of the Habsburg emperor.

1649 In January the royal family flee Paris. Mazarin besieges the city with an army led by Condé. On 1 April, peace is agreed between Mazarin and the Fronde. Louis XIV returns to Paris on 18 August, but there are already signs of future unrest, particularly from Condé, who now heads a faction of the nobility intent on depriving Mazarin of power.

Mlle de Scudéry begins publication of her *Artamène ou le Grand Cyrus* (1649–53), a massive novel in ten volumes which enjoys huge success.

1650 The arrest of Condé, his brother and brother-in-law precipitates the **princes' Fronde**. The court shifts from province to province in a desperate attempt to quell revolt and rally support.

1651 In January the princes' Fronde joins forces with the parliamentary Fronde, driving Mazarin out of Paris at the beginning of February. On 7 September, the 13-year-old king's majority is declared. Royal forces under **Turenne** are dispatched to fight Condé, who has raised an army in **Aquitaine**.

1652 Condé, defeated, flees to Brussels and takes service with the Spanish. On 21 October, the king re-enters Paris and immediately sets about restricting parliamentary power.

1653 Mazarin returns to Paris. **Nicolas Fouquet** is appointed joint Superintendent of Finances. By the end of the year, *intendants* are re-established throughout the kingdom. Answering only to the king and his principal minister, they become a prominent feature of Louis' system of government.

Jansenism

Taking its name from the Dutch bishop and theologian **Cornelius Jansen**, this Roman Catholic movement embraced the doctrines set out in his posthumous *Augustinus* (1640), which challenged the direction given to the Counter-Reformation by the Jesuits. In particular, the Jansenists emphasised the doctrine of **Original Sin**, accepting the concept of **predestination** and arguing that salvation was by **divine grace** rather than by human effort. In some respects this was a revival of the 5th-century controversy between St Augustine and Pelagius, but from the perspective of the Counter-Reformation the Jansenist return to Augustine's teaching now smacked of Calvinist heresy.

More troubling to government ministers was the moral rigour that made Jansenism independent of the concerns of the state. Richelieu and Mazarin wanted a Catholicism that could accommodate itself to the political needs of the moment – in accepting, for example, France's Protestant alliances during the Thirty Years War. The suppleness of the **Jesuits**, regarded by Jansenism as casuistry, was more congenial to the smooth operation of state policy. This was the start of a century of persecution, directed above all against the convent of **Port-Royal**, whose director, the **abbé de St-Cyran**, had made it the headquarters of Jansenist thought.

In spite of papal condemnation and the destruction of Port-Royal by Louis XIV, the influence of Jansenism persisted. Throughout his reign Louis XV continued to struggle against it, often in conflict with a *Parlement* that had strong Jansenist sympathies. Largely a spent force by the time of the Revolution, Jansenism survived into the 19th and 20th centuries as an ideal of moral integrity and spiritual independence.

'Le Roi Soleil'. Louis XIV in the role of Apollo – the source of his nickname

Pope Innocent X issues a papal bull condemning **Jansenism**.

Louis XIV appears as the sun god, Apollo, in Lully's *Le ballet de la nuit*, a performance which gives rise to his nickname **'Le Roi Soleil'**.

1654 Louis XIV is crowned at Reims. On the death of Jacques Lemercier, **Louis Le Vau** becomes the king's chief architect.

1655 On 13 April Louis holds a *lit de justice* to impose his financial edicts on a refractory *Parlement*. (It is on this occasion that he supposedly declares, *'L'État c'est moi'*.) These special sessions in which the king asserts his royal dominance over *Parlement* are later abandoned by Louis, who in 1673 withdraws the right of remonstrance altogether.

1656 In April the creation of the **General Hospital** in Paris provides a convenient means of containing the poor, who are ordered into it the following year. Similar establishments spread to the provinces. A decree is promulgated against begging.

1656–61 Fouquet begins building the great château at **Vaux-le-Vicomte** whose magnificence will contribute to his downfall.

1657 The treaty of Paris, arranged by Mazarin, allies France with **Cromwell**'s England against Spain.

1658 The **vicomte de Turenne** defeats Spanish forces allied with those of Condé at the **battle of the Dunes** (14 June), opening the way to the treaty signed in the following year.

1659 Fouquet takes over as sole **superintendent of Finances**.

The **treaty of the Pyrenees** (7 November) brings to an end a quarter of a century of hostility between France and Spain. Its central plank is the marriage of Louis XIV to the infanta of Spain, **Marie Thérèse**.

On 18 November, *Les Précieuses ridicules* enjoys a triumphant opening that marks the start of **Molière**'s success. Presented at court, it is seen three times by the king.

1660 Louis XIV marries Marie Thérèse (9 June).

1660–22 Persistently poor harvests result in **famines** severe enough to affect the population level.

1661 Mazarin dies on 9 March, the day after **Colbert** is appointed *intendant* of finances.

From the death of Mazarin to the Revolution 1661–1789

Thanks largely to the work of Richelieu and Mazarin, **Louis XIV** had a stable platform from which to launch his plans for a stronger France, and these were inextricable from his plans for a stronger French king. The troubles of the **Frondes** had broken out when Louis was 10, leaving the consequences of a recalcitrant *Parlement* and an over-powerful aristocracy etched in his mind. Accordingly, he chose his advisers – men like **Colbert** and **Le Tellier** – from the bourgeoisie rather than the nobility, and set about imposing royal authority with a determination that was to give France the most **absolute monarchy** in Europe. Everything proclaimed the same end, from the architecture of **Versailles** to a system of government that relied on ministers and administrators appointed by the king, dependent on the king, and answerable only to the king. The nobility was hobbled, the power of the *Parlement* to resist royal edicts was suppressed.

On the diplomatic front, Louis' **expansionist policy** seemed to be paying off. By the end of the **Dutch War**, France had secured its northern and northeastern borders. Across the same period the country was seeing a radical overhaul of its infrastructure. New roads and canals were built, new industries were started up, trade expanded both in Europe and overseas, a newly confident bourgeoisie grew and prospered. The rash of academies established to promote dance (1661), the sciences (1666), architecture (1671) and music (1672) were evidence of the ascendancy of **French culture**. In spite of numerous restrictions, the French publishing industry was on the way to becoming a dynamic force in the economy. But then came another age of costly, futile warfare, bleeding away the benefits of increased prosperity. First the **War of the League of Augsburg** and then the **War of the Spanish Succession** took their toll, pushing up taxes, stripping away the nation's overseas possessions, demoralising the population. By the time Louis died, France, which accounted for almost a quarter of the population of Europe, may not have been, as the preacher Fénelon claimed, 'just one great desolate hospital lacking provisions', but it had suffered a serious decline.

The rejoicing that greeted **Louis XV**'s accession did not last. More unprofitable foreign wars, more taxes, more suppression of dissent made him in the second half of his reign as unpopular as his predecessor. His occasional spasms of misdirected energy, as in his efforts to stamp out **Jansenism**, were if anything more damaging than his indolent pursuit of pleasure. Hampered by opposition from the privileged classes, a succession of more or less able ministers could make little impact on a worsening financial situation. By 1789 the well-meaning stupidity of **Louis XVI** had pushed crisis to the edge of revolution; the *ancien régime* was facing extinction.

But meanwhile France had enjoyed an extraordinary surge of cultural activity. This span of 130 years takes in many of the greatest artists and intellectuals in French history: in the theatre, Molière and Racine; in philosophy, Diderot, Voltaire and Rousseau; in painting, Watteau, Boucher and Fragonard;

in music, Lully, Couperin and Rameau; in science, Réaumur, Buffon and Lavoisier. These few names alone are an astonishing roll call that more than confirms France's dominant position in the culture of 17th- and 18th-century Europe.

1661 Louis begins to govern in his own right, reshaping the **High Council** to consist of three ministers who advise the king on all important matters of state and keep under review the decisions of subordinate councils.

On 5 September, three weeks after a lavish fête at his newly constructed château of Vaux-le-Vicomte, **Fouquet** is arrested on charges of corruption laid by **Colbert**. But the magnificence of his château has not been lost on the king. The team Fouquet has assembled – **Louis Le Vau** as architect, **Charles Le Brun** for design and decoration, **André Le Nôtre** in charge of landscaping – are recruited for work on **Versailles**.

Jean-Baptiste Lully is appointed master of the king's music.

1662 From May to July peasants in the region of **Boulogne** and **Calais** revolt against the *taille* – a tax to which only commoners are liable, because they do not bear arms.

On 27 November **Dunkirk** is bought back from Charles II of England for five million *livres*.

> [Louis XIV] was conscious that the substantial favours he had to bestow were not nearly sufficient to produce a continual effect; he had therefore to invent imaginary ones, and no one was so clever in devising petty distinctions and preferences which aroused jealousy and emulation.
>
> Saint-Simon, *Memoirs* (1788)

1663 In March **Bossuet** (1627–1704) preaches before Louis XIV. He will become a key figure in the spiritual life of the court, not least as an eloquent apologist for the ideology of absolutism.

Le Brun restores the **galerie d'Apollon** in the Louvre after a fire.

1664 Between May and August Colbert founds the *Compagnie des Indes orientales* and the *Compagnie des Indes occidentales*. His concern to expand France's commercial reach will lead him in 1669 to permit nobles to engage in maritime trade without losing their privileges. Two years later this will be extended to wholesale trade.

The **duc de La Rochefoucauld**'s *Maximes* are published. Worldly, cynical and formulated with consummate elegance, they are too honest not to be thought scandalous.

Molière's *Tartuffe* mounts a witty attack on the hypocrisy of elements among the *dévots,* who succeed in getting the play banned until 1669.

> **❝** We all have enough strength to bear the misfortunes of others. (19)
>
> One is never so happy or so unhappy as one thinks. (49)
>
> Hypocrisy is a homage vice pays to virtue. (218)
>
> Too much haste in repaying a favour is a form of ingratitude. (226)
>
> We often forgive those who bore us but never those who find us boring. (304)
>
> We acknowledge our small failings only to persuade people that we have no large ones. (327)
>
> In the misfortunes of our best friends, we always find something that does not displease us. (583) **❞**
>
> La Rochefoucauld, *Maximes* (1664)

1665 Colbert becomes **controller general of finances**.

1666 On 22 December Colbert establishes the *Académie des sciences*.

1666–81 The construction of the **Canal du Midi** links the Atlantic and the Mediterranean – a superb feat of engineering that transforms the economy of the **Languedoc**. This is one step in a general upgrading of the infrastructure, which, by improving food distribution, contributes to a marked population rise in the 18th century.

1667 In March, the *lieutenance générale de Police* is created in Paris, under the direction of **Gabriel Nicolas de La Reynie**. La Reynie will exercise wide powers of social control and surveillance. His brief to maintain public order also leads to improvements in the capital's lighting and paving.

Mme de Montespan replaces Louise de La Vallière as the king's *maîtresse en titre*.

Following the death of the king of Spain in 1665, Louis presses the claims of his wife Marie-Thérèse to the **Spanish Netherlands** (modern Belgium) on the basis of Devolution, the local custom by which daughters of a first marriage can inherit lands in preference to sons of a subsequent mariage. This marks the beginning of the **War of Devolution**.

The **Gobelins** is established by Colbert as the 'Royal Manufactory of Furnishings to the Crown', with Charles Le Brun at its head. Apart from the **tapestry weavers** responsible for its fame, it initially houses the workshops of cabinet-makers, gold- and silversmiths, and other artisans.

1667–72 The **Paris Observatory** is built. Under the direction of **Jean-Dominique Cassini**, it will play an important part in making the calculations about longitude necessary for France to become a maritime power.

1668 Resorting to diplomacy, perhaps in fear of retaliation from England and Holland, Louis negotiates the treaty of **Aix-la-Chapelle** (2 May), which brings the War of Devolution to an end, leaving France in possession of a number of Flemish towns, including Lille and Douai.

In September the Jansenist controversy is temporarily resolved by the '**Paix de l'Eglise**', a settlement based on various statements agreed by Jansenist theologians, the Crown and the pope.

Boileau's first nine *Satires* and **La Fontaine**'s first collection of *Fables* are published.

1670 Bossuet is appointed tutor to the 8-year-old dauphin.

Libéral Bruant is commissioned to build the **Hôtel des Invalides** in Paris.

1672 Louis initiates the **Dutch War** by invading Holland, partly in retribution for Dutch opposition in the War of Devolution, partly in pursuit of a generally expansionist foreign policy.

Lully's increasing control of French music is consolidated by his purchase of the exclusive right to produce opera.

1673 Spain joins an alliance with Germany and Holland against France, but over the next five years French forces maintain the upper hand with a series of victories at **Seneffe** (1674), **Turckheim** (1675), **Palermo** (1676) and **Cassel** (1677).

The musketeer **d'Artagnan**, later made famous by Alexandre Dumas, dies at the **siege of Maastricht**.

1673–74 The French establish a trading settlement in **India** at Pondicherry.

1675 The Jesuit **La Chaise** becomes Louis XIV's confessor.

The **marquis de Louvois** (1641–91), groomed for power by his father Le Tellier, overhauls the army's system of promotion, allowing commoners access to the highest ranks. As Louis' minister of war, Louvois will introduce the bayonet, standardize military uniform and oversee strategy for the next fifteen years. Together with his father, he builds an army of some 400,000 men, but at huge cost to the public purse.

Between April and October an uprising in **Brittany** against new taxes and government interference coincides with the revolt of the **'red bonnets'** in the countryside, where peasants are claiming new rights.

1676 On 17 July the **marquise de Brinvilliers**, who has poisoned numerous members of her family in pursuit of an inheritance, is beheaded and burnt the day after her conviction. The subsequent police investigation reveals the **'Affair of the Poisons'**, centring on Catherine Deshayes, known as **La Voisin**. In one of the great scandals of the 17th century, an extraordinary web of witchcraft and murder is uncovered that implicates Mme de Montespan in attempts to win back the king's favour through black magic. La Voisin will be executed in February 1680. By the time Louis puts a stop to further investigations, seven months later, 34 others have been executed and 150 more are waiting to appear before the tribunal. They are consigned to various dungeons for the rest of their lives.

1677 The failure of **Racine**'s *Phèdre*, as a result of a cabal against it, is followed by the author's decision to abandon writing for the stage. (At the prompting of Mme de Maintenon, he will later write *Esther* and *Athalie* for the pupils of her school at St-Cyr.) In October, he and Boileau are appointed royal historiographers.

1678 The war with Holland is brought to an end by the **treaties of Nijmegen**. France returns Maastricht to the Dutch and surrenders its footholds in the Spanish Netherlands but gains Artois and the Franche-Comté from Spain. This provides a more defensible northeastern frontier at a safer distance from Paris. Designated commissioner general of Fortifications, **Sébastien Vauban** (1633–1702), the foremost military engineer of his age, is given the job of defending France's borders with a line of fortifications.

Le Brun begins his decoration of the **Galerie des Glaces** at Versailles.

Mme de La Fayette publishes her novel *La Princesse de Clèves*.

The 17th-century theatre

The founding of the **Comédie-Française** in 1680 was in one sense yet another symptom of the relentless centralization that marked the reign of Louis XIV. **Molière**'s old troupe in the Palais-Royal had already merged by royal command with the company in the Marais to which **Corneille** had been attached. To form the Comédie-Française, Louis now ordered a further merger with the company based in the former Hôtel de Bourgogne which had presented many of **Racine**'s plays, including *Andromaque, Bérénice,* and *Phèdre*. But this act of royal patronage also reflected the growing status of drama as an aristocratic entertainment. Molière's work was performed at Versailles, and *Bérénice*, dedicated to Colbert, had been staged privately for the queen.

French drama, in the hands of Corneille and Racine, was not primarily a popular art form in the manner of the English theatre. With its emphasis on the **classical unities** of time, place and action, it appealed above all to a privileged elite, who could savour the eternal conflict between passion and reason, desire and duty, expressed in elegant verse that bridled emotion within the formal constraints of the **twelve-syllable alexandrine**. As in the Greek plays that were their models, the great works of French classical drama offered no sensational acts on stage. That Phèdre should so much as sit down is an indication of almost intolerable turmoil. Such drama was the product of a highly sophisticated culture, but also, perhaps, of a culture that had invested much in suppressing unwelcome passion.

In his last play, *Le malade imaginaire* (1673) Molière ridiculed the medical profession. By a strange irony, he died while playing the role of the hypochondriac, Argand

1679 The physicist **Denis Papon** invents a form of pressure cooker. His work on air pressure will later result in his design for the first practical steam engine.

1680 Marriages between Catholics and Protestants are prohibited.

The king founds the **Comédie-Française**.

1681 Louvois authorises the *'dragonnades'*. Dragoons are billeted on Protestant households in southern France, where they behave with an unchecked brutality that the inhabitants can only escape by converting to Catholicism. It is a policy that betrays the failure of Louis' attempts over the previous twenty years to stifle Protestantism by increasing the restrictions and exclusions to which its adherents are liable.

The Palace of Versailles

The rationale for spending over sixty million *livres* on **Versailles** was provided by **Colbert** when he remarked that buildings came next after battles as a way of increasing a king's prestige. More obviously than anything else, this massive palace reflects Louis' use of architecture for the purpose of self-aggrandizement. Versailles, with its ubiquitous **sun motif**, was designed to make a transcendent statement about the greatness of the French monarchy. Work began in 1661 and continued, at a pace that fluctuated according to the nation's finances, for the next fifty years. When **Louis Le Vau**, the chief architect, died in 1670, his position was filled for a time by one of his pupils, but it was **Hardouin-Mansart** who oversaw the project in the later years of the century. His *Galerie des Glaces* (Hall of Mirrors), where the treaty of Versailles was signed on 28 June, 1919, under the magnificent ceiling by **Le Brun**, remains one of the glories of the palace.

Once Louis had transplanted his court to Versailles, it became the focus for the elaborate system of **etiquette**, bounded by the ceremonies of the *lever* and the *coucher*, through which the king affirmed his semi-divine status and absorbed the energies of his courtiers. Only in the park, created by **André Le Nôtre**, was there a chance to escape the suffocating pressure of ritual, and it was here that Louis, at the request of his wife Mme de Maintenon, built the miniature palace of the **Grand Trianon** as a place of refuge. A monument to the power and glory of the Sun King, Versailles is, like its creator, both a marvel and a monster.

The Cour de Marbre (Marble Court) forms the heart of the Versailles complex. Designed by Philibert Le Roy in 1631, the façade was later ornamented by Louis Le Vau and Hardouin-Mansart

In September, the French seize **Strasbourg**. This is the culmination of Louis' 'reunion' policy, initiated two years earlier, which consists of claiming sovereignty, on dubious legal grounds, over the dependencies of his territories in Alsace, Lorraine and the Franche-Comté.

The creation of the *Ferme générale* unifies the system of tax farming by which the right to collect indirect taxes is sold to private individuals who pay the king a fixed amount based on expected revenues and can then enrich themselves by pocketing whatever they collect in excess of that sum.

On 1 October **Jules Hardouin-Mansart** is appointed royal architect.

1682 The Assembly of the clergy endorses Bossuet's *Déclaration des Quatre Articles*, which sets out the principles of **Gallicanism**, according to which the Church of France owes primary allegiance to the king rather than the pope.

Louis and his court move to Versailles, still under construction.

In the same year, **Robert Cavelier de La Salle** sails down the Mississippi and founds **Louisiana**.

1683 Death of Colbert (6 September).

In October, less than three months after the death of Marie-Thérèse, the king secretly marries **Mme de Maintenon** (1635–1719), the former governess of his illegitimate children by Mme de Montespan. Her Catholic piety exercises an austere influence on the court and fuels persecution of the Protestants.

Inordinately expensive works to supply water to **Versailles** are undertaken and will continue for the next ten years without being completed.

1684 In a move symptomatic of growing state authoritarianism, Louis extends to fathers the right to use *lettres de cachet*. Over the next century, this system, which allows those considered troublesome to be imprisoned by royal warrant without recourse to the normal judicial procedures, will be used with increasing arbitrariness as a way of suppressing political opposition.

1685 The '*Code Noir*' regulates the treatment of slaves.

In October the **Edict of Fontainebleau** revokes the Edict of Nantes, thus ending the limited toleration of Protestants. The resulting exodus of some quarter of a million Huguenots, who take with them a range of commercial, professional and manufacturing skills, leaves France impoverished economically and socially.

1686 From 28 to 29 May the '*grand carrousel*' is held at Versailles. In retrospect, this lavish festivity will mark the end of the glory days of France in the 17th century.

Austria, Spain, Sweden and the German princes, alarmed by France's aggressive foreign policy, form the **League of Augsburg** against Louis (9 September).

In Paris, the new **café Procope** in the rue des Fossés-St-Germain enjoys a popular success that heralds the start of a cultural trend.

1687–89 Hardouin-Mansart builds the **Grand Trianon**.

1688–97 The **War of the League of Augsburg** pits France against the alliance formed two years earlier. The brutality with which French forces, under the direction of **Louvois**, ravage the Rhineland helps to bring England and Holland into the war on the side of the alliance. In a conflict that widens to include the combatants' overseas colonies, France holds her own against the rest of Europe but achieves little.

1688 Jean de **La Bruyère**'s *Les Caractères*, an immediate success on publication, offers a devastating analysis of the social types created by the cross-currents of vanity, ambition, envy and lust in contemporary life.

> **❝** There are only three events in the life of man: to be born, to live, and to die. He is not conscious of being born, he suffers in dying and he forgets to live.
>
> The people have little intelligence, the great no heart ... If I had to choose, I would have no hesitation in wishing to be of the people.
>
> Everything has been said, and we are too late by more than seven thousand years of human life and thought. **❞**
>
> La Bruyère, from *Les Caractères* (1688)

1690 The composer **François Couperin** (1668–1733) publishes his *Pièces d'orgue*. Appointed court organist in 1693, he will become famous for his harpsichord compositions, uniting the French and Italian styles.

1693–94 A terrible winter followed by a poor harvest leads to **widespread famine**, almost doubling the normal mortality rate.

1694 The first edition of the *Dictionnaire de l'Académie française*, designed to set standards of good usage in the French language, is presented to the king.

1695 To finance the war, a **poll tax** is introduced which is supposed to be paid by all subjects, overriding the traditional exemptions enjoyed by privileged groups.

1697 The **treaties of Ryswick** (September–October) bring the War of the League of Augsburg to an end. France retains Strasbourg but surrenders most of the other territories acquired since the beginning of the reunion policy in 1679.

1700 Following the death of **Charles II** of Spain, Louis' grandson becomes king of Spain as **Philip V**, precipitating an international crisis. Although Charles II's will has appointed Philip his successor, the Holy Roman Emperor **Leopold I** presses the claim of his younger son, the archduke Charles. By accepting the provisions of Charles's will, Louis moves towards war with the Austrian Habsburgs.

1701–14 The **War of the Spanish Succession**.

1702 On 24 July the murder of the unpopular **abbé du Chaila** at Pont-de-Montvert launches the uprising of the *camisards* in the **Cévennes** against religious oppression.

The War of the Spanish Succession

France and **Spain**, with the support of the **electors of Bavaria** and **Cologne**, faced an alliance of **Austria**, most of the **German princes**, **England** and **Holland**. For once, Louis was not eager for war, but he had built up an impressive list of enemies – by supporting the claims of James Edward Stuart (the Old Pretender) against William III of England, by seizing Dutch border fortresses, and by demanding a monopoly on the lucrative Spanish trade with its American colonies. Linked to his dread of seeing an Austrian Habsburg back on the throne of Spain, there was enough material here to stoke the flames of war.

After a series of crushing defeats at **Blenheim** (1704), **Ramillies** (1706) and **Oudenarde** (1708), Louis was looking for peace, but the uncompromising stance of his enemies forced a continuation of the war, which in the end gave France the chance to stage a partial recovery. A decisive victory over coalition forces at the battle of **Denain** (24 July, 1712) staved off invasion and opened the way to a settlement. Under the **treaties of Utrecht** (11 April, 1713) and **Rastadt** (6 March, 1714) France lost most of her American colonies to England, but she maintained her national frontiers. As for the original cause of war, Louis' grandson was allowed to keep the throne of Spain, though with its foreign territories in Europe much reduced.

Working-class Protestants, they wage a form of guerrilla warfare that enables 4000 men to keep 20,000 soldiers engaged for the next two years. In spite of mass deportations from the area and a policy of harsh reprisals against the local population, it is not until late 1704 that the revolt is effectively suppressed, and even then periodic outbreaks continue for another six years.

1703 On 19 November the so-called **'Man in the Iron Mask'** dies in the Bastille after five years of imprisonment. (The mask was actually of velvet, but the mystery surrounding its wearer remains impenetrable.)

1704 To pay for the costly wars, **taxes increase**. Their burden exacerbates the effect of a second hard winter.

1709 Throughout January and February **famine** in the midst of a severe winter sets off widespread rioting.

The religious community of **Port-Royal** is dispersed on the orders of the king, and over the next two years the abbey buildings are razed.

1710 Louis d'Anjou, the future Louis XV, great-grandson of the king, is born at Versailles.

1711 Monseigneur, the Grand Dauphin, heir to the throne, dies of smallpox during an epidemic which sweeps the country.

1712 The **smallpox epidemic** kills in succession the second and third dauphins, leaving the young Louis d'Anjou heir to the throne.

1713 At the behest of Louis, Clement XI issues the papal bull *Unigenitus*, condemning **Jansenism**. It excites strong opposition, becoming a source of friction later in the century between Louis XV and the *Parlement*.

1715 Louis XIV dies at Versailles and is succeeded by his 5-year-old great-grandson, who reigns as **Louis XV**. In exchange for the return of its right to remonstrate against royal decrees, *Parlement* overrules the late king's will, which had provided for a council to take over the government during Louis XV's minority, and appoints **Philippe d'Orléans** as regent. He begins his regency by replacing ministers with a system of councils, each made up of seven members of the old nobility.

1716 Faced with the catastrophic **public debt** bequeathed by Louis XIV, the regent accepts a scheme proposed by the Scottish financier **John Law** to found a **national bank** that will relaunch the economy on the basis of paper money guaranteed by the state and backed by the riches expected to flow from the colonization of Louisiana.

1717 Peter the Great of Russia is received in fabulous style by the regent and Louis XV.

François Couperin is appointed court harpsichordist; in the same year he publishes his influential keyboard treatise *L'Art de toucher le clavecin*.

1718 New Orleans is founded in Louisiana, of which it will become the capital in 1722.

1720 After spectacular success, which has taken Law to the position of controller general of finances, his bank collapses. Law himself flees to Brussels, leaving behind him riots and **financial crisis**. Ironically, the bankruptcy that ruins so many families also has the effect, by clearing the weight of public debt, of providing the foundation for economic recovery.

1720–21 After gaining a foothold in Marseille in June 1720, **plague** spreads through Provence, ravaging the cities of Aix, Toulon and Arles. Of the population of Provence, 37 percent fall victim to the scourge, but it is prevented from spreading beyond the southeast by a ruthless policy of isolation that demonstrates the power of state organization.

1721 The Turkish ambassador is received by the king. In the same year, Montesquieu's *Lettres persanes* reflects both an exotic sense of a widening world and also sharp misgivings about social and political conditions in France itself.

Rococo

By the time of his death, Louis XIV was an unpopular king. The oppressive weight of his sovereignty was felt in everything from the burden of taxation to the monumental architecture of Versailles. It was in part as a reaction against this that the **rococo style** came to define a central aspect of the reign of his successor. Its origins, however, lie in the closing years of the Sun King. The chapel of Versailles itself, designed by **Pierre Le Pautre**, is an example of the beginnings of the new style. Lightness of touch in form, colour and decoration is the keynote of rococo. Against the pompous symmetry of the baroque, it set a more playful arrangement of curls and curves, characteristically decorated in white and gold. It was a style that painters such as **Watteau**, **Boucher** and later **Fragonard** developed into a captivating reflection of court life in the France of Louis XV.

The triviality of rococo subject matter is balanced by the delicacy of the execution, the frivolity by the lurking sense of fragility. 'No one who was not alive before 1789 knows the true meaning of *douceur de vivre*,' remarked Talleyrand, and it is impossible now to look at the painting and architecure of the rococo without an awareness of what the end of the century would bring. The scenes we glimpse in Watteau's *Les Champs Elysées* or Fragonard's *The Swing* have about them the transient beauty of a world only a few steps from annihilation. And this is perhaps partly why a label that was initially coined as a term of contempt quickly acquired a different kind of resonance. From France rococo spread to other European countries and beyond, particularly to Spain, Italy and the Catholic regions of the north, as well as to Russia, but its spiritual home was the French court of Mme de Pompadour.

The Swing (1767) by Jean-Honoré Fragonard epitomizes both the delicacy and frivolity of rococo painting

1722 The 4-year-old Spanish infanta, **Mariana**, is installed in the Louvre, following the signing of a marriage contract between her and Louis XV the previous year.

Louis is crowned at Reims (25 October).

René Réaumur (1683–1757) publishes *L'Art de convertir le fer forgé en acier* (*The Art of Turning Wrought Iron into Steel*), which has a significant influence on the development of the modern steel industry.

1723 At 13, Louis reaches his majority but retains the duc d'Orléans as his chief minister until the latter's death in December, when he is succeeded by the **duc de Bourbon**.

Restrictions on booksellers are introduced to regulate the circulation of printed material in Paris.

1724 **Begging** is curbed by a decree ordering the detention of the poor who are sick and the setting to work of those who are not.

1725 The infanta, who will be too young to bear children for some years, is sent back to Spain on the advice of the duc de Bourbon. Louis is presented with a new fiancée, **Marie Leszczynska**, daughter of the dethroned king of Poland. He marries her at Fontainebleau on 5 September.

1726 Louis undertakes to govern on his own, but much of the administrative power passes to his former tutor, the 73-year-old **André Hercule Fleury** (1653–1743), who becomes a cardinal in the same year. He exercises a stabilizing influence on financial and foreign policy until his death.

1729 Birth of the dauphin **Louis** (4 September).

In November the **treaty of Seville**, engineered by Fleury, temporarily eases the underlying tensions between France, England, Spain and Holland.

1730–32 Conflict between king and *Parlement* again flares up over the **Jansenist question**, when Fleury insists that the papal Bull *Unigenitus* be registered. In 1732 a total of 125 Jansenist members of the *Parlement* are exiled and then recalled.

1731 The **Abbé Prevost**'s novel *Manon Lescaut* foreshadows, in its stress on passion and sensibility, some of the later concerns of Rousseau and the Romantics.

1733 The death of the Polish king, **Augustus II**, leads to a succession crisis. When the candidature of Louis' father-in-law, Stanislas Leszczynski, is opposed by an Austro-Russian alliance, France is drawn into what becomes the **War of the Polish Succession**.

Rameau's first opera, *Hippolyte et Aricie*, challenges the model for French opera established by Lully with a work of heightened emotional power and harmonic daring.

1733–38 The cost of the war brings new taxes and the increased sale of offices and land titles. The *dixième*, a ten percent tax on all revenues, first imposed in 1710 to finance the War of the Spanish Succession, is reintroduced.

1735 François Boucher decorates the queen's room at Versailles.

1738 The **treaty of Vienna** (18 November) brings the War of the Polish Succession to an end. France gains the prospect of Lorraine, which will be inherited by Louis' wife on the death of her father.

1740–48 The death of the Holy Roman Emperor **Charles VI** (20 October, 1740) results in the **War of the Austrian Succession**. This complicated knot of European wars has three central strands: the Prussian emperor Frederick II's designs on the Austrian empire, which Charles VI has willed to his (Charles's) daughter Maria Theresa; France's age-old antipathy for the Austrian Habsburgs; and England's fears of French hegemony in Europe.

1743 The death of **Cardinal Fleury** (29 January) marks the beginning of Louis XV's personal reign.

1744 The regulations governing Paris booksellers are extended to cover the whole kingdom.

In Lyon, an uprising of **silk weavers**, angered by government restructuring and the threat of mechanization, is harshly suppressed. At about the same time, **Jacques de Vaucanson** is devising the first automatic silk loom.

1745 The French army, commanded by maréchal de Saxe and with Louis XV at its head, wins a celebrated victory over coalition forces of England, Holland, Austria and Hanover at the **battle of Fontenoy** (11 May).

Mme de Pompadour (1721–64) wins the favour of Louis XV and as *maîtresse en titre* immediately begins to exercise political influence. By the end of the year she has contrived the disgrace of the finance minister, **Philibert Orry**, and has set about finding places for her relations.

1746 The resumption of the *dragonnades* against Protestants in La Rochelle and Montauban signals a new wave of **religious oppression**.

Diderot publishes his *Pensées philosophiques*.

1748 On 28 October the **treaty of Aix-la-Chapelle** brings the War of the Austrian Succession to an end, leaving **Maria Theresa** in possession of most of her inheritance. On the Prussian side, Frederick II has gained Silesia. Louis XV, however, in a gesture that dismays French public opinion, hands back his conquests in the Austrian Netherlands to Maria Theresa. This clears the way for new political alignments but marks the end of Louis' period as '*le Bien-Aimé*' (the Well-Loved). An expensive war has brought no perceptible gain to France.

Montesquieu publishes his *Esprit des lois*.

1749 Machault d'Arnouville, controller general of finances, tries to impose the *vingtième* (a five percent tax) in place of the *dixième*, but with the provision that it should be collected on all revenues. This provokes resistance from clergy and *Parlement*.

Montesquieu

Born into a noble family in the Bordeaux region, **Charles Louis de Secondat, baron de La Brède et de Montesquieu** (1689–1755) trained as a lawyer and then married a wealthy Protestant woman before inheriting a comfortable estate from his uncle, along with the office of deputy president of the Bordeaux *Parlement*. In the event, he showed little enthusiasm for his wife and even less for a career in the law. His passion was study, and its chief fruits were the two works on which his fame rests. In 1721 he published (anonymously) the *Lettres persanes*, presented as a series of letters between two Persian travellers in Europe and their correspondents in Asia. It was a witty, iconoclastic satire on the institutions of contemporary France that spared neither court, church nor monarchy. When its authorship became known, Montesquieu enjoyed a celebrity that plunged him into the social and intellectual pleasures of salon life in the capital.

In 1728 Montesquieu left Paris for three years of travel that took him to Vienna, Hungary, Italy and England to meet statesmen, observe institutions, sample cultures and generally equip himself to write the book that finally appeared in 1748 as *De l'esprit des lois*. In short, clearly written sections, Montesquieu considers the principles that underlie human laws, examining different forms of government, making an influential case for the separation of legislative, executive and judicial powers, and discussing the effect of climate on attitudes and behaviour. It was a luminous, wide-ranging work that earned him the admiration of political thinkers across Europe and the enmity of the Vatican, which in 1751 put it on the Index of forbidden books. At one remove from the *philosophes*, Montesquieu none the less shared many of their values, and towards the end of his life contributed an essay on Taste to the *Encyclopédie*.

Denis Diderot is imprisoned for three months for the atheistical tendencies of his *Lettre sur les aveugles à l'usage de ceux qui voient* (*An Essay on the Blind for Those Who Can See*), which among other things anticipates the ideas on

The *Encyclopédie*

The *Encyclopédie*, or *Dictionnaire raisonné des sciences, des arts et des métiers*, is one of the outstanding achievements of the **Age of Reason**, and also one of its most representative monuments. Its creation was supervised by two men: **Diderot**, who was the driving force and managed the historical and philosophical parts, and **d'Alembert**, who oversaw the sections concerned with mathematics. Published between 1751 and 1772, it ran to 17 volumes of articles and 11 of illustrations. Its contributors included many of the great names of the century, among them **Voltaire**, **Rousseau** and **baron d'Holbach**, as well as Diderot and d'Alembert themselves; but it was important above all as the manifesto of a new age that set reason, philosophical enquiry and empirical investigation against tradition, orthodoxy and religious authority. 'Everything must be examined,' said Diderot, 'everything must be probed without exception and without reserve.' Compromises there were, of course. As soon as the first volume had appeared under royal licence, it was subjected to fierce and menacing criticism, not least from the Sorbonne. At a time when all books were subject to state control, it was not possible to execute a venture like this without occasionally bending before the wind, but the *Encyclopédie* remains an extraordinary feat of intellectual scope and daring that confirmed France's place at the centre of the **European Enlightenment**.

teaching the blind to read developed by Louis Braille in the 19th century.

The **comte de Buffon**, head of the Royal Botanical Gardens since 1739, begins publication of his 36-volume *Histoire naturelle* (1749–88).

1750 The first two volumes of the *Encyclopédie* are published.

1752–55 Further conflicts arise between the king and the *Parlement* over Louis' determination to stamp out Jansenism.

Diderot's *Encyclopédie* had articles on many trades and industries. This plate shows a *tapissier*, or upholsterer, at work

1752 Food shortages lead to peasant uprisings in southern France and elsewhere.

1754 The future Louis XVI is born to the dauphin at Versailles (23 August).

1755 Jacques-Ange Gabriel's design for the place Louis-XV (later renamed place de la Concorde) is approved.

1756 Work begins on **Jacques-Germain Soufflot**'s church of Ste-Geneviève, Paris (later the Panthéon), one of the first great examples of Neoclassical architecture.

The royal porcelain factory is moved from Vincennes to **Sèvres**.

1756–63 Growing tension between England and France in the North American colonies, combined with Austrian aspirations to recover Silesia from Prussia, leads to the **Seven Years War**. In a shake-up of traditional alliances, this ranges France and Austria against England and Prussia as the main combatants, with Sweden and Russia as allies of Austria.

1757 On 5 January **Robert François Damiens**, a former household servant who believes the king to be neglecting his duties, wounds Louis with a penknife at Versailles. The injury is slight, but the episode profoundly shocks Louis and marks a further stage in his alienation from the people. Damiens is tortured and executed on 28 March.

Robert Clive's victory at **Plassey** (23 June) on behalf of the London East India Company in Bengal heralds the end of French colonial and commercial expansion in India.

1758 The **duc de Choiseul**, a friend and protégé of Mme de Pompadour, becomes secretary of state for foreign affairs. For most of the next twelve years it will be he who shapes government policy.

1759 On 17 September the English take **Québec**. The French general **Montcalm** is fatally wounded in the battle.

At home, Louis has his silver plate melted down to contribute to the war effort.

Voltaire publishes *Candide*, which exposes with bitter irony the inadequacies of philosophical optimism in a world of inescapable suffering.

1760 Montréal, the last French stronghold in Canada, surrenders to the British (8 September).

1761 Fragonard returns to Paris from Italy. In the years that follow he will paint works such as *L'Escarpolette*, *La Fête à St-Cloud*, and *Le Verrou*.

1762 On 10 March **Jean Calas**, a Protestant merchant in Toulouse, is broken on the wheel, strangled and burnt for the murder of his son, whom he is supposed to have killed to prevent him from turning Catholic. Voltaire takes up the case with a deft propaganda campaign that secures the rehabilitation of Calas on 9 March, 1665, exactly three years after the original verdict. It is an Enlightenment triumph over prejudice, religious superstition and vested interests.

Jean-Jacques Rousseau publishes *Du Contrat social* and *Émile*.

1763 The **treaty of Paris** (10 February) brings the Seven Years War to an end. The fortunes of war in Europe have swung to and fro, giving neither side an overwhelming victory. In the colonies, France, after initial success, has

Voltaire

Born François-Marie Arouet, the son of a Paris lawyer, **Voltaire** (1694–1778) adopted his pseudonym in 1718 on the appearance of his first major literary work, the tragedy *Oedipe*. Its success launched him as a writer, and his stock at court was soon high enough for three of his plays to be staged at the marriage of Louis XV. A quarrel with the **chevalier de Rohan** in 1726 led to his exile in **England**, where he spent the next two and a half years. It was a formative experience. The contrast between what seemed to him a liberal, energetic Protestant country and the authoritarian Catholic country from which he was exiled became the basis of his *Lettres philosophiques* (1734), a work that caused scandal by its subversive religious and political views and was burned in France by the public executioner. Voltaire fled to **Cirey** in Champagne and the protection of the young and brilliant **Mme du Châtelet**, who remained his companion until her death in 1749. During his time at Cirey, Voltaire's studies and writings turned increasingly from plays to science and history.

Another period of royal favour in the 1740s (thanks to the protection of Mme de Pompadour) was followed by disgrace, and in 1750 he joined **Frederick II** of Prussia in Berlin. But Voltaire, though an adept courtier, had too critical an intelligence to remain welcome for long in the company of the great. After a rancorous break with Frederick, he stayed for a time near **Geneva**, where he worked on contributions to the *Encyclopédie*, before finally settling at **Ferney** in 1760. Here he lived the life of Europe's greatest man of letters, receiving a procession of the most eminent literary and intellectual figures of the day. Anti-Christian (though never atheist), anti-authoritarian and resolutely humane, Voltaire enjoyed a status that enabled him not just to write what he wanted in relative safety but also to intervene in public controversies, like the **Calas affair** of 1762, in a way that would have been impossible for anyone else. Against bigotry, prejudice and blind emotion, his voice still champions the claims of reason and humanity.

suffered a series of defeats. The terms of the treaty leave Prussia still in possession of Silesia and France bereft of most of its colonies, apart from the islands of Martinique, Guadeloupe and the western half of Santo Domingo.

1764 Death of Mme de Pompadour (15 April).

Louis decrees the expulsion of the **Jesuits** from France.

1765 **François Boucher** becomes principal painter to the king.

On 20 December, the dauphin Louis dies of consumption at Versailles.

Pierre-Marie-Jérôme Trésaguet formulates his method of road construction, which emphasizes strong foundations and good drainage.

1766 In February, on the death of Stanislas Leszczynski, Lorraine returns to France according to the terms of the treaty of Vienna.

In July the 19-year-old **Chevalier de La Barre** is tortured and executed for blasphemy, having refused to take off his hat at the passing of a religious procession and having allegedly mutilated a crucifix. For revolutionaries of the 18th and 19th centuries, he will become a symbol of resistance to bigotry.

In December **Louis Antoine de Bougainville** leaves on the three-year voyage recounted in his *Voyage autour du monde*. The goals of the journey are scientific rather than colonial, and his descriptions, especially of Tahiti, play a significant part in quickening 18th-century interest in the concept of the noble savage.

1768 **Genoa**, having failed to crush the **Corsican republic** established since 1755, sells the island to France.

Food shortages provoke riots.

'To dedicate one's life to the truth' (Vitam impendere vero) was the personal motto of Jean-Jacques Rousseau

1769 An invasion by French troops drives the Corsican nationalist leader **Pasquale Paoli** into exile, and Corsica becomes a French province.

Jean-Jacques Rousseau

A native of Geneva, **Rousseau** (1712–78) lost his mother at birth and was initially brought up by his watchmaker father before being handed over to the uncertain charity of relatives. At 16 he left Geneva for a life of wandering that led him to Savoy and the protection of **Mme de Warens**, a rich and cultivated woman with a taste for converting handsome young Protestants. In 1742 Rousseau reached Paris, where a friendship with Denis Diderot brought him into the company of the *philosophes* and established him as a contributor on musical subjects to the *Encyclopédie*. It was while going to visit Diderot, imprisoned in Vincennes, that he experienced the revelation which was to shape his thought: human beings, naturally good, had been corrupted by the progress of civilization. This was the basis from which he later went on to produce the three works that made him the most celebrated and reviled writer in Europe: the novel *Julie, ou la Nouvelle Héloïse* (1761), whose portrayal of virtuous passion enjoyed huge success across Europe; *Du Contrat social* (1762), in which Rousseau expounded his notion of society as a pact depending on the surrender of individual rights in exchange for civil rights guaranteed by the whole community; and *Émile* (1762), which inspired a sea-change in the philosophy of education and child-rearing.

The influence of these books – on the development of **Romanticism**, on the politics of the **Revolution**, on our concept of childhood – was immense and is still felt today, but Rousseau's arguments outraged the authorities in both France and Geneva. Forced abroad, he took refuge with a number of sympathisers, including the English philosopher **David Hume**, before returning to France, an increasingly bitter and paranoid figure, to live out his days in a series of restless wanderings during which he completed his posthumously published *Confessions* (1782 and 1789). He was survived by **Thérèse Levasseur**, the illiterate laundry maid who had been his companion for over thirty years and his wife since 1768. Of their five children, consigned by Rousseau to an orphanage, nothing is known.

'Marie-Antoinette, à la rose' is one of many portraits of the queen painted by
Elizabeth Louis Vigée-Le Brun

The king takes as his official mistress **Mme du Barry**, whose dislike of Choiseul soon leads to the minister's disgrace.

1770 On 16 May the 16-year-old dauphin marries **Marie-Antoinette**, daughter of the Austrian emperor. At the firework display held in the new place Louis-XV a fortnight later to celebrate the event, an accident results in explosions that kill 133 spectators.

1771 **René de Maupeou** (Chancellor), the **abbé Terray** (Controller General of Finances), and the **duc d'Aiguillon** (Foreign Secretary) form a ministerial triumvirate. Maupeou dissolves the Paris *Parlement* and imposes a programme of reform designed to restrict its functions to the purely judicial. With the support of the king, these reforms are extended to the provinces, and for a time it looks as though there may be hope of pushing through the fiscal measures that in the past have always been blocked by the *parlements*.

1774 Louis XV dies at Versailles and is succeeded by his 20-year-old grandson, who reigns as **Louis XVI** (crowned at Reims, 11 June, 1775). The new king, eager to be seen as a conciliator, dismisses Maupeou and recalls the *Parlement*, thereby extinguishing the prospect of any radical reform.

> ❝ When we returned from our walk we went up to an open terrace and stayed there half an hour. I cannot describe to you, my dear mamma, the transports of joy and affection which everyone exhibited towards us. Before we withdrew we kissed our hands to the people, which gave them great pleasure. What a happy thing it is for persons in our rank to gain the love of a whole nation so cheaply. Yet there is nothing so precious; I felt it thoroughly, and shall never forget it. ❞
>
> Letter of Marie-Antoinette to her mother, 14 June, 1773

Turgot, a liberal economist who has collaborated on the *Encyclopédie*, is appointed Controller General of Finances.

Antoine de Lavoisier, who has been working on the composition of air since 1772, discovers oxygen.

In Paris the first performance of **Gluck**'s opera *Iphigénie en Aulide* revolutionizes French opera by concentrating on narrative clarity rather than vocal display.

1774–76 **Turgot**'s decision to allow the free trade of grain results in price rises that cause serious rioting in Burgundy and the Paris region, the so-called *'guerre des farines'* (flour war). He goes on to propose a number of economic and social reforms, including changes in taxation and a relaxation of the laws that provide for internment of beggars and sanctions against Huguenots. His proposals run into overwhelming opposition from the entrenched interests of court, clergy and *Parlement*, and in May 1776 Turgot is dismissed.

1776 Towards the end of the year **Benjamin Franklin** arrives in Paris to seek French support for the American War of Independence against Britain.

Jacques Necker, a Swiss banker of more conservative inclinations than Turgot, is put in charge of the treasury, becoming Director General of Finances the following year.

1777 On 1 January Paris's first daily paper, *Le Journal de Paris*, is launched. It will continue publication until 1840.

In April the **marquis de La Fayette** arrives in America to support the fight for independence.

1778 France recognizes the sovereignty of the **United States** and enters the war against Britain, laying siege to Gibraltar and sending a fleet to America.

1780 With the abolition of the *'question préparatoire'* on 24 August, **torture** ceases to be an official part of French judicial procedure.

1781 Necker's attempts to reform the **financial administration** of the country run into opposition from the usual vested interests. When he loses the support of the king by revealing the expenses of the court, he resigns (19 May), leaving behind a financial situation that will steadily worsen as a result of constant borrowing.

Cornwallis's surrender to Franco-American forces at **Yorktown** (19 October) marks the defeat of Britain in the American War of Independence.

1782 Choderlos de Laclos publishes *Les Liaisons dangéreuses*, whose depiction of a corrupt and libertine aristocracy makes it an immediate *succès de scandale*.

The first part of Jean-Jacques Rousseau's *Confessions* is published, four years after his death.

1783 Charles Alexandre de Calonne is appointed Controller General of Finances. Over the next three years, he, like Turgot and Necker, will try to introduce fiscal and administrative reform, but like them he will be thwarted by opposition from *Parlement*, clergy and aristocracy.

On 3 September the **treaty of Paris** brings the American War of Independence to an end. The United States of America is recognized as a sovereign nation, and France acquires a number of Caribbean islands, including sugar-rich **Tobago**.

In November, the first manned free flight in the hot air **balloon** developed by the **Montgolfier brothers** takes place.

1784 After confinement in Vincennes, the **marquis de Sade** is imprisoned in the Bastille. His *120 Journées de Sodome* is published the following year.

Banned since 1781 and loathed by the king, **Beaumarchais'** *La Folle Journée ou Le Mariage de Figaro* is finally staged to huge popular acclaim (27 April).

Lavoisier identifies hydrogen and oxygen as the constituents of water.

1784–87 An **octroi wall**, ten metres high and 23 kilometres long, is built round Paris to facilitate the collection of taxes on goods entering the city. A source of deep resentment to Parisians, it symbolises the fiscal oppression of an incompetent government.

1785–86 The '*affaire du collier*', the last great pre-revolutionary scandal, acts as a focus for popular hatred of Marie-Antoinette. The **comtesse de La Motte** persuades the **Cardinal de Rohan** that he can gain the queen's favour by acting as intermediary in the secret purchase of a diamond necklace valued at over a million and a half *livres*. The queen herself knows nothing of what is in fact a criminal plot on the part of the countess and her accomplices to steal the necklace. When the affair comes to light, Louis XVI insists on a public trial of the cardinal. Rohan is finally acquitted, but the story of forged letters, night-time meetings and court intrigue, added to Louis' authoritarian handling of the affair, brings discredit on the royal family.

1785 The **comte de La Pérouse** leaves on the expedition that over the next three years will take him round the world, producing important cultural and cartographical observations about Easter Island, Hawaii, Macao, the Philippines, Korea and Kamchatka. In 1788, after leaving Botany Bay, he disappears in the south Pacific.

1786 **Jacques Balmat** and **Michel-Gabriel Paccard** reach the summit of Mont Blanc (8 August).

1787 Calonne is dismissed (8 April).

1788 As the state slides into bankruptcy, Louis, unable to impose his will on the *Parlement,* bows to popular pressure. Necker is recalled and a meeting of the **Estates General**, the first since 1614, is convened for 1 May, 1789.

6
The French Revolution and its aftermath

1789–1815

The **American War of Independence** had left the taste of **revolution** in the air. It was the last of a series of costly 18th-century wars into which France had poured money that could ill be spared. The attempts of successive finance ministers to redeem the situation had run into entrenched opposition from the *Parlement*, the clergy and the nobility, leaving the peasants at the mercy of an outdated feudal system and the rising bourgeoisie excluded from political power. Any measure of reform that affected the interests of the privileged classes was blocked, and there was no possibility of reform that did not affect their interests.

In response to this stalemate, and against a background of rising grain prices and popular unrest, **Louis XVI** agreed to recall the **Estates General** for the first time since 1614. What neither he nor *Parlement* had registered was the profound change in intellectual and political climate that had taken place through the years of the **Enlightenment**. The clergy and the nobility were ready enough to play their traditional roles, but the men elected to represent the **Third Estate** came to Paris with quite different expectations: their voice was going to be heard in the affairs of state. The ill-judged mixture of intransigence and reluctant conciliation with which they were handled tipped a crisis into a revolution.

For a while it looked as though the political changes might be contained within the new structure of a constitutional monarchy, but by the summer of 1792 the pressures were too great: the **Civil Constitution of the Clergy** had split the country, the war with Austria and Prussia was threatening national disaster, the working class was angry that its dream of social revolution had not been realized, the king was saluting the Revolution with one hand and embracing counter-revolution with the other. In an atmosphere of national panic and working-class resentment, the monarchy fell. The next few months saw a hardening of the radical line that led to the formation of the **Revolutionary Tribunal** and the **Committee of Public Safety**. Shortly afterwards, the reins of power in the National Assembly were snatched from the moderate **Girondin** party by the **Jacobins**. While Paris shuddered under the **Terror**, **civil war** raged in the provinces against the counter-revolutionary forces of western France. Abroad, the revolutionary army was faced by a coalition of European powers.

When military success had relieved some of the anxieties used as a justification for the Terror, a revulsion from the rule of the Jacobins brought a return to more moderate policies and the establishment of the **Directory**. But the tensions between royalist and revolutionary sympathies continued to dominate the political landscape, with the Directory openly flouting the democratic will when it seemed to pull too far in one direction or the other. Finally, it was **Napoléon Bonaparte** who put an end to the period of Revolution by establishing the **Consulate**, which within a few years had been translated into the **First Empire**. Meanwhile, France's policy of foreign conquest had united the European powers against her. Napoléon's disastrous foray into Russia gave them the opportunity they had been waiting for. Defeated by the forces of the coalition,

Napoléon was forced to abdicate and France was returned to its pre-revolutionary frontiers.

It was not on the whole a period that favoured cultural or intellectual pursuits. 'The Republic has no need for men of learning,' remarked the vice-president of the Tribunal grimly when **Lavoisier** asked for a fortnight's reprieve from the scaffold to complete an experiment. Writers and artists were expected to be in the service of the state. If they took another line they might well end up, like **André Chénier**, on the guillotine, like **de Sade**, in a madhouse, or like **Chateaubriand** and **Mme de Staël**, in exile. The real focus of cultural energy during these tumultuous years was on social change. Some of the reforms survived; many did not. What is certain is that this period of upheaval transformed for ever the social and political institutions that govern French life and set an enduring example to other radical movements in Europe and beyond.

1789 The rising cost of bread, now more expensive than at any time during the century, leads to **rioting** in several parts of the country. On 5 May, the **Estates General** holds its opening session in the hôtel des Menus-Plaisirs at Versailles.

> ❝ Walking up a long hill to ease my mare, I was joined by a poor woman, who complained of the times, and that it was a sad country. Demanding her reasons, she said her husband had but a morsel of land, one cow, and a poor little horse, yet they had a franchar (forty-two pounds) of wheat and three chickens to pay as a quitrent to one seigneur; and four franchar of oats, one chicken, and one franc, to pay to another, besides very heavy tailles and other taxes. ❞
>
> Arthur Young, From *Travels in France During the Years 1787, 1788 and 1789*

The Estates General

A consultative body made up of representatives of the nobility, the clergy and the commons, the **Estates General** had last met in 1614. The crucial question in 1789 was the role to be played by the commons or **Third Estate**. The difference in political climate between 1614 and 1789 was summed up by the abbé Sieyès: 'Therefore, what is the Third Estate? Everything; but an everything shackled and oppressed. What would it be without the privileged order? Everything, but an everything free and flourishing. Nothing can succeed without it, everything would be infinitely better without the others.'

Made up largely of middle-class professionals, the Third Estate was not a revolutionary body, but its interests were in conflict with those of the privileged classes, and this became the basis of a power struggle which the Third Estate, renamed the **National Assembly**, eventually won when the king agreed that the other two orders should join it. In October 1789, after the king had been brought back to Paris from Versailles, the Assembly followed. It was from the seating arrangements in their new hall – radicals on the president's left, conservatives on his right – that the terms 'left' and 'right' acquired their modern political significance.

On 1 October, 1791 the National Assembly was replaced by a newly elected **Legislative Assembly** in which the largest political grouping was formed by members of the Feuillant club, moderate breakaways from the more radical **Jacobins**. Among deputies from the provinces were a number of eloquent debaters from the Gironde who came to be known as the **Girondins**. Of the 745 deputies only 136 were Jacobins, but within a year the influence of the *sans-culottes* (see p.198), the growing unpopularity of the king and the unfavourable progress of the war against Austria and Prussia had shifted the political agenda onto an altogether more radical footing. Power had passed to an executive council and it was agreed that the Assembly should be replaced by a **National Convention**, elected by universal male suffrage.

Death of the 7-year-old dauphin (4 June).

On 17 June, the **Third Estate** renames itself the **National Assembly**, emphasising the fact that it represents the majority of the nation. Three days later, the members of the National Assembly, locked out of their meeting hall, adjourn to a nearby tennis-court where they swear the **tennis-court oath** (20 June), undertaking 'never to separate' until a constitution is agreed. On 21 June the Royal Council rejects **Necker**'s plan for financial recovery. Two days later the king holds a *séance royale* for all three orders at which he makes a number of concessions relating to taxation, freedom of the press and the use of *lettres de cachet* but fails to appease the members of the National Assembly, who refuse to leave the hall. **Mirabeau** declares: 'We are here by the will of the people; we shall leave only at the point of a bayonet.' After four days the king gives way, requesting the other deputies to join the National Assembly.

On 11 July the king dismisses Necker. Two days later, a bourgeois militia, soon to become the **National Guard**, is created by the committee of electors (the men who had made the final selection of Parisian deputies for the Estates General). On **14 July**, after two days of unrest, inspired by the dismissal of Necker, the high cost of bread and the concentration of troops around the capital, a crowd armed with weapons taken from the Invalides marches on the **Bastille**. Initial resistance by the defenders results in about a hundred deaths among the crowd before the governor surrenders and is himself killed and decapitated. As a symbol of victory over the oppressive forces of the *ancien régime,* the capture of the Bastille acquires huge importance. On the following day, the decision is taken to demolish the fortress.

The king's youngest brother, the **comte d'Artois** (later Charles X), emigrates to Germany (16–17 July). On 17 July, general euphoria greets news of the king's agreement

Prints depicting the events of the Revolution proved extremely popular. This one, of the storming of the Bastille, is by Pierre-Gabriel Berthault

to withdraw troops from Paris and Versailles. The new militiamen, now commanded by **La Fayette**, add a band of white, the king's colour, to their red and blue cockades, thus creating the *tricolore*.

Through July and August rumours of aristocratic plots and foreign invasion sweep the provinces, resulting in the **'Great Fear'**. Armed peasants attack and ransack châteaux, abbeys and government offices. In a frenzied session, later known as the **'night of 4th August'**, the deputies of the National Assembly vote to abolish privileges, including ecclesiastical tithes, thereby sweeping away a whole feudal system of property ownership. A number of measures carried in the heat of the moment are subsequently modified. On 26 August, the *Declaration of the Rights of Man and Citizen* proclaims a number of basic civil, political and religious freedoms, though its scope is largely restricted to men.

The first issue of **Jean-Paul Marat**'s newspaper, *Publiciste parisien*, appears on 12 September; its name is changed a few days later to *L'Ami du Peuple*. One of the most influential publications of the time, it will continue under this name until 21 September, 1792.

Popular anger at the price of bread results in a march of some 6000 women to Versailles (5–6 October). Amid a threatening clamour for the king to return to Paris, Louis agrees, and the royal family is escorted back to the capital. On 19 October, the *'Club des Amis de la Constitution'* installs itself in the former Dominican convent of the **Jacobins**, from which its members acquire their name.

To cope with the country's growing burden of debt, **Church property** is nationalized and sold off in small lots (2 November). The revenue is used as the basis for government bonds, *assignats*, which are issued the following month as a new form of currency.

On 1 December Dr **Joseph Ignace Guillotin**, a Paris deputy, proposes the introduction of a new instrument of execution. Intended as a humane alternative to the medieval barbarities of the wheel and the stake, the guillotine will first be used for common criminals before its employment, some months later, for political executions. Public dissatisfaction with the lack of spectacle leads to the development of the ritual of tumbril, drums and displayed head that will become a feature of the Revolution.

On 24 December, restrictions are lifted on the jobs open to Protestants.

Voices of the Revolution: Mirabeau and Marat

At the age of 40, Honoré Gabriel Riqueti, **comte de Mirabeau** (1749–91) had enjoyed a turbulent life marked by quarrels with his father, dangerous liaisons with a variety of women, and a dubious career as journalist, adventurer and secret agent. He had been rejected as a candidate for the Estates General by the nobility of Provence so turned to the Third Estate, who elected him as deputy for **Aix**. Ugly, passionate, eloquent and unscrupulous, he dominated the Assembly with his brilliant oratory. Instrumental in promoting the freedom of the press and the nationalization of the Church's wealth, he also helped to compose the *Declaration of the Rights of Man and Citizen*. But he was a defender of the monarchy as well as a revolutionary. While the king paid off his debts, Mirabeau argued cogently for the importance of royal authority. It was his good fortune to die before the extent of his double-dealing became apparent.

Two years after Mirabeau's burial in the Panthéon, his remains were displaced by those of **Jean-Paul Marat** (1743–93), the hero of the *sans-culottes*. (Literally meaning those without the breeches worn by the upper classes, in other words, the trouser-wearing working classes, the term *sans-culottes* actually embraced a range of ardent revolutionaries.) A society doctor in London and Paris before the Revolution, Marat turned from writing scientific papers to political journalism, using his newspaper *L'Ami du Peuple* to launch savage attacks on anyone, left or right, whom he perceived as a threat to the Revolution. Increasingly extreme in his calls for radical social measures and the elimination of the people's enemies, he earned the hatred of the Girondins, who had him arraigned before the Tribunal. They had miscalculated. It was Marat who triumphed and then played a leading role in bringing about their downfall at the hands of the *sans-culottes*. His murder by **Charlotte Corday**, in revenge for this action, ensured his status as a martyr of the Revolution.

> Mirabeau entered the chamber alone and took his place near the middle of the rows of backless benches which stretched one behind the other. There arose a very low but widespread murmur – a susurro – and the deputies already seated in front of him moved one bench forward, while those behind him moved back a little. He thus remained isolated in the middle of a very obvious space. Smiling contemptuously, he sat down.

Comtesse de La Tour du Pin, *Memoirs*

1790 In an important move to simplify the administrative arrangements of the *ancien régime,* the Assembly votes the division of France into 83 **départements** (15 January).

Lettres de cachet are abolished (26 March).

On 31 March **Maximilien Robespierre** becomes president of the Jacobin club. Less than a month later the *Club des Cordeliers* is founded by, among others, **Georges Jacques Danton** and **Jean-Paul Marat**.

Titles of nobility are abolished on 19 June, and the **Civil Constitution of the Clergy**, which brings the Church under the control of the State, is agreed by the National Assembly on 12 July. This document, stipulating a reduction in the number of bishoprics, the election of bishops and priests by popular vote, and a rejection of papal authority over the French Church, causes a split between those among the clergy who are willing to take a civic oath and those who are not. The king gives his reluctant assent to the Constitution, but its condemnation by the pope forces him to think again and appoint a non-juring priest as his confessor. Papal opposition to the Constitution intensifies feeling on both sides of the divide throughout the country.

On 14 July the *Fête de la Fédération*, marked by parades, banquets and games on the Champ-de-Mars, celebrates the progress of the Revolution and promotes a temporary mood of national unity that is soon undermined by conflict over the Civil Constitution of the Clergy. On 21 October France adopts *le drapeau tricolore* (the tricolour flag).

1791 On 19 February the **octroi tax** on goods entering Paris is abolished.

Pius V condemns the Civil Constitution of the Clergy (10 March). On 2 April **Mirabeau** dies and is buried in the Panthéon, to which the ashes of **Voltaire** are moved on 11 June.

The king, who has been under close watch in the **Tuileries** since Easter, when the crowd prevented him from leaving for St-Cloud, tries to escape with the royal family into Austrian territory but is arrested at **Varennes** and ignominiously brought back to Paris on 24 June. The order goes out: 'Whoever cheers the king will be beaten, whoever insults him will be hanged.' This is a turning point after which most of the population see the king as hostile to the Revolution.

On 17 July, the National Guard, under the command of La Fayette, fires on a crowd in the **Champ-de-Mars** demanding the deposition of the king.

In **St-Domingue**, the French-controlled area of Santo Domingo (present-day Haiti), a slave revolt breaks out in August, later headed by François Dominique Toussaint (known from 1793 as **Toussaint Louverture**).

The **Declaration of Pillnitz** (27 August), by the king of Prussia and the Austrian emperor, proclaims in vague terms a willingness to support a constitutional monarchy in France but has the effect of giving fresh impetus to the mood of revolution.

In September, **Olympe de Gouges** publishes her *Declaration of the Rights of Woman and Citizen*. Its affirmation of sexual equality points up a major failing in the parallel declaration published the previous August. An opponent of the Jacobins, Olympe will go to the guillotine two years later.

On 4 September, the first **Constitution** is promulgated, making France a **constitutional monarchy**. Legislative power rests with an assembly elected by adult male taxpayers over 25, and the king's power of veto extends to a maximum of four years. After nine days, the king swears allegiance to the new Constitution. The legislative **Assembly** meets for its first session on 1 October.

On 9 November the Assembly passes a decree ordering the return of *émigrés*, which is vetoed by the king two days later.

Marquis de Sade publishes *Justine*.

The sculptor **Jean-Antoine Houdon** creates his busts of Voltaire and Mirabeau.

1792 The Assembly confiscates the possessions of *émigrés* for use by the nation (9 February). On 15 March, the **Girondins** gain power in the Assembly after the decline of the more conservative Feuillants. Partly in response to a perception by the Girondins that an external enemy is needed to sustain the Revolution and prevent it from being destroyed by internal divisions, France declares war on **Austria** (20 April). War with **Prussia** soon follows.

During the *'journée révolutionnaire'* (day of revolution) of 20 June, *sans-culottes* invade the palace of the Tuileries and force the king to don the **red bonnet** of the revolutionaries. Three weeks later, on 11 July, the ill success of the war and the threat of an Austrian invasion lead the Assembly to declare a state of emergency – *'la Patrie en danger'*.

On 25 July a manifesto signed by the **Duke of Brunswick**, commander of the enemy army, threatens

Paris with retribution if any harm comes to the king, and warns the National Guard not to resist the Austro-Prussian advance. The effect is to harden sentiment against the monarchy.

On 30 July volunteers from **Marseille**, the *fédérés*, arrive in Paris singing the *Chant de guerre pour l'armée du Rhin*. Composed a few months earlier by **Joseph Rouget de Lisle**, a young army officer, it becomes known after this as the *Marseillaise*. *Sans-culottes* invade the palace of the Tuileries again on 10 August, forcing the king and his family to take refuge with the Assembly. Under the eyes of the **Insurrectionary Commune** newly formed by the *sans-culottes*, the Assembly votes for the king to be arrested and detained. The following day, government passes to an executive council of six ministers, of whom Danton, as minister of Justice, is the most influential. It is agreed to replace the Assembly with a **Convention**, elected by universal male suffrage, which will establish a new Constitution.

On 23 August, after scant resistance, the town of **Longwy** in Lorraine falls to the Prussians, giving rise to talk of treachery. **Verdun** is besieged (2 September). To save France, urges Danton, the nation requires *'de l'audace, encore de l'audace, toujours de l'audace'*. Over the next four days (2–6 September) the tense atmosphere in Paris erupts in the **'September massacres'**. Some 1200 inmates of the prisons, among them the queen's friend the princesse de Lamballe, are brutally murdered. A similar wave of killings spreads to the provinces. On 20 September Generals **Kellerman** and **Dumouriez** defeat the Prussians at **Valmy**. Little more than an artillery skirmish, the 'Valmy cannonade' is of great psychological importance to the French. Goethe witnesses the battle: 'At this place, on this day, there has begun a new era in the history of the world; and you can all claim to have been present at its birth.' Next day, at its first meeting, the Convention votes for the abolition of the monarchy.

Having adopted 22 September as the start of Year 1 of the Republic, the Convention decrees a new calendar, which will be finally established on 24 November, 1793. Abroad, Valmy is followed by a further victory at **Jemmapes** (6 November). A week later the French enter Brussels and on 19 November issue a decree promising 'help to oppressed peoples'.

On 20 November a strongbox is discovered in the Tuileries containing correspondence that makes clear Louis' contempt for the new constitution and the duplicity of many of his responses to the Revolution. Three months of military success are crowned on 27 November by the **annexation of Savoy**. On 11 December, the **trial** of Louis XVI begins.

The National Convention

Composed of 749 deputies, about a quarter of whom had been members of previous assemblies and most of the rest drawn from similar backgrounds, the **National Convention** fell into three distinct, though by no means unified, groupings: the moderate **Girondins**, who made up about twenty percent of the total; the radicals, who sat on the higher benches and in consequence came to be known as **Montagnards** (about 35 percent); and the **deputies of the Plain**, who sat between them and held the balance of power. An important influence on the Convention was the pressure exerted by the will of the *sans-culottes*. It was their intervention, orchestrated by Marat and the leaders of the radical *Enragés*, that led to the downfall of the Girondins and ushered in the second phase of the Convention, dominated by the Montagnards.

Although a new **Constitution** had been approved on 23 June, 1793, its adoption was deferred on grounds of present danger to the Revolution at home and abroad. To meet the emergency, executive powers were placed in the hands of the **Committee of Public Safety**. The fall of **Robespierre** on 9 Thermidor (27 July, 1794) brought in the so-called **Thermidorian Convention**, which saw the reinstatement of surviving Girondins and a general suppression of Jacobin radicalism, leading finally to the establishment of the **Directory**.

1793 In January Louis XVI is found guilty of treason and an appeal to the people rejected. The deputies vote by a narrow majority for execution, and he is guillotined on 21 January in the place Louis-XV, now renamed **place de la Révolution** (the present-day place de la Concorde). Acknowledging the inevitable, France declares war on **England** and **Holland** (1 February), and France annexes the principality of **Monaco** on 14 February. Ten days later, the Convention decides to draft 300,000 men into the army. This conscription, combined with serious economic problems and resentment at religious reforms, provokes widespread protest, notably in the **Vendée** where royalist and Catholic forces rise against the Revolution in March.

On 10 March, against the advice of more moderate elements in the Convention, a **Revolutionary Tribunal** is set up to deal with suspected enemies of the Revolution.

Hampered by directives from the Convention, **Dumouriez**, commander of the French army in the north, is defeated by the Austrians at **Neerwinden** (18 March). He contemplates marching on Paris with Austrian support to restore the monarchy but is unable to persuade his army to follow him. Early in April he goes over to the enemy. This act of treachery, combined with the threat from counter-revolutionary uprisings in the provinces, contributes to the onset of the **Terror**. In response to growing alarm for the future of the Revolution, the **Com-**

mittee of Public Safety is formed on 6 April, with Danton among its nine members. Under attack from the Montagnards for their association with Dumouriez, the Girondins respond by having Marat, president of the Jacobin club, brought before the Revolutionary Tribunal. He is triumphantly acquitted on 24 April.

Architects of the Terror

An aspiring lawyer at the outbreak of the Revolution, **Georges Jacques Danton** (1759–94) had been one of the founders of the Club des Cordeliers and had voted for the execution of the king. Unmoved by the bloodshed in the early years of the Revolution, he reached the height of his power in the spring of 1793 as the dominant figure on the **Committee of Public Safety**, but by the end of the year he was calling for moderation. Damaged by charges of corruption and also by his association with the traitorous **General Dumouriez**, he was brought to the guillotine a few months later in the company of **Camille Desmoulins** (1760–94), the romantic idealist who had rallied the Parisians to arms in the Palais-Royal on 12 July, 1789.

For all his faults, Danton was thoroughly human – not a comment often made about the man who now took charge of the Revolution. **Maximilien Robespierre** (1758–94), another lawyer who moved to Paris from the provinces, had been president of the Jacobin club and had followed Danton onto the Committee of Public Safety. The austere qualities that earned him the nickname 'The Incorruptible' also enabled him to preside with equanimity over the bloodiest phase of the Revolution. Supported by **Antoine Quentin Fouquier-Tinville** (1746–95), the Public Prosecutor who dispatched the business of the Terror with exemplary severity, and **Louis Antoine Léon Saint-Just** (1767–94), whose commitment to the Revolution could make even apathy a capital crime, Robespierre pursued a path that seemed to many to be leading towards tyranny rather than liberty. Inexorably, the Revolution's tendency to devour its children caught up with him.

Counter-Revolution in the Vendée

Aside from minor episodes in the early years of the Revolution, the first and fiercest stage of the war in the **Vendée** began in March 1793, when smouldering discontents at religious repression, social interference and the worsening economic situation were fanned into flame by the threat of conscription. A powerful alliance of **royalist** and **Catholic** counter-revolutionary forces captured a number of towns in the region before turning northeast to take **Saumur**. Atrocities were commonplace. Among the figures who passed into folk history was the 13-year-old drummer boy **Joseph Bara**, shot by the Vendéens for refusing to hand over horses.

It was only in the autumn that government troops regained the initiative and inflicted a series of crushing defeats on the rebels at **Cholet** (17 October), **Le Mans** (12 December) and **Savenay** (23 December). The ensuing repression was savage enough to ensure that the conflict would not be laid to rest: men, women and children were mutilated and murdered in what was virtually a war of annihilation. (In February 1794 the government representative was recalled from Nantes because the Loire had become so polluted with corpses that disease threatened.) For most of the next three years a bitter guerrilla struggle was carried on with the aid of the **Chouans**, another association of rebel groups in the west, called after their leader's nickname (*chouan* = screech owl). Until the beginning of the next century there were flickerings of resistance in a landscape devastated and depopulated by the horrors of this civil war.

The **cost of grain** is fixed by the setting of a maximum price (4 May).

On 24 May, having failed to secure the conviction of Marat, the Girondins try to consolidate their hold on power by arresting a number of more radical members of the Convention, including **René Hébert**, editor of the newspaper *le Père Duchesne*. This incurs the wrath of the extremist *Enragés* and the *sans-culottes*, who on 27 May invade the Convention demanding the release of the prisoners. Between 31 May and 2 June the Girondins fall, and 29 of their leaders are proscribed. Power passes to the **Jacobins**, whose takeover, resented in the provinces, gives rise to federalist revolts on the part of Girondins in **Normandy** and **Bordeaux**. On 13 July Marat is assassinated by **Charlotte Corday**, who holds him responsible for the fate of the Girondins. Later in the year *The Death of Marat* is painted by **Jacques-Louis David**.

On 17 July all **feudal rights** are abolished. Ten days later, **Robespierre** takes a seat on the Committee of Public Safety. On 17 September the **Law of Suspects**, which authorizes the arrest of a wide range of people suspected of counter-revolutionary sympathies, marks the beginning of the **Terror**.

Year II of the Republic begins on 22 September. Popular discontent over rising prices leads to a general **'Law of the Maximum'** (29 September), which fixes the price of essential goods.

> ❝ As we were locked up every evening about five o'clock, and the door not opened until near ten the next morning, a tub was placed in the room ... We had with us a tolerably good physician, who advised us to burn incense every night before we went to bed, in order to purify the air, and to take a mouthful of brandy every morning as soon as we got up, as a preventive against infection... At twelve o'clock every night we used to be visited by three or four turnkeys, with as many great dogs. With large staves they used to thump against the ceiling, open the windows, and with an iron hammer beat against the bars to see that all was safe and sound. ❞
>
> Sir William Codrington on his imprisonment in the Conciergerie (1795)

Cultural Revolution

After a period of relative social calm, the transfer of power from Girondins to Jacobins saw the beginning of a **cultural revolution** driven by the *sans-culottes* who were keeping the Jacobins in power. They had two principal goals: greater **social equality** and a **secularization** of the state. It was during this period that 'citizen' became the standard form of address, the use of '*tu*' replaced '*vous*', a revolutionary calendar was introduced, towns were renamed, education overhauled, and a concerted effort made to reshape the social life of a whole nation. (It was a project the 20th century revisited more than once in upheavals such as the Communist revolutions in Russia, China and Cambodia.) But radical atheism was never on Robespierre's agenda, and by the end of 1793 he was attacking it along with Catholicism. His desire to give the Revolution a moral focus was partly responsible for the **Festival of the Supreme Being** in June the following year, but this ambitious and faintly absurd spectacle failed to recapture the spirit of national unity of the 1790 *Fête de la Fédération*. In the long run, the cultural goals of the Revolution were probably unrealistic, but the attempt to reach them left a permanent mark on French society.

From October to December Republican forces under **Jean-Baptiste Kléber** inflict a decisive series of defeats on the Vendéen rebels at Cholet, Le Mans and Savenay. On 10 October, a decree establishes 'revolutionary government until peace'.

Marie-Antoinette follows her husband to the guillotine in the place de la Révolution (16 October). Her execution is another symptom of *sans-culotte* pressure on the ruling Jacobins. The execution of the **Girondin leaders** on 31 October marks a further stage in the relentless purges that characterise the Terror. On 5 November the Convention orders the closure of all women's revolutionary clubs in Paris, reflecting the generally conservative Jacobin view of women's proper role in the Revolution. Three days later, **Mme Roland**, an influential associate of the Girondins, is guillotined. On the scaffold she famously declares, 'Liberty, what crimes are committed in your name.'

In December, **Napoléon Bonaparte** distinguishes himself in the recapture of Toulon from the English and is made a general.

1794 In a celebrated speech on 5 February Robespierre speaks of 'virtue, without which terror is deadly; terror, without which virtue is impotent'. On 24 March **Hébert**, one of the most brutal champions of the Terror, is executed along with nineteen of his followers. After eight months in hiding, the philosopher and mathematician **Condorcet** is arrested for his Girondin sympathies and dies in prison, probably by poisoning himself (27–28 March). On 5 April **Danton** goes to the guillotine. Along with him are **Desmoulins** and a number of other supporters, known as the *Indulgents* because they, like Danton himself, have begun to advocate clemency rather than violence. With the Hébertistes cleared away on one side and the *Indulgents* on the other, Robespierre and his allies are left in control of the Committee of Public Safety.

Twenty-seven tax farmers (see p.166), among them **Lavoisier**, are executed (8 May). On 8 June, four days after Robespierre's unanimous election as president of the Convention, the **Festival of the Supreme Being** (whose existence was recognised by decree the previous month) is organised by the painter David. Two days later, Robespierre extends the definition of 'enemies of the people', instituting the *'Grande Terreur'*. On 26 June the French army, expanded by conscription, defeats the Austrians at **Fleurus**, opening the way to a reoccupation of Belgium. The poet **André Chénier**, whose early enthusiasm for the Revolution has given way to horror at its excesses, expressed in dangerously outspoken articles, is guillotined (25 July).

27 July (9 thermidor) marks the fall of **Robespierre**, who is executed the following day along with 105 of his supporters, among them **Louis Saint-Just**, one of the principal executives of the Terror. Robespierre is brought down partly by a revulsion from the Terror, which no longer seems justified by the military situation, partly because too many deputies fear that accusations may be laid against them. On 1 August **Fouquier-Tinville**, the public prosecutor, is executed. On the same day the repeal of the Law of Suspects marks the end of the Terror. A week later, 478 prisoners are released.

In October the *École normale supérieure* is founded. An institute of higher education for France's academic élite, it will number among its alumni such names as Louis Pasteur, Henri Bergson, Emile Durkheim, Jean-Paul Sartre and Michel Foucault. The following month, the Jacobin club is closed. On 24 December, the Law of the Maximum, which has regulated prices at the cost of stifling commerce, is repealed.

1795 In January the progress of the French army continues with the occupation of **Holland**.

> ❝ Danton was the last to appear on the platform, soaked with the blood of his friends. Night was falling. At the foot of the horrible statue whose mass stood out against the sky in a dreadful silhouette, I saw, like a shade from Dante, the tribune standing, dimly lit by the dying sun, as though emerging from the tomb instead of about to enter it... I recall the full force of my feeling at Danton's last words, which I did not hear myself but which were passed round with horror and admiration: 'Make sure you show my head to the people; it's worth seeing.' ❞
>
> Arnault on Danton's last moments

At home, reaction against the excesses of the Revolution, intensified by the royalist desire for revenge, leads in February to a **'White Terror'**, which spreads from Paris to the provinces. Reprisals, particularly savage in Lyon and the Midi, carry on through the spring and summer. In April, a demonstration by *sans-culottes* calling for 'bread and a return to the Constitution of 93' is put down by the National Guard. Later in the month, the Paris *sections* (the 48 districts into which the city has been divided for administrative purposes) are disarmed in a move to narrow the opportunities for political violence.

The **treaty of Basel** (5 April) between France and Prussia puts France in control of the left bank of the Rhine. The following month the **treaty of the Hague** (16 May) brings Holland, now the **Batavian Republic**, into a forced alliance with France.

Another series of **revolutionary demonstrations** by *sans-culottes* is suppressed (20–23 May). At the end of the month the Revolutionary Tribunal is abolished. A **massacre of Jacobins** at Marseille on 5 June is further evidence of anti-revolutionary sentiment. On 8 June 'Louis XVII', the 10-year-old son of Louis XVI, dies in the Temple prison. On 24 June the **comte de Provence**, Louis XVI's brother, proclaims himself king Louis XVIII in the **manifesto of Verona**. The **second treaty of Basel** (22 July), between France and Spain, gives France control of the whole of Santo Domingo. On 22 August the **Constitution of Year III**, voted by the Convention, provides for a bicameral legislature with executive power in the hands of a five-man **Directory**. On 5 October (13 vendémiaire) an attempted **royalist coup** is crushed by Napoléon. Three weeks later, the Directory comes to power, with Napoléon in charge of internal affairs.

1796 On 2 March Napoléon is given overall command of the army in Italy, which faces an Austrian force of almost double its size. Following a victory over the Austrians at **Lodi**, Napoléon enters Milan (15–16 May). On 17 November he defeats the Austrians at the **pont d'Arcole**.

1797 Napoléon wins a decisive victory over the Austrians at **Rivoli**, near Verona (14 January). On 16 May **Venice** is occupied by the French. **'Gracchus' Babeuf** and his supporters, convicted of a left-wing conspiracy to overturn the Directory, go to the guillotine (27 May). A veteran of the Revolution, who narrowly escaped death during the Terror, Babeuf is noted for his proposals on agrarian reform. On 6 June **Genoa** is declared a Republic. Three weeks later a **Cisalpine Republic** is declared, with Milan as its capital.

Royalist success in the elections of 4 September prompts a government-inspired *coup d'état* that annuls the elections in 49 *départements* and reintroduces measures against *émigrés* and the clergy. Without consulting the Directory, Napoléon imposes on Austria the **treaty of Campo-Formio** (17 October), which recognizes the French annexation of Belgium and the establishment of the 'sister republics' in northern Italy but cynically hands Venice back to Austria. Napoléon then returns to Paris in triumph.

1798 Jacobin success in the elections of 11 May leads again to their annulment and a further erosion of democracy by the Directory.

On 19 May, Napoléon leaves for **Egypt**. Aware that an invasion of England is impracticable as long as the English fleet commands the sea, he has decided to combine his dream of an eastern empire with an attempt to undermine England's prosperity by occupying Egypt, which will give him control of the trade route to India. Initial successes in taking Malta, Alexandria and the Nile delta are followed by the disastrous battle of the Nile in **Aboukir Bay** (1 August) during which **Nelson** destroys the French fleet.

1799 Between February and May Napoléon invades **Syria** but is checked by the British at **Acre** and forced to retreat into Egypt again.

Against a background of unrest at home and abroad – rebellions in Switzerland, Belgium and Italy, continuing hostilities with England, counter-revolutionary uprisings in France itself, and resistance to yet another conscription law – the **abbé Sieyès**, one of the early champions of the Revolution and a skilled survivor, organises a coup, on 18 June, that brings Jacobins temporarily back to power in the Directory as a bulwark against counter-revolutionary forces.

On 9 October Napoléon lands in France, where the failures of his Egyptian campaign are largely unknown.

On 14 October the **Chouan rebels** take Le Mans. Alongside the Vendéens, they have been fighting a counter-revolutionary guerrilla war in western France for the past five years.

On 9 November (18 brumaire), in collusion with Sieyès, Napoléon stages a *coup d'état* to overthrow the Directory, replacing it with a **Consulate**. This consists of a triumvirate of consuls: Sieyès, Ducos and, in effective control, Napoléon himself.

The **Constitution of the Year VIII** is proclaimed (15 December). Republican in appearance, this in fact concentrates power in the hands of the First Consul, Napoléon, who appoints ministers and officials and presides over the State Council. Realising the need to heal divisions and restore domestic peace, Napoléon offers a pardon to the remaining Vendéen rebels in exchange for laying down their arms. Most of the leaders accept the offer and sign the **peace of Montfaucon**, bringing the conflict to an end.

Napoléon Bonaparte

Born in **Corsica** on 15 August, 1769, the son of a lawyer of noble ancestry, Napoléon must have looked set for a fairly undistinguished career as a soldier when he graduated from the military academy in Paris ranking 42 in a class of 58. It was at the **siege of Toulon**, where royalist troops with the British in support were holding out against republican forces, that Napoléon rose to prominence. His command of the artillery between September and December 1793 was decisive in driving out the British and facilitating the capture of the town. Bonaparte himself was made a brigadier general.

In disfavour after the fall of Robespierre, Napoléon recovered his standing when called upon to suppress a royalist uprising against the National Convention on 5 October, 1795 (13 vendémiaire). Five months later, two days after marrying **Joséphine de Beauharnais**, he left Paris as commander-in-chief of the army of **Italy**. A series of brilliant victories against the Austrians turned Napoléon into a popular hero, making him largely independent of the will of the **Directory**. After his campaign in **Egypt** – which received better publicity at home than it deserved – he returned to participate in the coup that ended the Directory and set the **Consulate** in its place.

Standing between the Jacobins and the royalists, Napoléon was well positioned: for those who feared the Revolution, he represented stability and a guarantee against revolutionary excess; for those who feared another monarchy, he represented a guarantee against losing the gains of the Revolution. When a royalist attempt was made on his life, there was widespread support for his establishment of a hereditary empire to fend off any bid to restore the Bourbons. Napoléon's own dynastic aspirations reflected a character that was increasingly dictatorial. The full apparatus of the state was deployed to suppress opposition and burnish his imperial image, while the various European sovereigns he had put in place, usually from his own family, were treated as little more than pawns on a diplomatic chess board. The failed blockade against England

and his ill-fated campaign in Russia left him prey to a legacy of European resentments that were finally enough to bring about his downfall at **Waterloo**. When he died on **St Helena** on 5 May, 1821, he bequeathed a legend of military and administrative genius that has given France one of the indisputably great figures of history.

Napoléon was a brilliant general, whose 'presence on the field,' according to Wellington, 'made the difference of forty thousand men.'

1800 In January, 60 out of Paris's 76 **newspapers** are suppressed. On 13 February the **Banque de France** is established. Four days later, the **Local Government Act** does away with elections for local office. Each *département* will now be run by a centrally appointed prefect.

Women's fashion in the post-Revolutionary period became increasingly simple and classically-inspired. This fashion plate is from the *Journal des dames et des modes* c.1803

Having secured his position in France, Napoléon again turns his attention to **Italy**, crossing the Alps in May. In the first week of June, French forces occupy Milan and Genoa before moving on to win a difficult but decisive victory over the Austrians at **Marengo** (14 June). On 1 October Spain restores **Louisiana** to France. A further French victory over the Austrians at **Hohenlinden** in Germany (3 December) forces them to accept the **treaty of Lunéville** (February, 1801), which leaves France in control of the left bank of the Rhine and recognizes her domination of the Austrian Netherlands, Switzerland and Italy. On 24 December, following Napoléon's rejection of Louis XVIII's pleas for a restoration of the monarchy, a royalist attempt is made on his life. Napoléon, unhurt, uses it as an opportunity to deport both Jacobins and royalists, thereby furthering his general policy of eliminating any source of political dissent.

1801 On 22 February, under pressure from France, Spain declares war on England's ally **Portugal**.

A concordat between Napoléon and **Pope Pius VII** (15 July) reaffirms the public right of worship but effectively ratifies the nationalization of Church property during the Revolution. Clergy will now be salaried by the state.

Following an invasion by British and Turkish forces, France withdraws from **Egypt** at the beginning of September.

1802 The **peace of Amiens** (25 March) brings a truce between France and England, both of them war-weary, but its failure to deal with the questions of Belgium and the Rhineland leaves the way open for future conflict.

On 26 April most of those on the list of *émigrés* benefit from an **amnesty**. Napoléon creates the order of the *Légion d'honneur* for services to the state (19 May). On 2 August he is declared **consul** for life.

In the same year, **Louis Joseph Gay-Lussac** (1778–1850) formulates his laws on the expansion of gases, and **François René de Chateaubriand** (1768–1848) publishes *Le Génie du christianisme*. The latter, a celebration of Christianity, owes its fame partly to the success of two short narratives contained within it, *Atala* and *René*, which establish Chateaubriand as a leader of the French Romantic movement.

1803 On 7 April **Toussaint Louverture**, deported to France the previous year after his surrender to Napoléon's forces, dies in captivity at the fort of Joux in the Jura. On the same day, the **franc**, which has been a unit of currency since 1795, is fixed by law in relation to gold and silver. A week later, the Banque de France is given the sole right to issue bank notes.

After a number of minor treaty violations, the rivalry between France and England breaks out in renewed hostilities. On 2 May, the agreement is signed for the **Louisiana Purchase**, by which France sells Louisiana to the United States.

1804 On 15 March Napoléon has the **duc d'Enghien**, wrongly suspected of complicity in a royalist conspiracy, kidnapped from Germany. A week later, to international dismay, the duke is summarily executed. The fear that Bonaparte, seen as guardian of the revolutionary heritage, might be a victim of royalist assassination is an important factor in winning popular support for the establishment of a hereditary empire to consolidate his position.

On 21 March Napoléon's *Code civil des Français*, known from 1807 as the **Code Napoléon**, comes into force. Two months later, on 18 May, he is proclaimed **emperor**. The **coronation** of Napoléon and Joséphine takes place at Notre-Dame de Paris (2 December). The event is later commemorated in a huge canvas by Jacques-Louis David, Napoléon's official painter.

Code Napoléon

For centuries the French legal system had relied on a mixture of **Roman law** in the southern parts of the country and **customary law** in Paris and the north, with much that concerned family life coming under the control of the Church. The period following the Revolution, when so much of the old order, and the privileges enshrined in it, had been demolished, was an ideal moment to formulate a new **civil code** based on principles of reason rather than on the prejudices and special interests of the past.

Napoléon set up a four-member commission, subject to frequent interventions by himself, to carry this out. The three books of the code deal respectively with the law of **persons**, of **goods** and of **contracts**. The operation of the law is separated from political or ecclesiastical considerations, and central to it is the principle of equal rights and equal treatment for all citizens. (This was rather less exciting news for women, who were classed as minors in what is a fundamentally conservative document.) Written in clear, accessible language, the code enjoyed a success that long outlasted Napoléon's empire and has been a formative influence on legal systems across the globe from Luxembourg to Latin America. It was Napoléon himself who, looking back across a career of legendary military and material achievement, affirmed on St Helena: 'My true glory…, what nothing will efface, what will live for ever, is my Code civil.'

1805 On 9 March an **office of censorship** is set up to ensure that nothing is printed against Napoléon or 'the interests of the state'. This is part of a wider strategy of control over what is written, said and printed in the empire. Two of France's most celebrated writers, Chateaubriand and Mme de Staël, will be forced into temporary exile from Paris by the new order.

On 8 April the **treaty of St Petersburg** creates an alliance between England and Russia which, with the addition of Austria, becomes the **third coalition** against France.

Napoléon is crowned **king of Italy** (26 May). On 20 October he defeats the Austrians at the **battle of Ulm**, but on the following day the French fleet is destroyed by Nelson at the **battle of Trafalgar**, putting an end to Napoléon's hopes of invading England. On 13 November the French occupy **Vienna**. On 2 December Napoléon defeats the Russians and Austrians at the **battle of Austerlitz**.

1806 The **revolutionary calendar** is abandoned (1 January).

In response to the formation of a **fourth coalition**, Napoléon turns his armies against Prussia and inflicts a severe defeat on them at the **battle of Jena** (14 October) before moving on to occupy Leipzig, Potsdam and Berlin. **Marshal Joachim Murat** then advances into **Poland**, occupying Warsaw on 27 November. Napoléon undertakes to **blockade** Europe against trade with England. In the event, the effects of the blockade weigh as heavily on some of the participants, starved of raw material from England's colonies, as on England herself.

Napoléon commissions the **Arc de Triomphe** to commemorate his military victories.

1807 The French army defeats the Russians at the **battle of Eylau** (8 February), which leaves a scene of slaughter that shocks even Napoléon. Four months later, after a second defeat at **the battle of Friedland** (14 June), Tsar Alexander I agrees the **treaty of Tilsit**, which isolates England and dismembers Prussia. In October the French invade **Portugal**, which has proved reluctant to join the blockade against England.

In the same year, **Mme de Staël** publishes *Corinne*, which becomes one of the most popular novels of the Romantic age, exercising a profound influence on 19th-century European attitudes to Italy.

The Departure of the Volunteers of 1792 by François Rude is one of four sculptural reliefs decorating the Arc de Triomphe

1808 Events across Europe offer faint signs of a turn in Napoléon's fortunes. The occupation of **Rome** by French troops intensifies a quarrel with Pius VII over papal jurisdiction in France. In Spain, the imposition of Napoléon's brother **Joseph Bonaparte** as king provokes a rebellion that marks the start of the **Peninsular War** and enables the British under **Sir Arthur Wellesley** (later Duke of Wellington) to establish a bridgehead in Portugal. On 30 August, the French surrender to the British at **Cintra** in Portugal and are forced to evacuate.

A large painting of the **Battle of Eylau**, by Napoléon's official battle artist **Antoine-Jean Gros**, shocks viewers with its graphic depiction of the dead and injured.

1809 In January **Charles Maurice de Talleyrand-Périgord**, probably France's most able diplomat, is disgraced after the discovery that he has been advising Russia not to side with Napoléon against Austria. In April, Austria joins England in the **fifth coalition** against the French.

On 6 July Napoléon defeats the Austrians, though with heavy losses, at the **battle of Wagram**. On the same day, the pope is arrested on Napoléon's orders and held in captivity. This follows Pius VII's excommunication of Napoléon for his **annexation of the Papal States** in May.

On 28 July the French are defeated by British forces at **Talavera** in Spain, but the British, unable to reach Madrid, then withdraw into their fortified Portuguese base behind the lines of **Torres Vedras**.

On 16 December Napoléon divorces Joséphine de Beauharnais, who has not borne him a child.

1810 Napoléon marries **Marie-Louise**, daughter of the defeated emperor of Austria (2 April). Increasingly despotic in outlook and action, Napoléon thinks ever more strongly in terms of founding a dynasty.

With 130 *départements* and control over much of Europe, France is at the zenith of her power, but in Spain a series of **guerrilla actions** (the modern meaning of guerrilla, Spanish for 'little war', originates in this conflict) is draining French resources.

1811 A son, given the title king of Rome, is born to Napoléon and Marie-Louise (20 March).

The French under **Masséna**, defeated by Wellington, finally abandon Portugal in May.

1812 In March hunger among the poor leads to **riots** in Caen.

On 12 June Napoléon annuls the Concordat and transfers the pope to **Fontainebleau**.

NAPOLEON'S EMPIRE, 1812

- Ruled by Napoleon
- Ruled by Napoleon's relatives
- Dependent state

NORWAY
SWEDEN
RUSSIAN EMPIRE
DENMARK
Copenhagen
REPUBLIC OF DANZIG
PRUSSIA
Hamburg
Berlin
DUCHY OF WARSAW
Warsaw
UNITED KINGDOM
Amsterdam
WESTPHALIA
London
Leipzig
Erfurt
Prague
Brussels
CONFEDERATION OF THE RHINE
AUSTRIAN EMPIRE
Paris
Vienna
Buda
Pest
FRANCE
Bern
Munich
HELVETIA
Lyon
Milan
Venice
Illyrian Provinces
Belgrade
Marseille
ITALY
OTTOMAN EMPIRE
LUCCA
Corsica
Papal States
Rome
MONTENEGRO
PORTUGAL
Madrid
Naples
NAPLES
Lisbon
SPAIN
SARDINIA
Balearic Islands
SICILY
0   200 km
MOROCCO
ALGERIA
Tunisia

After making alliances with Austria and Prussia against Russia, which has suffered from the blockade and distanced itself from France accordingly, Napoléon crosses the **Niemen** with an army of over half a million men (24 June). By 14 September, having won the costly **battle of Borodino**, the French are in **Moscow**. But there the campaign stalls. In a city all but destroyed by the huge fire that breaks out on the day of his arrival, Napoléon waits for offers of surrender that do not come. The Russians fade back into the vastness of their country, leaving only a burnt and hostile landscape. On 23 October the French begin their retreat. The terrible rigours of winter are aggravated by the guerrilla attacks of **Prince Kutuzov**'s Cossack cavalry. By the time it reaches Vilna on 9 December, Napoléon's *Grande Armée* numbers a pitiful 5000 men. Napoléon himself has already left, heading back to Paris four days earlier to face rising discontent. Encouraged by his disasters, the European powers are already preparing to strike.

1813 On 16 March **Prussia** declares war on France. In Spain, the defeat of the French at the **battle of Vitoria** (21 June) is followed by the withdrawal of Joseph Bonaparte. The way is open for Wellington to fight his way into France. In August, Austria declares war on France after a failure to agree terms at the **Congress of Prague**. Napoléon is defeated by coalition forces at the **battle of Leipzig** (16–19 October) and retreats from Germany.

> ❝ I have come to finish off, once and for all, the Colossus of Northern Barbarism. The sword is drawn. They must be thrust back into their snow and ice, so that for a quarter of a century at least they will not be able to interfere with civilized Europe. ❞
>
> Napoléon on his invasion of Russia, from the *Memoirs* of General de Caulaincourt

> I go, but you, my friends, will continue to serve France. Her happiness was my only thought. It will still be the object of my wishes. Do not regret my fate; if I have consented to survive, it is to serve your glory. I intend to write the history of the great achievements we have performed together. Adieu, my friends. Would I could press you all to my heart.

Napoléon taking leave of the imperial guard, 20 April, 1814

1814 With France under attack from all directions, Napoléon's position becomes increasingly desperate. When the coalition armies reach Paris, Talleyrand, as head of the provisional government, proclaims the deposition of Napoléon and opens negotiations with Louis XVIII, brother of Louis XVI. On 6 April, yielding to the inevitable, **Napoléon abdicates**. Two weeks later, after his farewell to the imperial guard in the courtyard of the château de Fontainebleau (the *adieux de Fontainebleau* of 20 April), he leaves for exile on the island of **Elba**.

Louis XVIII enters Paris (3 May). On 4 June he accords the French a 'Charter' that tries to strike a balance between an absolute and a parliamentary monarchy. In August Pope Pius VII, released earlier in the year, re-establishes the order of the **Jesuits**.

In September the European powers meet for the **Congress of Vienna**. Over the next nine months, they redraw the map of Europe in a way that maintains the balance of power but fails to take account of the nationalist aspirations that will undermine their achievement. Representing the France of Louis XVIII, Talleyrand acts skilfully to mitigate the political consequences of defeat.

In the same year, **Ampère** makes his first studies of atoms and molecules.

1815 On 1 March Napoléon returns to France, disembarking near Cannes. Three weeks later he is in Paris, Louis XVIII having prudently decamped.

On 31 May the **treaty of Vienna** seals a new coalition between England, Prussia, Austria and Holland. On 16 June, Napoléon defeats the Prussians under **Blücher** at the **battle of Ligny** and fights an indecisive action against Wellington at **Quatre Bras**. An ill-executed pursuit of the defeated Prussians allows the main part of Blücher's army to escape, while almost a third of the French army is held down by Blücher's rearguard and prevented from rejoining Napoléon. On 18 June Napoléon's depleted army of about 72,000 men meets a combined Anglo-Dutch and Prussian force of about 113,000 men at **Waterloo**. After a battle lasting for around seven hours, during which Blücher's army arrives just in time to tip the scales, the French are defeated. Altogether, over 50,000 men are killed or wounded. On 22 June, two days after his return to Paris, Napoléon again abdicates, this time finally, and is exiled to the island of **St Helena**.

7
France in the 19th century
1815–1914

The restoration of the monarchy in the wake of Napoléon's fall brought with it an ultra-royalist majority in the elected chamber. There were scores to be settled, and a period of '**White Terror**' followed. **Louis XVIII**, however, was intelligent enough to realize that in a country split between those who wanted to build on the achievements of the Revolution and those who wanted to erase all trace of it, only some form of political compromise would ensure survival. Accordingly, he refused to abandon the **Charter of 1814** and replaced the ultra-royalist administration with a more moderate one. The **assassination of the duc de Berry** and the accession of the intransigent **Charles X** swung the pendulum so far back towards the ultras that opposition stiffened into rebellion. In **1830**, three days of revolution, *Les Trois Glorieuses*, toppled the monarch and set **Louis-Philippe** in his place. Eighteen years later, the so-called July monarchy, which had provided relative stability but had mishandled the rising tide of liberal opposition, was itself overturned by the **revolution of 1848**. The nephew of Napoléon Bonaparte, who had already staged two coup attempts against Louis-Philippe, saw his chance. Elected President of the new Republic, **Louis-Napoléon Bonaparte** converted it four years later into a new empire, ruling as Napoléon III until France's defeat in the **Franco-Prussian War** of 1870 led to the **Paris Commune** and the establishment of the **Third Republic**.

As always, there were significant regional differences within

France, but in spite of periods of economic crisis and popular unrest, these were for the most part years of comparative prosperity, characterized by a more gradual process of **industrialization** than in England. **Railway networks** spread across the country, production of coal, iron and steel increased rapidly in the second half of the century, and technological innovations transformed certain areas of manufacture such as the **cotton industry**; but France remained a predominantly **agricultural society**, relying on small-scale enterprises.

Meanwhile, the political seesaw from right to left was reflected in social legislation that swung between the authoritarian and the progressive, until the advent of the Third Republic shifted policy decisively towards the liberal, anticlerical bias of the majority of deputies. Overall, France benefited from a foreign policy that, with the devastating exception of the Franco-Prussian War, tended to steer clear of serious embroilment in international disputes. A more attractive alternative was the rich seam offered by **colonial expansion**, where economic gain could be combined with a cultural *mission civilisatrice*. The mid-century conquest of **Algeria** was followed in the early years of the Third Republic by a burst of activity in **Indochina**, the **Pacific** and **West Africa** that laid the foundations of France's 20th-century colonial empire.

Culturally, the roll call of France's achievements between the fall of Napoléon and the start of World War I is staggering. The writings of **Hugo** and **Chateaubriand**, the music of **Berlioz** and the paintings of **Delacroix** represent only part of the French contribution to **Romanticism** alone. Such names as **Stendhal**, **Balzac**, **Flaubert**, **Zola**, **Baudelaire**, **Rimbaud** and **Verlaine** in literature, **Saint-Saëns**, **Bizet**, **Offenbach**, **Franck**, **Debussy** and **Ravel** in music, **Monet**, **Manet**, **Degas**, **Rodin**, **Renoir**, **Gauguin**, **Cézanne**, **Braque** and **Matisse** in art suggest some measure of the range and genius of what France gave the world during these years. And this artistic energy was paralleled by the advances in science and medicine made by **Pierre** and **Marie Curie**, **Louis Pasteur**, **Marcelin Berthelot**, **Jean Martin Charcot** and others. Against a political backdrop that was for much of the century anything but heroic, France once more asserted her cultural pre-eminence in Europe.

1815 From June to September **ultra-royalist** forces institute a second **'White Terror'**, especially in the south, where it persists for much of the following year in spite of efforts by **Louis XVIII** to moderate its excesses. On 6 July the **Prussians** enter Paris, two days ahead of King Louis XVIII.

The imperial army is demobilised (1 August). In elections to the **Chamber of Deputies** (14–21 August), the ultra-royalists ('ultras') sweep to victory. Because such a royalist majority had seemed out of the question, this is known as the *'chambre introuvable'*.

On 24 September **Talleyrand** resigns and is succeeded as first minister by the **duc de Richelieu**.

Under the second, and harsher, **treaty of Paris** (20 November), imposed after Napoléon's Hundred Days, France is returned to its pre-1790 frontiers and obliged to pay a large indemnity, with foreign occupation of eastern parts of the country until payment is made.

Carême publishes *Le Pâtissier pittoresque*.

1816 On 12 January an **amnesty** is voted for revolutionaries, with the exception of a few regicides. **Divorce**, already made more difficult by Napoléon's *Code civil*, is abolished in May.

On 2 July the French ship the *Medusa* is wrecked off the coast of West Africa. Of 149 passengers who escape onto a raft, only 15 survive. **Théodore Géricault**'s painting of the subject, *The Raft of the Medusa* (1818–19), causes uproar both for its horrifying realism and for its implied criticism of the royalist navy's incompetence.

Marie-Antoine Carême and French gastronomy

Abandoned by his father while still a child, **Carême** (1784–1833) found work in the kitchen of a cheap Paris restaurant. From these beginnings he went on to become the creator of French *grande cuisine*. The son of a stonemason, he had an irrepressible interest in architecture that permeated his attitude to **gastronomy**. This was reflected not just in the spectacular table decorations, *pièces montées*, for which he is famous – meticulously constructed Greek temples, bridges, classical monuments and the like – but also in his concern to bring structure and planning to meals that had previously been a random clutter of sometimes ill-assorted dishes. He sought a combination of elements that was pleasing to the eye as well as the taste. After working for Talleyrand, he went on to take service with the Tsar of Russia, with England's Prince Regent and finally, back in Paris, with Baroness Rothschild. Along with **Anthelme Brillat-Savarin**'s *Physiologie du goût* (1825), his *Le Pâtissier pittoresque* (1815) and *L'art de la cuisine au dix-neuvième siècle* (1833) mark the beginnings of a modern literature of French gastronomy.

In the early 20th century **Prosper Montagné**, who was responsible for the *Larousse Gastronomique* (1933), abandoned the more elaborate aspects of Carême's cuisine, switching the emphasis towards the simpler menus and more efficient methods of preparation promoted by **Auguste Escoffier**. It was Escoffier (1847–1935), dubbed the Emperor of Chefs, who laid out the principles of French *grande cuisine* in a number of books he wrote with Philéas Gilbert. The past half century has seen a reaction against the traditions of *grande cuisine* towards a **nouvelle cuisine** that tends to eschew heavy dishes and thick

Recognising that the **extreme policies** of the ultras will merely divide the country, Louis dissolves the *chambre introuvable* in September. New elections bring victory for the

sauces in favour of small, sometimes tiny, quantities of carefully selected foods, displayed with elaborate artistry.

'A well ordered kitchen': frontispiece to the 3rd edition of *Le Cuisine Parisien* (1825)

more **moderate royalists**, inaugurating a period of fragile stability during which the liberals make steady gains in the annual elections of one fifth of the legislative chamber.

On 8 December **Marshal Ney** is executed for having rallied to Napoléon after his escape from Elba.

Joseph Niepce develops the first camera, and successfully produces a heliographic image of a landscape.

1817 A serious **grain shortage**, continuing from the previous year, causes rioting in the provinces.

In February restrictions, based on age and level of taxation, are placed on the right to vote or be elected.

The passage des Panoramas becomes the first site in Paris to be lit by **gas**.

1818 On 10 March a new law on military recruitment provides for a **volunteer army** to be brought up to strength by conscription by lot.

In October both **La Fayette** and the writer **Benjamin Constant** win seats in elections to the Chamber. In the same month, the **treaty of Aix-la-Chapelle** ratifies arrangements for the payment of France's indemnity, which brings the allied occupation to an end two years ahead of schedule.

1819 In May liberal laws are passed relaxing controls on the **press**.

In November the moderate **Elie Decazes**, who enjoys the king's confidence and has wielded effective power for some time as minister of the interior, forms a new administration.

Forced by financial troubles to take lodgings in the former convent of the Abbaye-aux-Bois, **Mme Récamier** re-establishes her salon, where **Chateaubriand** will later hold court.

1820 On 13 February the assassination of Louis XVIII's nephew, the **duc de Berry**, by a fanatical Bonapartist upsets the political balance. Decazes is forced to resign and the ultras regain the political initiative. Laws are introduced restricting civil liberties and the freedom of the press. Those who pay the most taxes are given a double vote.

The Greek statue (c.150 BC) known as the **Venus de Milo** is found on the Aegean island of Melos and brought to France.

1821 **Napoléon** dies on St Helena (5 May).

In the October elections, the right reinforces its majority. Liberal reaction to the increasing power of the ultras leads in November and December to the renewal of the republican secret society known as the *charbonnerie*, based on the Italian Carbonari.

In December a new administration is formed under one of the leaders of the ultras, the **comte de Villèle**.

1822 In March further restrictions are placed on the press.

On 21 September the **'four sergeants of La Rochelle'**, implicated in an attempted *charbonnerie* uprising earlier in the year, are executed.

In December **Chateaubriand** becomes Foreign Minister.

Jean-François Champollion deciphers the **Rosetta stone**, thereby providing the key to ancient Egyptian hieroglyphics.

1823 In April France intervenes in Spain to restore the authority of **Ferdinand VII**, who has been forced by a liberal revolt to accept a parliamentary monarchy. The **capture of Madrid** the following month enhances the popularity of the ultras.

1824 The right wins an overwhelming victory in the elections (February–March).

In June the length of **military service** is increased from six to eight years.

Louis XVIII dies (16 September), and is succeeded by his brother as **Charles X** (crowned at Reims 29 May, 1825).

At the Salon of 1824, **Ingres**' Raphaelesque *Vow of Louis XIII* is seen to exemplify the virtues of academic classicism in opposition to **Delacroix**'s arch-Romantic *Massacre of Chios*.

1825 In April Charles immediately sets out to turn back the clock by introducing two laws central to the ultra cause: **émigrés** are to be indemnified for the loss of their property; **sacrilege** becomes a capital offence. These are the first of a series of measures designed to wipe out the legacy of the Revolution and restore the authority of Church and king.

1827 In April the **Dey of Algiers**, the local ruler, strikes the French consul with a fan. This insult – unprovoked, according to the French; a response to consular insolence, according to the Algerians – provides the pretext for a **French blockade**.

Liberal gains in the November elections turn the Villèle administration into a minority government.

1828 In January the more moderate **Martignac administration** replaces Villèle's. Laws on the press are liberalized in July.

The first **French railway**, drawn by horses, opens between St-Etienne and Andrézieux. In Paris, **horse-drawn omnibuses** come into operation.

1829 In August Charles X dismisses Martignac, replacing him by the **prince de Polignac** at the head of a diehard ultra administration.

Louis Braille publishes details of his system of tangible writing for the blind.

Gas lighting comes to the streets of Paris.

The influential political literary magazine the **Revue des Deux Mondes** is founded to establish a cultural, economic and political bridge between France and the USA. Its contributors will include Chateaubriand, Delacroix, Baudelaire, Hugo, Taine, Sainte-Beuve and Michelet.

1830 On 18 March conflict between Charles X and the liberal deputies of the Chamber results in **'the address of the 221'** to the king, reminding him of the principles of Louis XVIII's Charter.

Their blockade having proved fruitless, the French land an expeditionary force in **Algeria** (16 June). On 5 July the Dey surrenders and Algiers is taken.

Elections held in June and July reinforce the **liberal majority**. The king responds by dissolving the Chamber, narrowing the suffrage and placing further restrictions on the press.

The decrees, published on 26 July, lead directly to **revolution**. From 27 to 29 July *Les Trois Glorieuses* (the Three Glorious Days) usher in a revolution which, at the cost of about 1000 dead in the fighting, brings the Bourbon dynasty to an end. With barricades in the streets, regiments of the army in open mutiny, and Paris in the hands of the rebels, it looks for a time as though the days of the republic are about to return, but a powerful group of deputies and journalists, headed by **Adolphe Thiers**, persuades the duc d'Orléans, **Louis-Philippe**, to accept the role of constitutional monarch. On 31 July Louis-Philippe appears on the balcony of the Hôtel de Ville and receives the theatrical endorsement of **La Fayette**, who embraces him, wrapped in a tricolour flag. Three days later, Charles X abdicates and leaves for England. The July revolution is immediately commemorated by **Delacroix** in his famous painting *La Liberté guidant le peuple*.

Louis-Philippe is proclaimed king on 9 August, having agreed to reign under a revised charter that stipulates a broader suffrage, the abolition of censorship and a reduced

La Liberté guidant le peuple (Liberty leading the people) by Eugène Delacroix was inspired by the events in Paris of 1830 which the artist witnessed first-hand

constitutional status for the Catholic Church. On 2 November a government of broadly liberal tendency is formed under **Jacques Laffitte**.

Earlier in the year, the first night of **Victor Hugo**'s melo-drama *Hernani* (25 February) results in a pitched battle between the adherents of classicism, who oppose the play, and the revolutionary forces of Romanticism, led by the writer **Théophile Gautier**, who support it.

Honoré de Balzac publishes *Les Chouans*, the first of his great series of interlocking novels (called collectively *La Comédie humaine*) which explore and analyse contemporary French society.

Hector Berlioz's *La Symphonie fantastique*, which attempts to tell a story through music, extends the symphonic form into something more emotive and subjective.

Barthélemy Thimonnier invents a sewing machine capable of making 200 stitches per minute. He wins a contract to make uniforms for the French army but his factory is later attacked and destroyed by irate tailors.

In the dance halls of Montmartre the French **can-can** makes its appearance.

Stendhal's novel *Le Rouge et le Noir* paints an unsparing picture of society in Restoration France.

1831 On 9 March Louis-Philippe creates the French **Foreign Legion**, the *Légion étrangère*.

Casimir Périer heads a new government, replacing that of Laffitte (13 March).

In November an uprising of **silk workers** in Lyon is harshly suppressed.

The occupation of Oran, Bône and Bougie marks a further stage in the **colonization** of Algeria.

The Foreign Legion

It was not by chance that the creation of the *Légion étrangère* in 1831 coincided with France's first major attempt at colonization in the 19th century. Having taken **Algiers** in the previous year, the nation had now embarked on a course that would lead to the acquisition of a new empire. The legion, set up to accommodate foreign mercenaries who were already cut off from their roots, was well adapted to the process of colonial expansion. With its headquarters at **Sidi-Bel-Abbès**, it played a central part in the conquest of Algeria and went on to serve France's colonial interests across the world, as well as participating in a range of national conflicts from the Franco-Prussian War to World War II. Its recruits, whose oath of allegiance was not to France but to the legion, were drawn from a variety of (mostly European) countries and an even greater variety of backgrounds; few questions were asked about a man's past. With its white *képi* and red epaulettes, the uniform of the legionnaire became a symbol of romantic adventure thanks to a series of novels and films in the 1920s and 1930s, most famously P.C. Wren's *Beau Geste* (1925) and its sequels. At its peak in the early 1950s the legion numbered some 35,000 men. Although its headquarters are now in France, it continues to have a role in many of the nation's military actions abroad.

On 4 November **Charles Philipon** begins publishing a weekly satirical newspaper, *La Caricature*, which employs a brilliant team of artists including **Honoré Daumier**. The following year he starts a daily satirical paper, *Le Charivari*.

1832 In February a **legitimist** conspiracy in Paris is foiled. This is one of a number of plots and assassination attempts against Louis-Philippe from both the legitimists (as the ultras are now known) and the republicans. A couple of months after this, the widow of the **duc de Berry** lands in France in the vain hope of rallying support for the duke's posthumous son. Her arrest in September puts an end to the attempt.

In March **cholera** breaks out in Paris. The continuing danger of cholera will add force to Napoléon III's decision in the middle of the century to reconstruct Paris.

1833 On 28 June **François Guizot**, as minister of education, introduces an important reform (the *loi Guizot*) that increases the provision of schools, establishing the principle of general **primary education**.

1834 **Workers' unrest** leads to riots in Paris and Lyon.

A general government is created for French territories in **North Africa**.

Founding of the association that later becomes the **Jockey Club**, one of the most exclusive circles of 19th-century Paris's high society.

1835 On 28 June French forces are defeated by the Algerian leader **Abd el-Kader** at the start of a 12-year conflict.

Giuseppe Fieschi makes an unsuccessful attempt on the life of Louis-Philippe that leaves 18 people dead (28 July).

In January **Pierre François Lacenaire** is guillotined. A well-educated bourgeois, Lacenaire has chosen a life of theft and murder. The piquant combination of respectability, dandyism and calculated viciousness turns him into one of French history's most celebrated criminals.

1836 At the end of October **Louis-Napoléon Bonaparte** launches a failed *coup d'état* from Strasbourg. A week later, on 6 November, Charles X dies in Austria.

An obelisk transported from **Luxor** is erected in the place de la Concorde, in Paris.

1837 On 13 October the Algerian city of **Constantine** is taken by the French.

Elections in November reinforce support for Louis-Philippe.

A **railway** is laid from Paris to Versailles. Between the middle of the century and the outbreak of World War I the French rail network will expand from under 4000 to around 40,000 kilometres.

Berlioz writes his *Grande Messe de Morts*, a state-commissioned requiem. The work's vast scale – one section alone employs four brass bands – makes Berlioz the target of critical ridicule.

1838 **Louis-Jacques Daguerre** develops the photographic process that creates the daguerreotype, much used for portraits in the mid-19th century.

The composer and pianist **Frédéric Chopin**, resident in Paris since 1831, begins his relationship with the free-thinking novelist Aurore Dudevant (better known as **George Sand**). While holidaying with her in Majorca, Chopin writes his 24 *Préludes* for piano.

1839 Two revolutionaries, **Armand Barbès** and **Auguste Blanqui**, lead an unsuccessful insurrection against the government of Louis-Philippe (12 May).

Publication of **Stendhal**'s novel, *La Chartreuse de Parme*, which initially has little success but is highly praised by Balzac in a celebrated article for his short-lived journal *Revue parisienne*: 'Never before have the hearts of princes, ministers, courtiers and women been depicted like this…'

1840 On 6 August, in the wake of another failed coup attempt, Louis-Napoléon is imprisoned at the **fort of Ham**, where he will remain until 1846.

At the end of October a **new administration**, in which François Guizot is the guiding force, inaugurates a period of relative stability.

On 15 December **Napoléon's ashes**, which have been returned to France, are deposited in Les Invalides.

1841 A law, widely disregarded in practice, is passed to restrict **child labour** in factories.

1842 France occupies the **Marquesas**, **Wallis** and **Gambier islands** in the Pacific and declares a protectorate in **Tahiti**.

August Comte (1798–1857) completes the publication of his six-volume *Cours de philosophie positive* (1830–42), an exposition of positivist philosophy which lays the groundwork of modern sociology.

1843 A meeting at Eu between **Queen Victoria** and Louis-Philippe establishes cordial relations between France and England that are undermined two years later when Guizot, as Foreign Minister, promotes a marriage between the duc de Montpensier and the Spanish infanta which **Lord Palmerston** considers hostile to British interests.

1844 In August a French victory over Moroccan forces at **Isly** marks a further stage in the continuing war against the Algerian leader Abd el-Kader, who has now taken refuge with the Moroccans.

Publication of *Les Trois Mousquetaires* by **Alexandre Dumas** (père).

1846 Louis-Napoléon **escapes** from the fort of Ham (25 May).

A **deteriorating social situation**, due to poor harvests, industrial unrest, peasant uprisings in the west and south, and a rash of bankruptcies, heightens resentment against the government.

The inequities of the *status quo* are highlighted by **Proudhon**'s *Système des contradictions économiques, ou Philosophie de la misère*.

Charles Baudelaire's *Le Salon de 1846*, with its eulogy of the painter **Eugène Delacroix**, proclaims the natural opposition between the artist and bourgeois society – a theme that

Daumier's caricature of Louis-Philippe as a pear (*poire* also means fool)

catches the critical mood of work by writers such as **George Sand**, **Eugène Sue** and **Alphonse de Lamartine**, as well as artists like **Honoré Daumier** and **Gustave Courbet**.

Louis-Philippe grows more authoritarian, and Guizot, now Prime Minister, steadfastly resists calls to broaden the suffrage.

1847 Faced with a government ban on public political meetings, the leaders of the **liberal opposition** begin a campaign of **'banquets'** to provide a forum for expressing political discontent.

In October, the capture of Abd el-Kader brings one phase of the conquest of Algeria to an end. The brutal 'pacification' of the **southern Sahara**, on which France embarks shortly afterwards, will continue until 1857.

Théodore Rousseau rents a house in the village of **Barbizon** near the Forest of Fontainebleau, where he becomes the leading figure in a school of landscape artists who paint directly from nature.

1848 A ban on the large political banquet scheduled for 22 February leads to **demonstrations** in the Latin Quarter and across the eastern part of Paris. Barricades go up in the streets, and a surge of revolutionary activity brings the

---

Pierre Joseph Proudhon

Born into a working-class family in Besançon, **Pierre Joseph Proudhon** (1809–65) became the most influential of a generation of French socialist thinkers. In his first major work, *Qu'est-ce que la propriété?* (1840), he proclaimed himself an anarchist and made the statement with which his name has ever since been somewhat misleadingly associated: 'Property is theft'. In fact, Proudhon's target was property ownership as a system of exploitation, rather than the principle of private ownership itself. Libertarian in outlook (though conservative in the role he envisaged for women), he saw reform as a process that should emerge from the peaceful economic action of groups of workers rather than through violent revolution.

The clash between his ideas and the authoritarian thinking of **Karl Marx** led the latter to respond to Proudhon's *Système des contradictions économiques, ou Philosophie de la misère* (1846) with *Misère de la philosophie*. Imprisoned between 1849 and 1852 for his criticisms of Louis-Napoléon, Proudhon was again threatened with imprisonment after the publication of *De la justice dans la révolution et dans l'Eglise* (1858) but escaped by fleeing to Belgium. His lasting importance is twofold: through his influence on **Mikhail Bakunin**, in particular, he became the father, or at least the patron, of the anarchist movement; by his promotion of a form of anti-authoritarian, decentralized socialism, he made a significant contribution to French working-class radical thought.

downfall of Louis-Philippe, who abdicates and leaves for exile in England. On 25 February a **Republic** is declared, with the poet **Alphonse de Lamartine** as one of the leaders of the provisional government. Political clubs spring up to debate ideas for radical social reform, and a series of liberal measures are voted, including universal male suffrage (5 March) and the establishment of '*ateliers nationaux*' (national workshops) for the benefit of unemployed workers.

In April the tide begins to turn against the revolutionaries. A socialist demonstration is put down by the National Guard, and the elections on 23 April produce a clear majority for **the moderate republicans**. On 27 April **Victor Schoelcher** is responsible for the abolition of slavery in French territories.

As the assembly veers to the right, the expensive '*ateliers nationaux*', which provide money for the unemployed, are disbanded (21 June). Over the next five days a revolt of workers and students is bloodily suppressed by **General Cavaignac**. Apart from the thousands killed in street-fighting, 1500 are shot without trial, 25,000 arrested and 11,000 imprisoned or deported.

On 12 November a **new constitution** is established which provides for the election of a president for a four-year term by universal male suffrage. A legislative assembly will also be elected, but the balance of power between president and assembly remains unclear. **Louis-Napoléon**

> ❝ The red flag has done no more than go round the Champ-de-Mars, trailing through the blood of the people. The tricolour flag has gone round the world, carrying the name, the glory and the liberty of the nation. ❞
>
> Lamartine arguing successfully against replacing the tricolour with the red flag (1848)

Bonaparte, who has returned from exile, wins the presidential election on 10 December by a large majority.

Publication of *La dame aux camélias* by **Alexandre Dumas** (fils), a novel (later a play) that causes controversy by treating the story of a courtesan in a highly sympathetic manner.

1849–50 Elections to the legislative assembly (13 May, 1849) confirm the **swing to the right**. Political and personal freedoms are curbed by a number of measures, including restrictive press laws, the suspension of the right of association, a narrowing of the suffrage, and harsher penalties for political crimes. Teachers come under closer government supervision and the Church is given a dominant role in education. The political scientist **Alexis de Tocqueville** serves briefly as minister for Foreign Affairs, but in 1851 he retires from politics following Napoléon's coup.

1850 Three paintings by **Gustave Courbet** exhibited at the Salon – *The Burial at Ornans*, *The Peasants of Flagey* and *The Stonebreakers* – establish the artist as a leader of the new Realist school.

1851 On 15 September Louis-Napoléon, the Prince-President, lays the first stone of a new covered market, **Les Halles**, whose structure, designed by **Victor Baltard**, makes innovative use of a metal framework.

Prevented by the royalist majority from changing the constitution to allow himself a second term as president, Louis-Napoléon mounts a *coup d'état* in December, dissolving the Assembly, restoring universal male suffrage and announcing a plebiscite on a new constitution. The republican riots that follow this move result in 27,000 arrests and 10,000 deportations to Algeria. Held on 21–22 December, the plebiscite produces a 76 percent majority in support of the coup.

1852 On 14 January the new Constitution is promulgated, extending the president's term to ten years and giving him greatly increased powers.

Following a triumphal tour of the provinces and some carefully stage-managed petitions, a **second plebiscite** (21 November) gives overwhelming support to the restoration of the empire. Louis-Napoléon bows to the will of the nation.

On 2 December the **Second Empire** is proclaimed, and Louis-Napoléon Bonaparte adopts the title emperor **Napoléon III**.

The launch of the **Crédit mobilier** reflects new developments in the banking industry, which sees the founding over the next twelve years of the Crédit Industriel et commercial, the Crédit Lyonnais and the Société générale.

Paris gets its first **department store** with the opening of *Au Bon Marché*. In spite of competition from *Printemps*, opened in 1865, and *Samaritaine*, opened in 1870, this will remain the largest department store in the world until World War I.

1853 In January Napoléon III marries **Eugénie de Montijo**.

Baron Haussmann and the transformation of Paris

Paris in the mid-19th century was still a semi-medieval city of narrow, crowded streets and huddled buildings. Drainage was primitive, light and air were at a premium. In 1853 **Georges Haussmann** (1809–91) was appointed Prefect of the Seine with a brief from Napoléon III to create a new capital – grander, healthier and more beautiful than the old. Haussmann acted with ruthless decision, demolishing whole areas of the city in his pursuit of modernization. The **Île de la Cité** was swept clear of its warren of picturesque, menacing streets and given a new identity, heavy with the weight of official architecture. Wide, tree-lined **boulevards** cut through the old quarters; large squares acted as hubs for a network of radiating streets; urban parks opened out the city still further; grand public buildings such as **Charles Garnier's** new opera house proclaimed the prosperity and prestige of Napoléon's empire. Paris was to be a capital adapted to the social and commercial needs of the modern world, where goods and people could be carried efficiently along the main arteries to and from the city's strategically placed railway stations. The rich were no longer expected to live cheek by jowl with the poor, who were increasingly dispersed to the city's rim.

In addition, there was a **political agenda** that the events of 1830 and 1848 had brought to the fore. Cluttered districts like the faubourg St-Antoine had yet again proved dangerously suitable for revolutionary barricades and close-quarter fighting. What Napoléon III had in mind was an urban layout, epitomised by a street such as the boulevard de Sébastopol, that favoured the tactics and fire-power of an organised military force. Haussmann's mixture of personal energy and administrative efficiency enabled him in the space of less than 20 years to transform the city in ways that were later copied around the world. It was a controversial process, not least because the speculative opportunities gave rise to widespread corruption. Haussmann's programme came at a cost, both social and aesthetic, but it was he, none the less, who did more than anyone else to create modern Paris.

In June **Georges Eugène Haussmann** is appointed Prefect of the Seine.

In September France occupies **New Caledonia**.

1854 In need of both allies and prestige in Europe, Napoléon III joins England in declaring war on **Russia**, ostensibly in defence of the Ottoman Empire (27 March). Apart from victories at the battles of **Alma** (20 September) and **Inkerman** (5 November), the **Crimean War** gives little cause for celebration, but France emerges with honour intact and increased diplomatic influence, reflected in her role as host for the **treaty of Paris** (1856) that brings the war to an end.

1856 On 16 March the birth of the **prince imperial** seems to assure the continuance of the dynasty.

Gustave Flaubert's first novel, *Madame Bovary*, is published. Flaubert's tale of a bored, provincial doctor's wife who seeks romantic fulfilment in adultery, and ultimately kills herself, shocks many readers by the author's detached tone and apparent lack of moral judgement.

1857 Charles Baudelaire publishes *Les Fleurs du mal*, a collection of poems that explores with unprecedented directness the complexities and perversities of love. Within

> " Baudelaire had supper at the table next to ours. He was without a cravat, his shirt open at the neck and his head shaved, just as if he were going to be guillotined. A single affectation: his little hands washed and cared for, the nails kept scrupulously clean. The face of a maniac, a voice that cuts like a knife, and a precise elocution that tries to copy Saint-Just and succeeds. He denies, with some obstinacy and a certain harsh anger, that he has offended morality with his verse. "
>
> From Edmond and Jules de Goncourt's *Journal*, trans. Robert Baldick

Charles Baudelaire photographed by Nadar

a few months of each other, both *Les Fleurs du mal* and *Madame Bovary* are prosecuted for offending religion and public morals. That two of the greatest literary works of the century should fall foul of the authorities is an indication of the restrictive and illiberal character of the early years of the Second Empire.

1858 On 14 January an **assassination attempt** is made on the emperor and empress by the Italian patriot **Felice Orsini** in the hope of starting a revolution that will spread to Italy. Orsini is guillotined on 13 March.

Between February and July the **Virgin Mary** appears to Bernadette Soubirous (1844–79) at **Lourdes**. The cult that later grows up around these apparitions turns Lourdes into one of the world's main sites of Catholic pilgrimage.

On 13 July Napoléon III and the Italian first minister **Cavour** meet at Plombières in the Vosges and agree a strategy to expel the Austrians from northern Italy.

Charles Worth, the 'father of *haute couture*', opens his own shop. Worth brings a new level of tailoring to women's fashion, and becomes internationally famous after being taken up by the Empress Eugénie.

1859 The occupation of **Saigon** marks a further stage in France's colonial expansion (18 February). Over the next eight years a substantial part of Indochina will be brought under French control.

On 3 May a declaration of war against **Austria** is followed by costly Franco-Piedmontese victories at **Magenta** (4 June) and **Solferino** (24 June), but fears of Prussian intervention, as well as Catholic opposition from within Italy, bring the conflict to an early end. Peace negotiations begin with a meeting between Napoléon III and the Austrian emperor **Franz-Joseph** at Villafranca in July. Lombardy is transferred from Austria to France, which passes it on to Piedmont, and the way is opened for the emergence of the **kingdom of Italy** in March, 1861.

An amnesty for **political exiles** heralds a move towards more liberal domestic policies.

Offenbach's satirical operetta *Orpheus in the Underworld* ridicules the ruling class. It also confirms the popularity of the can-can, which will become a symbol of the risqué attractions of 19th-century Paris.

First performance of **Charles Gounod**'s opera *Faust*.

1860 A **free-trade agreement** is negotiated with England in January, but the lowering of protectionist barriers dismays the business community that had previously supported the emperor.

Under the **treaty of Turin**, France regains possession of Nice and Savoy after a referendum – the price agreed between Cavour and Napoléon III for French support in the war against Austria.

A Franco-British expedition to China (August–November) results in the **capture of Beijing**.

1861 **Pierre Michaux** and his son **Ernest** invent the first usable **bicycle**.

1861–62 While France continues its conquest of Indochina, it also mounts an expedition, in conjunction with the English and Spanish, to protect its economic interests in **Mexico**. France is soon left on its own, and Napoléon's subsequent attempt to establish an empire under the Austrian emperor's brother, **Maximilian**, ends in embarrassing failure five years later when French troops are driven out of Mexico and Maximilian himself is executed (19 June, 1867). The execution is later depicted in a series of paintings and prints by **Edouard Manet**.

1863 On 11 April **Cambodia** becomes a French protectorate.

Publication of *La Vie de Jésus* by philosopher and historian **Ernest Renan**. The book causes controversy by rejecting the divinity of Jesus.

Manet shows his *Déjeuner sur l'herbe* at the first **Salon des Refusés**, which has been set up to exhibit those artists rejected by the official Salon. Manet's painting scandalizes the artistic establishment by its irreverent use of classical models as well as by its depiction of nudity in an unconventional setting, but it provides a beacon for the group of young painters who will later launch the Impressionist movement.

1864 The right of workers to **strike** is recognized by law (25 May).

1865 **Stéphane Mallarmé** writes *L'après-midi d'un faune*, an evocative, elusive poem in free verse that later inspires an orchestral piece by Debussy.

1866–67 Napoléon tries unsuccessfully to claim territory from the **Prussians** in return for the friendly neutrality he has shown over their war with Austria. His diplomatic mishandling of the situation leaves a legacy of ill-feeling that is tinder for the Franco-Prussian War of 1870.

1867 **Jules Michelet** (1798–1874) completes his 17-volume *Histoire de France*, on which he has been working since 1831. Along with his *Histoire de la Révolution française* (1847–53), this monumental synthesis of French history will have an incalculable influence on future historians of France.

Claude Monet completes his *Women in the Garden*, a large canvas painted out of doors over several months. Concerned to replicate specific light conditions, Monet has the canvas lifted by pulleys in and out of a trench.

1868 Laws are passed relaxing controls on the press and recognizing the **right of assembly**.

The bones of **Cro-Magnon man** (see p.3) are discovered during the construction of a new railway line in the Dordogne.

1869 On 16 November the empress Eugénie opens the **Suez canal**, which, under the direction of **Ferdinand de Lesseps**, has taken ten years to build.

Publication of **Victor Hugo**'s epic novel of injustice *Les Misérables* and of **Gustave Flaubert**'s *L'Education sentimentale*.

The *Folies–Bergère* variety theatre is founded in Paris, and the **café de Flore**, which in the 1940s will become a centre of French intellectual life, opens its doors for the first time.

1870 In January **Emile Ollivier** is appointed by Napoléon III to head a new government that looks set to take the empire towards a more liberal, parliamentary regime, but the projects for reform are overtaken by events.

On 19 July, France declares war on **Prussia**. Relations between France and Prussia have been strained since the Prussian defeat of Austria in 1866. France sees the balance of power in Europe shifting too much in Prussia's favour, Prussia sees France as the main obstacle to a unified Germany. A disagreement over the succession to the throne of Spain gives Bismarck the chance he wants. By publishing an amended and insulting version of the **Ems telegram**, which details the king of Prussia's response to Napoléon's request for assurances that no member of the Hohenzollern family will seek the Spanish throne (and thereby create the possibility of a hostile alliance between Spain and Prussia), **Bismarck** manoeuvres France into taking the role of aggressor. Within a month, a series of defeats at the hands of the Prussian general von Moltke leaves half the French army cornered in Metz, the other half in Sedan.

On 2 September Napoléon III, encircled with his army at **Sedan**, surrenders. Without allies and faced by a superior army, the French have been fighting against the odds, but this ignominious collapse results in the immediate fall of the empire.

The **Third Republic** is proclaimed on 4 September and a provisional government formed. A fortnight later, Paris is besieged by the Prussians. On 7 October **Léon Gambetta**, minister of the interior, escapes from the capital by balloon to raise an army against Prussia.

1871 One by one the armies raised in different parts of France with phenomenal energy by Gambetta are defeated. On 28

January **Paris surrenders** and an armistice is agreed with the Prussian forces. The National Assembly, elected on 8 February and meeting in Bordeaux, appoints **Adolphe Thiers** to head a predominantly conservative administration. Towards the end of the month, the terms of a peace treaty (finally signed, with slight modifications, on 10 May as the **treaty of Frankfurt**) are agreed at Versailles. Its provisions – the loss of Alsace and most of Lorraine, an indemnity of five billion francs, and the cost of maintaining an army of occupation in the east until this is paid – will be a source of resentment that festers on until World War I.

Early in March, the Assembly takes the decision to move from Bordeaux to Versailles. On 18 March a government attempt to disarm the Paris National Guard provokes bloodshed and rebellion, signalling the start of the **Commune**. Thiers withdraws from Paris, and the city is again besieged, this time by the forces of the French government. From 21 to 28 May the *semaine sanglante* (week of blood) sees the murderous suppression of the Paris Commune by government troops. With the prospect of revolution dead, voters are more willing to support republican candidates, who make gains in the by-elections in July. The following month, Thiers is confirmed as president of a conservative republic.

Emile Zola publishes *La Fortune des Rougon*, the first in his long series of *Rougon-Macquart* novels anatomising the society of the Second Empire in a supposedly 'scientific' fashion.

> ❝ What a week since last Sunday! No week during the siege was anything to be compared with it. My heart has been full of anguish… Madame Sabatier this morning gave us a good déjeuner, a roast with carrots. After we had finished she told us that it was a morsel of the horse of an insurgent commander, which had been killed near her son's house. ❞
>
> William Gibson on the *semaine sanglante*, from *Paris during the Commune*

The Commune

After the surrender of Paris, elections were held to provide a government that would make terms with the Prussians. Headed by **Adolphe Thiers**, this reflected the conservative bias of the provinces. Paris republicans were already angry at the signing of the armistice and suspected the new Assembly of planning a restoration of the monarchy. An attempt by Thiers to disarm the Paris workers who made up the majority of the **National Guard** led to a bloody incident on 18 March when troops were sent to seize the cannons situated on the high ground around Paris. The affair turned violent, and two generals were summarily executed on the Butte de Montmartre. Paris was once again in a state of revolution.

Municipal elections on 26 March, 1871 confirmed the revolutionary character of the **Commune**, marking the start of two hectic months of idealistic but uncoordinated government that set out to introduce measures on workers' rights, social reform and the conduct of education. But the forces of the Versailles government were meanwhile being swelled by prisoners of war released by Bismarck at the request of Thiers. The sister communes that had sprung up in southern and central France were rapidly suppressed.

On 21 May began the *semaine sanglante* that saw the end of the Paris Commune. Street by street government troops (the *Versaillais*) reclaimed the city, crushing the Communards, or *Fédérés,* with an indiscriminate savagery that makes the excesses of Robespierre's Terror pale in comparison. Resistance finally ended among the graves of the Père-Lachaise cemetery on 28 May when the last combatants were shot in front of the *mur des Fédérés*. Some 25,000 Parisians were dead, as against about 750 of the *Versaillais*. Buildings across the city, including the Hôtel de Ville and the palace of the Tuileries, were in ashes, burnt by the Communards. It was a brief, horrifying episode that left a permanent mark on the political and psychological landscape of France.

1872 Sarah Bernhardt gives an acclaimed performance as the queen in Hugo's *Ruy Blas* (1838). This, and her performance as Racine's Phèdre two years later, establish her as the leading actress of the age.

1873 In May the monarchist majority in the Assembly overthrow Thiers, replacing him with the royalist general **Mac-Mahon**. The desire for a restoration of the monarchy,

Impressionism

It was a painting by **Monet**, *Impression, soleil levant*, that gave the movement its name. In the spring of 1874 thirty or so artists put on an exhibition in the former studio of the photographer Félix Nadar. A derisive journalist latched on to Monet's title and dubbed them 'Impressionists'. The focus of the exhibition was a group of painters who had for some years been accustomed to meet at the café Guerbois in **Montmartre**, among them Monet, Pissarro, Sisley, Bazille, Renoir and Cézanne. Other contributors included Degas and Berthe Morisot. Although they belonged to different studios, and had different priorities, these artists were the core of the Impressionist movement. Alienated from the artistic establishment, they were reacting against the large emotions and historical dramas that had been the stock-in-trade of Romanticism and also against the glossy photographic realism of contemporary *Art Officiel*. Above all, they wanted to capture reality as it strikes the eye. The revolution this brought to painting was partly a question of technique – the pursuit of ways to catch transient effects of light that led several Impressionists to paint outdoors – and partly a question of subject matter, since it put on canvas a whole range of commonplace scenes that had previously been classified as inappropriate to art. Many of the painters associated with the movement later took different paths, others who are not thought of primarily as Impressionists, such as Gauguin, Lautrec and Matisse, none the less went through an Impressionist phase. Between them, the eight **Impressionist exhibitions** of 1874–86 laid the foundations of what we think of as modern art.

Monet's *Poplars on the Epte* (1891) shows the increasingly abstract quality of his later work

however, founders on the unsuitability of the main candidate, the **comte de Chambord**, grandson of Charles X, who rejects any form of constitutional monarchy and will accept restoration only under the white flag of the Bourbons.

In September the Prussian occupation ends after early payment of the indemnity.

1874 In May **child labour** is made illegal below the age of 12. A maximum of twelve hours a day is introduced for those under 16.

Between January and July laws are passed to establish a **new constitution** for the Republic. The **president**, who will have powers similar to those of a constitutional monarch, is to be chosen by two chambers: a **Chamber of Deputies**, elected by universal male suffrage, and an indirectly elected **Senate**, designed to restrain any excesses on the part of the Chamber of Deputies.

In a foretaste of the economic and social difficulties of the next twenty years, **phylloxera** begins to spread through the French vineyards, causing a crisis in the wine industry which reaches its peak in the 1880s.

1875 Completion of **Charles Garnier**'s Paris *Opéra*, a building that exemplifies the exuberant and eclectic Beaux-Arts style.

Georges Bizet's opera *Carmen* receives it premiere (3 March). Based on a novella by **Prosper Merimée**, it brings a new degree of realism to the opera house, merging spoken dialogue with intense local colour.

The publication of the definitive edition of the *Dictionnaire raisonné de l'architecture française du XI au XVI siècle* (1854–68) by **Viollet-le-Duc**, consolidates the Gothic revival in French architecture.

1876 Elections to the Chamber of Deputies produce a **republican majority** that immediately comes into conflict with the monarchist president Mac-Mahon.

Gustave Moreau's jewel-like painting *Salome Dancing before Herod* is exhibited at the Salon where it is greatly admired by the writer J.K. Huysmans.

1877 Mac-Mahon dissolves the Chamber of Deputies in June, but the electorate returns another republican majority.

The **Grand Orient**, the leading French Masonic Obedience, removes from its constitution the requirement to believe in a Supreme Being and the immortality of the soul. For the next forty years **Freemasonry** will be an important force on the left of French politics, nourishing the Third Republic's anti-clericalism.

Auguste Rodin's life-size sculpture of a nude man, *The Age of Bronze*, causes consternation at the Salon because of its extreme naturalism, which gives rise to accusations that he has cast it from a live model.

1879 When January elections give the republicans a majority in the Senate, Mac-Mahon's position becomes untenable and he resigns. From this point on, the Republicans, whether **Opportunists** (the name given to the moderate faction) or **Radicals**, hold the reins of power, and the balance swings significantly in favour of the Chamber as opposed to the president.

1880 This year sets the tone for the next two decades in terms of liberal legislation, colonial expansion, industrial enterprise, and the general secularisation of society: former Communards are amnestied, progressive educational reforms are undertaken (including a Bill for the secondary education of girls), **Tahiti** and the **Society islands** are annexed, the company for the construction of the **Panama canal** is founded, and the requirement that Sunday be a day of rest is abandoned.

Louis Pasteur (1822–95) successfully protects chickens against fowl cholera by inoculating them with a weaker strain of the microorganism responsible for the disease. Thereafter he is able to adapt the principle of **vaccination** for use against other diseases.

Alphonse Laveran, working in Algeria, discovers the parasite that causes malaria.

1881 In May **Tunisia** becomes a protectorate.

Under the premiership of **Jules Ferry** further liberal reforms include laws on freedom of the press, freedom of assembly, and free primary schooling. The republican left makes gains in the elections of August–September.

French bicyclists form their own organisation, the *Union vélocipédique française*. An increasingly prominent feature of the emerging society, the **bicycle** gives more social freedom to women and provides a means of escape into the country for workers.

1882 On 28 March Jules Ferry makes **secular schooling** compulsory for all 6- to 13-year-olds. The emphasis placed both on education and on the need to prise it away from the control of the Church is central to the ethos of the Republic during these years.

The French occupy **Madagascar** and force **Vietnam** to accept the status of a protectorate.

The death of the **comte de Chambord** brings to an end any lingering hope among royalists of a restoration of the monarchy (24 August).

In November the Prefect of the Seine, **Eugène Poubelle**, introduces a system of containers for household and public refuse that dramatically improves the cleanliness of Paris streets.

1883 Reforms are enacted legalizing **divorce** again (see p.229) and approving the election of **provincial mayors** by universal male suffrage.

In March **trade unions** are legalized.

A **miners' strike** in Anzin, which will form the basis of Zola's novel *Germinal* (1885), is one of a number of violent labour disputes in the 1880s and 1890s that demonstrate a growing resistance among workers to exploitative pay and conditions.

Claude Monet settles at **Giverny** (about 50 miles from Paris), where he creates an ornamental lily pond that will be the subject of a remarkable series of his late paintings.

Joris-Karl Huysmans (1848–1907) publishes *A Rebours*, whose hero Des Esseintes perfectly expresses the mood of *fin-de-siècle* decadence that influences much of the literature, art and music of the period.

1884 The *Société des Artistes Indépendants* is formed by, among others, **Seurat** and his follower **Paul Signac** as a forum for avant-garde artists. The *Salon des Artistes Indépendants* becomes the main showcase for **Post-Impressionism**.

1885 Following his death on 22 May, **Victor Hugo** (b.1802) receives a state funeral that excites a massive public display of respect and affection (1 June). His coffin is placed under the Arc de Triomphe before being transported to the Panthéon.

The **Peugeot family** set up a shop to make bicycles.

Louis Pasteur experiments with the first **vaccination** against rabies.

At the hospital of Salpêtrière, **Jean Martin Charcot**'s course of lectures on the function of the brain are attended by **Sigmund Freud**.

1886 In January gains by the left-wing **Radicals** in the previous autumn's elections to the Chamber enable them to insist on the appointment of General **Georges Boulanger** (whom they wrongly take for a republican) as Minister of War. He earns immediate popularity among the workers by refusing to use the army against striking miners in the Aveyron coalfield. An energetic, though not especially capable, minister, he promotes a number of reforms to the army, introducing the repeating rifle and boosting patriotic morale. His vigorous calls for revenge on Prussia add to his popularity but alarm his political colleagues.

Publication of *Les Illuminations* by **Arthur Rimbaud**. This collection of vivid and often obscure prose poems, written in the early 1870s, will have an important influence on modern poetry.

First performance of *Symphony No. 3* (Organ Symphony) by **Camille Saint-Saëns**. In the same year he writes *Le Carnaval des Animaux* as an amusement for his friends.

Georges Seurat completes his *Sunday Afternoon on the Island of La Grand Jatte*, a large painting in which colour is applied in small dots to secure greater luminosity. This technique, later known as **Pointillism**, is called by Seurat **Divisionism**.

1887 Dismissed from the government, Boulanger becomes a focus for various elements disenchanted with the republican administration. In December the president of the Republic is forced to resign when it is discovered that his son-in-law has been selling decorations for the *Légion d'honneur*.

1888 First performance of the *Symphony in D minor* by the Belgian composer **César Franck**. Franck, who has lived in France since 1848, is an inspirational teacher of several important French composers.

First performance of **Gabriel Fauré**'s *Requiem*, at the church of the Madeleine where he is organist. Fauré later adds two further movements and re-orchestrates the work.

The Dutch painter **Vincent van Gogh** moves to **Arles** where he hopes to found an artists' colony. Over the next year he produces an extraordinary number of canvases, marked by a use of brilliant colour and swirling lines that reflect his increasing distance from the visual realism of Impressionism.

1889 Boulanger's sweeping success in the Paris elections in January brings him to the edge of staging a *coup d'état*, but he pulls back, giving the administration time to charge him with plotting against the state. To avoid arrest, he flees to Brussels, bringing to an end the phenomenon of *boulangisme*, which slides into extinction at the autumn elections.

In February the failure of the **Panama Canal Company** swallows the savings of many French investors.

Henri Bergson publishes his *Essai sur les données immédiates de la conscience* (Time and Free Will), in which he suggests a crucial difference between time as experienced by human consciousness, and time as measured chronologically. His ideas were to have a notable influence on the writings of **Marcel Proust**.

For the Universal Exhibition, **Gustave Eiffel** constructs the **Eiffel Tower**. Over 300 metres high, it stands as a

ROBERT HARDING

The Eiffel Tower was initially ridiculed by many leading figures of the day. Huysmans called it 'a half built factory pipe . . . a funnel-shaped grill, a hole-riddled suppository.'

symbol of the new age of technology and is vilified and revered accordingly. The traffic problems created by some thirty million visitors to the exhibition give rise to the project for building an underground rail network, the **Paris métro**.

The *Moulin Rouge*, a dance hall and cabaret that becomes a focal point of *Belle Epoque* Paris, opens in Montmartre, Paris. Its dancers – among them, La Goulue and Jane Avril – are immortalized by the artist **Henri de Toulouse-Lautrec** in a number of prints and paintings.

1891 On 1 May troops fire on striking workers at **Fourmies** in the north of France, killing nine of them.

Two weeks later, **Pope Leo XIII** issues his encyclical *Rerum novarum*, which formulates a shift to the left in the Church's position on social matters, facilitating a rapprochement between socialism and Catholicism.

In August, following the collapse of the Russo-German alliance, **Russia** enters a loose alliance with France, less important in itself than as a symptom of future changes in the European balance of power.

The French automobile industry is launched when two companies – **Panhard and Levassor**, and Peugeot – produce petrol-driven cars using the engine developed in Germany by Daimler. In the same year, the **Michelin** brothers invent the inflatable tyre, which will be adapted for cars in 1895. By 1900 France will have produced some 6000 vehicles, more than ten times the number produced in Britain or Germany.

Paul Gauguin leaves France for **Tahiti**, where he develops an increasingly simplified and anti-naturalistic style of painting. His life in the South Seas will quickly become central to a western mythology of escape into the primitive and the exotic.

1892 On 11 January **Jules Méline** extends the range of protectionist tariffs introduced in the 1880s to defend French agriculture.

On 30 March the anarchist **Ravachol** is arrested for a bombing campaign against those involved in the trial of a worker arrested for his part in the Fourmies demonstration of 1 May, 1891. Condemned to life imprisonment, Ravachol will be executed in July for murders committed previously. After his death he becomes a symbol of protest against society, the patron saint of **anarchists** responsible for a wave of bombings that take place over the next few years.

In November, following discoveries by the anti-Semitic journalist **Edouard Drumont** about extensive bribery of politicians and journalists to keep the Panama Canal Company afloat, a judicial enquiry is undertaken which implicates, among others, Clemenceau, Eiffel and de Lesseps. This episode contributes to growing cynicism about a political establishment already tainted by scandal.

The engineer **François Hennebique** patents his system of building in reinforced concrete.

1893 The Panama scandal boosts support for the **socialists** in elections to the Chamber (August–Sptember).

Maxime Gaillard opens a restaurant in the rue Royale, Paris. *Maxim's* soon becomes a highly fashionable rendezvous for the *beau monde*.

1894 The president of the Republic, **Sadi Carnot**, is assassinated by the anarchist **Caserio** (24 June). Against the opposition of socialists and radicals, laws are passed in July to restrict the freedom of the press and to facilitate the pursuit of anarchists. As their opponents suspect, these will in time be used as a weapon against other political targets, notably socialists and pacifists in the run-up to World War I.

The Dreyfus Affair

In September 1894 a document was recovered from the **German embassy** in Paris which showed that secret information about **French armaments** had been passed to the Germans. On the basis of an apparent similarity between his handwriting and that on the document, Captain **Alfred Dreyfus** (1859–1935), a Jewish officer from a wealthy family of textile manufacturers in Mulhouse, was convicted of treason (22 December, 1894). On 5 January, 1895, in the courtyard of the **Ecole Militaire**, he underwent the ceremony of degradation – his epaulettes were torn off and his sword broken, while a crowd outside screamed anti-Jewish slogans – before being transported to the harsh conditions of the penal colony on **Devil's Island**, off the coast of Guiana.

It was more than a year later, when lieutenant-colonel **Georges Picquart** discovered evidence suggesting that major **Ferdinand Walsin-Esterhazy** was the true author of the treasonous document, that the case for Dreyfus's innocence began to receive serious consideration. What followed was a series of extraordinary contortions to cover up the truth by the army, the Ministry of War and Esterhazy himself, clamorously supported by anti-Semitic sections of the press, notably Edouard Drumont's *La Libre Parole*, and also by a significant proportion of the clergy. Against them were ranged Dreyfus's family and the journalist Bernard Lazare, joined later by an increasingly outraged body of journalists, intellectuals and left-wing politicians, including Charles Péguy, Anatole France, Marcel Proust, Léon Blum, Jean Jaurès and Georges Clemenceau, for whom neither the convenience of the state nor the reputation of the army could be allowed to override the rights and liberties of the individual.

The battle between Dreyfusards and anti-Dreyfusards reached a defining moment on 13 January, 1898, when **Emile Zola** published a 'Letter to the president of the Republic' entitled 'J'Accuse…!' in *L'Aurore*. Zola was prosecuted for libel and had to go briefly into exile to avoid imprisonment, but his indictment of the army and the Ministry was a dramatic step towards the final quashing of Dreyfus's conviction in July 1906. The affair had split France in two, exposing the depths of popular anti-Semitism but also revealing the political and social lines of force that would shape the country's destiny in the 20th century. Dreyfus himself, broken in health by his four years on Devil's Island, was rehabilitated and awarded the *légion d'honneur*. Recalled to the army during World War I, he reached the rank of lieutenant-colonel before retiring into obscurity.

Captain Dreyfus is charged with high treason. Engraving from the magazine *L'Illustration*

On 22 December **Alfred Dreyfus** is found guilty of treason and condemned to the penal colony of **Devil's Island**.

France completes its conquest of the **Sudan**.

Baron Pierre de Coubertin proposes the revival of the **Olympic Games** which are relaunched two years later in Athens.

The **'Bal des Quat'z'Arts'**, which becomes notorious as an annual bacchanalia, is held for the first time.

1895 The **CGT** (*Confédération générale du travail*), France's General Labour Federation, is founded in September.

On 28 December, the **Lumière brothers** put on the first public film show. The **Cinématographe**, their combined camera and projector, will give rise to the word cinema.

Entrepreneur Siegfried Bing opens *La Maison de l'Art Nouveau*, a shop selling furniture and jewellery by designers such as **Eugène Gaillard**, **Emile Gallé** and **René Lalique**, who favour a decorative style in which curving lines and sinuous forms predominate. This style, strikingly exhibited in **Hector Guimard**'s entrances for the Paris métro, becomes known as **Art Nouveau**.

Following his first one-man show in Paris, **Paul Cézanne** receives greater recognition and becomes an inspirational figure to younger artists.

1896 **Madagascar**, designated a protectorate some ten years earlier, becomes a French colony following a military expedition to overthrow the local administration and occupy the island.

The first **automobile race** – from Paris to Marseille – takes place.

1897 **Emile Durkheim** (1858–1917) publishes *Le Suicide* (*Suicide*). Along with his doctoral thesis *De la division du travail social* (*The Division of Labour in Society*, 1893) and *Les*

Règles de la méthode sociologique (*The Rules of Sociological Method*, 1895), this establishes him as the father of the French school of sociology.

1898 On 13 January, **Zola**'s 'J'Accuse' is published on the front page of *L'Aurore*, the newspaper founded by Georges Clemenceau the previous year.

In September the **Fachoda incident**, in which French and British dispute the occupation of territory in the Upper Nile, brings relations between the two countries to a point of crisis. The French withdraw.

In Paris, **Pierre** and **Marie Curie** discover radium.

JOE STAINES

The Abbesses métro stop in Paris, showing Guimard's ornate Art Nouveau entrance

> As for those I accuse, I do not know them, I have never met them, I have for them neither rancour nor hatred. For me, they merely represent the spirit of social wrongdoing. And my action here is no more than a revolutionary means of hastening the explosion of truth and justice. My only passion is for the light, in the name of that humanity which has suffered so much and which has the right to happiness.
>
> Emile Zola, from 'J'Accuse'

1899 The *Action française* movement is founded. Born partly in response to the humiliation of the Fachoda incident and the ramifications of the Dreyfus affair, it is a reactionary force – Catholic, anti-Semitic, hostile to Freemasonry and Protestantism – that will exercise considerable influence in French social and political life, most obviously through its newspaper *l'Action française*, founded by **Charles Maurras**, **Léon Daudet** and **Jacques Bainville**.

1900 France takes part in the international expedition to put down the **Boxer rebellion** in China (May–September).

The first line of the **Paris métro** is opened.

Paris hosts the second **Olympic Games** and mounts another universal exhibition.

1901 On 1 July the **Associations Law** allows free association to all but religious groups, whose recent activities, overwhelmingly anti-Dreyfus and often vocally anti-Semitic, have made them suspect.

1902 **Elections** to the Chamber of Deputies (April–May) are won by a coalition of radical groups known as the *'Bloc des gauches'*. Over the next three years, the new administration, which has a strongly anti-clerical agenda, brings in a number of reforms affecting education, working conditions, social security, military service and the separation of Church and state.

First performance of **Debussy**'s opera *Pelléas et Mélisande*, seven years after its completion.

Georges Méliès, who founded the first European film studio in 1897, produces his most famous film *Le Voyage dans la Lune*.

1903 The first **Tour de France** bicycle race is held.

Henri Becquerel, who has discovered radioactivity in the form of rays emitted from uranium salts, wins the Nobel prize for Physics in conjunction with Pierre and Marie Curie.

The *Salon d'Automne* is founded as an alternative to the official Salon and the *Salon des Indépendants*.

Couturier **Paul Poiret** opens his own fashion house. Poiret revolutionizes fashion by liberating women from corsets, and introducing an element of exoticism influenced by the Ballets russes.

1904 Following a visit to Paris the previous year by King Edward VII, France and Britain sign the *Entente cordiale* on 8 April. Primarily a resolution of colonial rivalries, it allows Britain a free hand in Egypt while leaving France to pursue her ambitions in Morocco.

A strike by **agricultural workers** in the south is just one instance of the industrial unrest that becomes widespread over the next few years, as political awareness among the working classes continues to grow, and strikers fight to improve pay and conditions.

Jean Jaurès, the socialist leader, founds the daily paper *L'Humanité*.

Completion of **25b Rue Franklin**, a Paris apartment block. Designed by **Auguste Perret**, which is the first multistorey building to use a reinforced concrete frame.

Jean Jaurès

Born into a petit-bougeois family in the Tarn district of southern France, **Jean Jaurès** (1859–1914) proved a brilliant student and seemed destined for a career in teaching. In 1885, however, a passionate interest in politics led him to seize the opportunity of entering the Chamber of Deputies as a **republican**. Defeated in 1889, he continued to pursue a political career, and his developing allegiance to the socialist movement was crystallized by his support for the striking miners of **Carmaux** in 1892. In the following year he was elected deputy for that district. His support for **Dreyfus** cost him his seat in 1898, but he was re-elected in 1902 and remained a Deputy for the rest of his life.

A moderate and a conciliator, he was more concerned with seeing social reforms enacted than preserving the ideological purity of a particular doctrine, and he worked tirelessly for the unification of different strands of socialist thought. Aided by a remarkable gift for oratory, he established himself as the most prominent figure in French socialism and one of the leaders of the **SFIO** (see 1905). Among his voluminous writings were his *Histoire de la Révolution française* (1898) and *Histoire socialiste 1789–1900* (1901–08). An opponent of **colonialism**, he was also an **anti-militarist** and devoted much effort in the years before 1914 to averting war. In doing so, he earned the hatred of the nationalists. It was one of them, **Raoul Villain**, who assassinated him on 31 July, 1914. Ten years later, on 23 November, 1924, the ashes of Jaurès were transferred to the Panthéon.

1905 Socialist groups form a united political party as the **SFIO** (*Section française de l'Internationale ouvrière*).

On 9 December the **Law of Separation** of Church and State puts an end to Napoléon's Concordat of 1801 and establishes a secular state which guarantees freedom of worship but gives no special recognition to any religious group. The law is condemned by the pope in the following year.

At the *Salon d'Automne* the term **Fauvism** is coined for a new group of artists, headed by **Henri Matisse**, whose work is characterized by an extremely vivid and non-naturalistic palette.

Claude Debussy's symphonic composition *La Mer* receives its first performance. Debussy's concern with atmosphere leads some critics to describe his compositions as a form of musical Impressionism.

1906 Following German attempts to block French aims in Morocco, the **conference of Algeciras** results in a diplomatic victory for France. Although she cannot declare a protectorate, her economic rights in the country are supported by Russia, England, Spain and Italy. Germany is isolated.

Strikes and **demonstrations** across the country repeatedly end in violent repression by the authorities.

On 25 October a new administration is formed under **Georges Clemenceau**. Long known as a Radical, Clemenceau will be faced with a period of **industrial agitation** which, whatever the merits of the workers' cause, seems to him to threaten the authority of the State. On several occasions over the next three years he will respond by calling in troops or arresting strikers and union leaders – measures which put him at odds with former colleagues on the left.

> **❝** The Republic neither recognizes nor salaries nor subsidises any religion. In consequence, from the first of January following the promulgation of the present law, all expenses relative to the exercise of religions shall be suppressed in the budgets of the state, departments, and communes. **❞**
>
> The Law of Separation, from Title I

A major retrospective of **Gauguin**'s work is held at the *Salon d'Automne*.

1907 In June a massive uprising erupts in the **Languedoc** among wine-growers whose livelihood has been damaged by the practice of importing cheap Algerian wine, begun during the phylloxera crisis. Troops are called in but refuse to open fire.

On 31 August France, Britain and Russia sign the **Triple Entente**.

The Spanish artist **Pablo Picasso**, now living in Paris, completes *Les Demoiselles d'Avignon*, a revolutionary painting, influenced both by African sculpture and the late work of Cézanne. This marks a crucial stage in the history of **Cubism**, a new way of painting – developed by Picasso and **Georges Braque** – in which objects are fragmented into facets, as if viewed from different perspectives simultaneously.

1909 Clemenceau is succeeded as Prime Minister by **Aristide Briand**, who continues the policy of repressive opposition to striking workers.

On 25 July **Louis Blériot** makes the first Channel crossing by plane.

Sergei Diaghilev causes a sensation in Paris with his Russian ballet company, the Ballets russes. Diaghilev's inspired use of painters, composers and dancers perfectly expresses the artistic vitality that makes the French capital the cultural centre of Europe.

1911 **Marie Curie** is awarded the Nobel prize for Chemistry.

1912 **Morocco** becomes a French protectorate. The subsequent uprising of Moroccans is crushed by the French army under the command of **General Lyautey**.

The Ballets russes give the first performance of *Daphnis et Chloë* to a specially commissioned score by **Maurice Ravel**.

> We have made [France] understand the glory that there is for a nation to undertake the education of so many peoples still immersed in barbarism. We have explained that there was cannibalism to suppress, slavery to destroy, the awful tyranny of bloody kinglets to repress. We have been told that by appearing thus as the great liberating power, we would prodigiously enhance our moral prestige as well as our economic prosperity, and that the curiosity of these people, awakened, would turn toward us in order to draw upon our reasoning, our methods and our tastes, and thus steeped in our genius without dreaming of an impossible assimilation, they would continue magnificently France overseas...

Maurice Viollette in 1912, quoted in Alice L. Conklin, *A Mission to Civilize* (1997)

1913 On 17 January **Raymond Poincaré** is elected President of the Republic.

On 29 May the premiere of **Igor Stravinsky**'s uncompromisingly modern and dissonant *Le Sacre du Printemps*, performed by the Ballets russes at the Théâtre des Champs-Elysées, causes uproar.

In August the period of **military service** is extended to three years despite opposition from Jaurès.

On 23 September **Roland Garros** makes the first flight across the Mediterranean.

The artist **Marcel Duchamp** invents the idea of a 'ready-made', a mass-produced object, presented as a work of art. These include a bicycle wheel, a bottle rack and a urinal.

1914 On 17 March the wife of the former Prime Minister **Joseph Caillaux** murders **Gaston Calmette**, editor of the *Figaro*, to prevent him publishing her husband's love letters as part of a smear campaign. Her trial, which leads to an acquittal, is one of the great *causes célèbres* of prewar years, enthralling the nation and provoking much commentary on the nature and status of women.

On 28 June **Archduke Franz-Ferdinand** of Austria is murdered at Sarajevo by a Serb nationalist hoping to strike a blow against Austro-Hungarian rule in the Balkans. A month later, on 31 July, Jaurès, who has been a leading campaigner against the slide towards war, is murdered in Paris. On 1 August the government decrees general **mobilization**.

8
World War I to the Liberation
1914–1944

Decades of international tension had divided the major European powers into two rival camps: on one side, the **Triple Alliance** of Germany, Austria-Hungary and Italy; on the other, the **Triple Entente** of France, Russia and Great Britain. No more than a spark – **Franz–Ferdinand**'s assassination – was needed to set the continent alight. In spite of the internal divisions of the previous few years, France went to war as a more or less united force, confident of a quick victory. Within two months that confidence had evaporated and the war had ground to a standstill. Four years later, France did emerge the victor but with a tragically depleted population and a shattered economy. It had lost 1.3 million men, proportionately more than any of the other warring nations.

For the next ten years the country's political history is played out against a backdrop dominated by two interconnected features: the need to restore economic prosperity and the continuing struggle with Germany over war **reparations**. The work force, augmented by a stream of **immigrants** to fill the place of the dead, was discontented but too ill-organised for effective protest. After initial concessions on an eight-hour working day, the government stood firm against further demands, and the wave of strikes in 1919–20 was put down with crushing brutality. The membership of the **CGT** (*Confédération générale du travail*) fell off, and in 1920 the **Socialist Party** was torn apart when a majority of its members voted to transform themselves into the **French Communist Party**. Until 1924 the centre right *Bloc national* retained its hold on power, but the question of reparations was a running sore. Bitterly resentful of the treaty that had been forced on it, Germany defaulted on its payments. In 1923 the Prime Minister **Raymond Poincaré** sent in French troops to occupy the Ruhr valley. The result was resistance among the Germans and dissatisfaction among the French, whose taxes had to be increased to pay for this new occupation.

By 1924 the left had managed to regroup itself as the *Cartel des gauches*, which won power in the elections that year. But the franc was under increasing pressure, and the Cartel's lack of consensus on economic management resulted in a series of rapidly changing cabinets, none of which had the strength to resolve the situation. Only in 1926, when the left-wing Chamber called on the right-wing Poincaré to form an administration of national unity to 'save the franc', did some sort of financial stability return. For a while the outlook was fair. Abroad, **Aristide Briand**, the long-serving Foreign Minister, operated a successful policy of accommodation with Germany, agreeing a renegotiated programme of reparations and sponsoring her inclusion in the **League of Nations**; at home, Poincaré was able to preside over a brief economic upturn.

But it was only a matter of time before the aftershock of the **Wall Street crash** would reach France. From 1931 the economy began to slow down, unemployment to get worse and the budgetary deficit to increase. This was fertile ground for the extreme right-wing groups that were becoming a feature of the political scene. In the wake of the **Stavisky financial scandal**, which had implicated members of the government, social tensions exploded in a bloody demonstration on 6 February, 1934 that brought down the government. Successive administrations pursued a deflationary economic policy in defence of the franc, but this led merely to a further slowdown in the economy and victory for the left-wing *Front populaire* in the 1936 elections. Led by **Léon Blum**, the new administration introduced a range of worker-friendly social measures known as the **Matignon agreements**, but these reforms were expensive and, from the perspective of the markets, unwelcome. The financiers quickly began to take their capital elsewhere, and in 1938 another centre-right coalition was back in power, pursuing more conservative policies under **Edouard Daladier**. By this time, however, the clouds had begun to gather over Europe. Hitler's Germany was looking westward for revenge.

The four years following France's rapid military defeat were among the darkest in her history. Whether they were living under **German occupation** or the **Vichy regime**, the French were faced with hard choices between resistance that to many seemed futile, and collaboration that meant the daily acceptance of evil as a condition of survival. It was their good fortune that in the heroism of the Resistance movement and the determination of **Charles de Gaulle** to preserve a Free France there was enough to salvage the nation's pride.

Throughout this period, French culture – its literature in particular – continued to flourish. In France, as in England and Germany, writers produced a number of classic indictments of the pointless carnage of World War I, notably **Henri Barbusse**'s *Le Feu* (1916). More obliquely, the work of **Louis-Ferdinand Céline** reflects the experience of these years in a nihilistic vision that offers us a world bleached of moral purpose. At the same time **Marcel Proust** was following quite other artistic goals as he worked towards the completion of *A la recherche du temps perdu*. The writings of **Guillaume Apollinaire**, who died in the flu epidemic at the end of the war, look forward to the emergence of the surrealist movement in the middle of the 1920s. In the same decade, the **Art Deco** movement was beginning what would become a revolution in style. The influence of its sweeping, streamlined look spread from upper class *objets de luxe* to the department stores of Paris and out into the design centres of western Europe and America. The pressure of political events in the 1930s is evident in, for example, the work of **André Malraux** on the left and **Robert Brasillach** on the right. Meanwhile, writers such as **François Mauriac** and **André Gide** continued to produce work that added to their international standing. By the time of the Liberation, two young writers, **Albert Camus** and **Jean-Paul Sartre**, had emerged as dominant figures, both of whom would play a central role in the intellectual life of the postwar years.

1914 On 3 August, two days after its declaration of war on Russia, **Germany** declares war on France and immediately invades Belgium. The next day a government of **national unity** (the *Union sacrée*) is formed under the presidency of **Raymond Poincaré**, with **René Viviani** as prime minister. On the same day, Britain enters the war in fulfilment of its commitment to defend Belgian neutrality.

On 20 August, having swept through Belgium, the Germans enter France and by the end of the month are threatening Paris. The **French government** retreats to Bordeaux on 2 September, leaving **General Gallieni** in charge of the capital. Between 6 and 12 September, Gallieni comandeers some 2000 Paris taxis to ferry troops to the **battle of the Marne**, where the Germans are driven back and Paris saved.

From 18 September to 4 November the Germans make for the coast in an outflanking manoeuvre. To prevent them, allied forces do the same. This 'dash for the sea' ends with the German occupation of **Ostend** on 15

> And now to arms, all of us! I have seen weeping among those who cannot go first. Everyone's turn will come. There will not be a child of our land who will not have a part in the enormous struggle. To die is nothing. We must win. And for that we need all men's power. The weakest will have his share of glory. There come times, in the lives of nations, when there passes over them a tempest of heroic action.
>
> Georges Clemenceau's call to arms, 5 August, 1914

October, swiftly followed by the allied arrival at Calais. The result is stalemate as the two sides dig in for what becomes four years of **trench warfare**. By the end of 1914 the French have already lost over 300,000 men, among them the writers **Charles Péguy** and **Alain-Fournier**, both killed in September.

On 1 November **Turkey** enters the war on the side of Germany. In December, the government returns to Paris.

1915 On 4 February **Kaiser Wilhelm II** inaugurates **submarine** warfare.

On 16 February, in an effort to relieve Turkish pressure on the Russians, the allies embark on what proves to be a disastrous campaign in the **Dardanelles**.

On 22 April Germany uses **poison gas** at Ypres. This weapon, already tested against the Russians in January, will become one of the horrors of the war.

The torpedoing of the liner *Lusitania* by a German submarine on 7 May results in the death of 1198 passengers and crew, including 128 Americans. It causes outrage in **America** and shifts public opinion towards intervention in the war. American protests have the effect of severely restricting German use of submarine warfare.

> The gaseous vapor which the Germans used against the French divisions near Ypres last Thursday, contrary to the rules of the Hague Convention, introduces a new element into warfare. The attack of last Thursday evening was preceded by the rising of a cloud of vapor, greenish gray and iridescent. That vapor settled to the ground like a swamp mist and drifted toward the French trenches on a brisk wind. Its effect on the French was a violent nausea and faintness, followed by an utter collapse. It is believed that the Germans, who charged in behind the vapor, met no resistance at all, the French at their front being virtually paralyzed.
>
> New York *Tribune*, 27 April, 1915

Towards the end of October, **Aristide Briand** forms a new administration, replacing that of **René Viviani**. On 2 December, General **Joseph Joffre** is appointed commander-in-chief of the French armies. By this stage, the policy of drafting large numbers of natives from France's colonies in Africa and Indochina as cannon fodder has triggered a revolt in **Upper Volta**.

The writer **Romain Rolland**, author of the long 'roman-fleuve' *Jean-Christophe*, is awarded the Nobel prize for Literature. A pacifist, whose internationalist sympathies are out of tune with the times, he excites patriotic outrage during the war by advocating peace with Germany.

The satirical magazine *Le Canard enchaîné* is founded.

In a move that parallels British restrictions on the sale of alcohol, the French government bans **absinthe**.

1916 The year is dominated by the **battle of Verdun**, which lasts from February to December. For the French, this is the defining episode of the war. The **battle of the Somme** (July–October), which looms so large in British memories, is of concern to the French primarily in so far as it relieves pressure on Verdun.

On 12 December General **Robert Nivelle** takes over command of the French armies from Joffre, whose strategy has proved costly and ineffective.

The battle of Verdun

At 8 o'clock on the morning of 21 February, 1916, the German army unleashed a bombardment more terrible than any before: over a thousand pieces of artillery thundered their missiles across the River Meuse. It was the start of the **battle of Verdun.** During the next ten months 60 million shells would be expended on this little piece of ground. Against artillery, gas, flame-throwers, and machine guns firing up to fifteen rounds a second, the ordinary soldier could rely only on the protection of waterlogged foxholes or muddy trenches constructed out of sandbags and cemented with corpses. This was the reality of modern war. By the end of the battle, almost three quarters of a million men would be dead or wounded. The strategy of **Erich von Falkenhayn**, the German general, was to 'bleed the French army white', forcing them to throw in every man they had.

Within four days the Germans had advanced far enough across the fortified area around Verdun to take the fort of **Douaumont**. It was at this point that **General Pétain** was given command of the sector and famously declared, 'We shall not yield an inch of French soil.' With a tenacity beyond reason the French troops held on. By the summer it was clear that the attack had failed, and Pétain emerged as the hero of Verdun. In the second half of the year a French offensive commanded by **General Nivelle** recovered the lost forts, leaving the Germans little to show beyond a roll call of dead almost as long as their enemy's. In this, as in so much else, the battle of Verdun had become an epitome of the larger tragedy of four years of fruitless conflict.

French troops attacking German trenches at the battle of Verdun

> The opposing French and German trenches, their parapets hard frozen, were so close that they were actually within hearing of each other. Towards dawn a rapid thaw set in. The parapets melted and subsided, and two long lines of men stood up naked, as it were, before each other, face to face with only two possibilities: wholesale murder on the one side or the other, or a temporary unofficial peace for the making of fresh parapet protections. The situation was astounding and unique in the history of trench warfare. The French and German officers, without conferring and unwilling to negotiate, turned their backs so that they might not see officially so unwarlike a scene, and the men on each side rebuilt their parapets without the firing of a single shot.
>
> Lord Northcliffe on Verdun, 4 March, 1916

The posthumous publication of **Ferdinand de Saussure**'s (1857–1913) *Cours de linguistique générale* lays the foundations for later work on linguistics and also for the development of structuralism.

1917 In January **strikes** and **pacifist demonstrations** bear witness to a growing disillusionment with the war.

On 1 February Germany declares all-out submarine warfare in the hope of breaking the **allied blockade** that threatens its food supplies. Two days later the **United States** breaks off diplomatic relations with Germany. On 2 April it enters the war on the side of the allies.

On 16 April Nivelle launches the futile **'Chemin des dames'** offensive between Laon and Soissons on the Aisne front. Intended to produce the longed-for breakthrough, it grinds to a halt in mid-May after appalling loss of life. This costly failure acts as a catalyst for the **mutinies** that begin to break out on the western front, affecting in total some 40,000 men. Brought in to replace Nivelle as commander-in-chief, **Pétain** suppresses the mutinies but also improves living conditions and leave arrangements for the troops.

On 28 June the first **US division** arrives in France. By the end of the year there will be 365,000 US troops in France.

The air ace **Georges Guynemer**, with 53 victories to his credit, is shot down over Belgium (11 September).

The *Union sacrée* founders when socialists and Catholics break ranks with the government (12 September).

The **Russian Revolution** brings the Bolsheviks to power (6–7 November).

On 16 November **Georges Clemenceau** forms a new administration, determined, against increasing opposition, to fight on.

Georges Clemenceau

To say that **Clemenceau** (1841–1929) founded a journal in the 1860s and could still go tiger hunting in the 1920s is to give some measure of the range and energy of this extraordinary life. Born in the Vendée, Clemenceau studied medicine in Paris, where he mixed in republican circles hostile to the Second Empire, earning a short spell in prison for his activities as a **radical journalist**. After qualifying as a doctor, he spent almost four years (1865–69) in the United States. Shortly before his return to France, he married an American, from whom he separated seven years and three children later.

At the time of the **Franco-Prussian** War Clemenceau resisted the armistice and then tried to negotiate between the Commune and the National Assembly. His political career under the Third Republic was that of a permanent spokesman for the opposition. Anti-clerical and anti-colonialist, he was instrumental, through a mixture of eloquence, intelligence and tenacity, in bringing down a series of administrations, but he continued to refuse all invitations to form one himself. Involvement on the margins of the **Panama scandal** left him vulnerable to his enemies, and he lost his seat in the elections of 1893.

Having returned to journalism, he was brought back into prominence – and political favour – by his support for **Dreyfus**. As Minister of the Interior and then, from 1906 to 1909, Prime Minister, Clemenceau was faced with a number of labour disputes, in which his sympathy with the demands of the workers was outweighed by his concern for the authority of the State. **'Le Tigre'** (The Tiger), as he became known, showed a readiness that would have dismayed his younger self to use the machinery of state repression against protesting strikers. It was when France was at its lowest ebb in 1917 that he was called by **President Poincaré** to form a new administration. At 76 he displayed a ruthless determination to prosecute the war to a successful conclusion that won him the title **'Father Victory'**. After handling France's side of the treaty negotiations, he was defeated in the Presidential elections of 1920 and retired to travel and write.

Henri Matisse moves to the Riviera. The boldly coloured and sensuous canvases he paints over the next two decades confirm his international reputation.

Apollinaire's proto-surrealist drama *Les Mamelles de Tirésias (The Breasts of Tiresias)* is performed for the first time. In the same year the *Ballets russes* have another *succès de scandale* with the absurdist ballet *Parade*, devised by **Jean Cocteau** with music by **Erik Satie** and Cubist costumes by Picasso.

The anarchic, 'anti-art' movement known as **Dada**, (founded by Tristan Tzara in Zurich) establishes itself in Paris with the support of the poet **Louis Aragon** and the writer **André Breton**.

1918 On 8 January US President **Woodrow Wilson** lays out the 'Fourteen Points' that should be the basis of a post-war peace settlement.

On 3 March the **treaty of Brest-Litovsk** between Russia and Germany ends Russian involvement in the war. March–July: Aware that America's entry into the war has tipped the balance against Germany, **General Erich Ludendorff,** von Hindenburg's chief-of-staff, tries for a quick victory with a series of offensives on the Somme and then in Champagne and Lorraine. The Germans get close enough to bombard Paris with the long-range cannon known as **Big Bertha**, sited on the edge of the forest of Compiègne, but, in spite of considerable territorial gains, fail to make a decisive breakthrough.

On 26 March General **Ferdinand Foch**, a more attack-minded soldier than Pétain, is appointed commander-in-chief of allied forces.

During March and April a series of strikes interrupt production at **munitions factories** in Paris and St-Etienne. At the end of May, the first Renault **tank** comes into service. Hazardous and somewhat unreliable, tanks will none

This equestrian statue of Marshal Foch, by Georges Malissard, was unveiled by the Prince of Wales in London in June 1930

the less play an important part in the final months of the war.

On 18 July Foch launches a successful **counter-offensive** in Champagne, forcing a German retreat. Pressing home the allied advantage, the British 4th Army mount another offensive north and south of the Somme on 8 August. The collapse of German divisions in the face of this advance convinces Luddendorf that the war is lost.

In September another **allied offensive** between the Meuse and the North Sea drives the exhausted German army back to the Hindenburg line.

During October and November an epidemic of **Spanish**

flu, probably brought over by American troops earlier in the year, gathers intensity as it sweeps through Europe.

On 29 October discussions on the terms of an **armistice** open in Paris. On the following day the Ottoman Empire capitulates.

On 9 November Kaiser Wilhelm II **abdicates**. Two days later, on 11 November, the armistice is signed in a railway carriage at **Rethondes**, ending World War I.

1919 France's main concern now, apart from future security, is **reconstruction**, but with so many of its potential work-force dead, it faces a serious manpower shortage. Over the next few years it brings in some two million **immigrant workers**, mostly from Italy, Spain and Poland.

In response to growing union demands, the government reduces the **working day** to eight hours (23 April), but then hardens its line as industrial action spreads. The threat of a general strike is averted when the CGT, to the disgust of many of its members, does a deal with Clemenceau.

On 18 January the **peace conference** opens in Paris with disagreement among the Allies over the question of **reparations**.

Mutiny breaks out aboard French ships sent to the Black Sea to support the White Russian counter-revolution (19–21 April). The sailors refuse to fight against the Bolsheviks.

At the end of April it is agreed at the Paris peace talks that the **League of Nations** should be formed to provide mechanisms for resolving international disputes without recourse to war. On 28 June the **treaty of Versailles** is signed with Germany.

On 16 November, partly as a consequence of the year's industrial troubles, the **centre-right coalition**, the *Bloc national*, wins a clear majority in elections to the Chamber of Deputies. One result of this is the 'blue horizon' Chamber, so-called on account of the blue military uniforms worn by the many deputies who are war veterans.

Fashion designer **Madeleine Vionnet** reopens her Paris store. Cutting cloth on the bias (against the grain of the material) enables her to create a distinctively flowing and sculpted look.

The treaty of Versailles

There were four main players at the **Paris Peace Conference**: Clemenceau for France, Lloyd George for Britain, Woodrow Wilson for America, and Vittorio Emanuele Orlando for Italy. They started from the **fourteen points** that Wilson had set out as the basis for a just peace, but these had to contend with competing national interests and an overriding concern for the future security of Europe. The upshot was a series of provisions that left Germany, which had not been invited to participate, feeling betrayed and discriminated against. Its colonies were forfeit to the Allies, Alsace and Lorraine were to be returned to France, and the Rhineland demilitarised. All this was bad enough, but worse was the **'war guilt' clause** which declared Germany the aggressor and insisted on reparations. This was not what the Germans had been led to expect when the armistice was signed. The huge sum of money required for reparations – in 1921 it was set at $30 billion – was never going to be payable, and it proved a source of fierce resentment through the rest of the decade.

The **League of Nations**, which came into being under the provisions of the treaty, could do little to prevent the drift towards a resumption of hostilities. Moreover, an undertaking by Britain and America to come to the help of France in case of attack was rendered meaningless by the refusal of the American Senate to ratify the treaty. In the end, this treaty which had been designed to ensure that a war of such magnitude could never take place again went some way towards ensuring the opposite.

> The Allied and Associated Governments affirm and Germany accepts the responsibility of Germany and her allies for causing all the loss and damage to which the Allied and Associated Governments and their nationals have been subjected as a consequence of the war imposed upon them by the aggression of Germany and her allies.
>
> Article 231 (the 'war guilt' clause) from the treaty of Versailles

Founding of the **FFF** (*Fédération française de football*) with **Jules Rimet** as its first president.

1920 Defeated by **Paul Deschanel** in the January elections for president of the Republic, Clemenceau resigns his premiership and retires from politics. He is replaced as prime minister by **Alexandre Millerand**.

A wave of **industrial unrest**, from February to May, culminates in mass demonstrations and the start of a general strike (1 May). After violent repression, the CGT calls off the strike on 21 May.

In July **abortion** is outlawed. Like the prohibition on the sale of contraceptives, which is passed at the same time, this is partly a response to the need for an increase in the birth rate.

On 21 September Alexandre Millerand replaces Deschanel as president.

The tomb of the **Unknown Soldier** is inaugurated at the Arc de Triomphe in Paris (11 November).

In December, at the **Congress of Tours**, the French left, formed into a single socialist party in 1905 (the SFIO – *Section française de l'Internationale ouvrière*), splits in two. The majority become the new **French Communist Party** (PCF – *Parti communiste française*), leaving the rump to reconstitute themselves as a depleted SFIO under **Léon Blum**.

Stravinsky's ballet *Pulcinella* (created for the *Ballets russes*, with designs by Picasso) initiates his Neoclassical style, which is to have a marked influence on French music.

The publication of *Chéri* marks the emergence of **Colette** as a major novelist.

Fashion designer **Gabrielle 'Coco' Chanel** opens a *maison de couture* in rue Cambon, Paris. Her designs, inspired by men's tailoring, provide women with clothes that are both simple, practical and chic.

1921 A new administration is formed by **Aristide Briand** (16 January).

Les Mariés de la Tour Eiffel is written for the Swedish ballet to a scenario by **Jean Cocteau**. The music is composed by five members of *Les Six*, a group of young composers (including **Darius Milhaud**, **François Poulenc** and **Arthur Honegger**) united in their admiration of Erik Satie and their antipathy to Romanticism.

1922 Viewed as too conciliatory towards the Germans, Briand is forced to resign in January. He is succeeded as Prime Minister by **Raymond Poincaré** whose hardline policy leads to the rejection later in the year of German demands for a moratorium on reparations.

Death of **Marcel Proust**. His novel *A la recherche du temps perdu*, whose final volume is not published until 1927, becomes one of the most influential works of European fiction in the 20th century. 'So disconcerting is the suppleness of his style,' writes André Gide, 'that alongside it every other seems stilted, dull, imprecise, perfunctory, lifeless.'

1923 On 11 January French troops occupy the **Ruhr** in retaliation for Germany's failure to keep up the payment of reparations.

On 1 April the length of **military service** is reduced to eighteen months.

In September the German authorities call on the local population to support a policy of **passive resistance** to the French occupation of the Ruhr.

Darius Milhaud composes the ballet *La Création du Monde*, the first major jazz-inspired score by a classical composer.

1924 In April, in response to pressure from American bankers reluctant to finance a loan to France without greater international stability, an Anglo-American commission headed by the American banker Charles Dawes publishes the **Dawes Plan**, which sets out a reduced programme of reparations.

France resumes diplomatic relations with the Vatican (May).

Elections to the Chamber of Deputies in May result in a victory for the *Cartel des gauches*, a left-wing coalition of Socialists and Radicals led by **Edouard Herriot** and **Léon Blum**. Herriot, the Prime Minister, accepts the Dawes plan and initiates a conciliatory policy towards Germany which is successfully continued over the next few years by Aristide Briand as Foreign Minister. Herriot's proposed **tax on capital**, however, runs into opposition from the markets. He resigns on 27 October.

Between 1924 and 1926 the intractable nature of France's economic problems results in a dizzying number of changes of Cabinet (seven in all) on the part of the Cartel.

In July the **8th Olympic Games** are held in Paris. The first **Winter Olympics** are held in Chamonix.

On 29 October France recognises the **USSR**.

Release of **René Clair**'s humorous, surrealist film, *Entr'acte*, with music by **Erik Satie**.

André Breton publishes the **Surrealist Manifesto**.

'I do not see the woman hidden in the forest'. In this collage, Magritte's painting is surrounded by Surrealist artists, all with their eyes closed. They are (clockwise, from bottom right): Albert Valentin, André Thirion, Yves Tanguy, Georges Sadoul, Paul Nougé, Camille Goemans, Max Ernst, Salvador Dali, Maxime Alexandre, Louis Aragon, André Breton, Luis Buñuel, Jean Caupenne, Paul Eluard, Marcel Fourier and René Magritte

Surrealism

Although it emerged in the mid-1920s, the **Surrealist movement** was in some ways a product of World War I. Marching under the banner of reason, enlightened men seemed to have led western civilization straight to the muddy carnage of Verdun. In 1916 the **Dadaists** had expressed a ferocious rejection of this culture of rationalism, creating a nihilistic form of anti-art that exalted absurdity and unreason. For the poets who formed the nucleus of the Surrealist movement, notably **André Breton**, **Louis Aragon** and **Paul Eluard**, this offered a cue for something more positive. Clearly influenced by the work of Sigmund Freud, the manifesto that Breton published in 1924 stressed above all the importance of the subconscious. Dream, instinct, coincidence, unexplained juxtaposition and psychic automatism were keys to a higher awareness. But rather than simply rejecting mundane reality, the aim was to infuse it with these other, sexually charged, subconscious realities in order to create a 'surreality'.

Though the theorists of Surrealism were writers, its fruits were most evident in painting. Artists from across Europe such as **Salvador Dali**, **René Magritte**, **Paul Delvaux**, **Max Ernst**, **André Masson** and **Yves Tanguy** bear witness to the range of its influence, as, in other art forms, do the photographs of **Man Ray** and the films of **Luis Buñuel**. Political differences soon fragmented the movement but it has remained central to the story of 20th-century culture, both in the emphasis it gave to the unconscious and in the importance it ascribed to content at a time when formal concerns were dominant.

1925 In April **Abd el-Krim**, the Moroccan leader who has declared an independent Republic in the mineral-rich **Rif district** of Spanish-held Morocco, mounts an offensive against French Morocco. Marshal Pétain is sent to oppose it and assembles a vast Franco-Spanish force that devastates the area in pursuit of the rebel leader. The episode is a taste of colonial wars to come.

In July French troops evacuate the Ruhr.

> I believe in the future resolution of these two states – outwardly so contradictory – which are dream and reality, into a sort of absolute reality, a surreality, so to speak. I am aiming for its conquest, certain that I myself shall not attain it, but too indifferent to my death not to calculate the joys of such possession.
>
> From *Le Manifeste du Surréalisme*, 1924

In October, under the **Locarno Pact**, France and Germany agree to respect each other's frontiers.

In November George Valois, a former member of *Action française*, founds **le Faisceau** which over the next year builds up a membership of some 26,000. This fascist group is one of a number of extreme right-wing organisations founded in the wake of the left's electoral victory in 1924. Taking their inspiration from Italy, where Mussolini has been in power since 1922, they include *Action française*'s *Camelots du roy* and Pierre Taittinger's *Jeunesses patriotes*.

The *'Exposition des Arts décoratifs'* launches **Art Deco**, a self-consciously modern style of decorative art and interior design characterized by elegant and attenuated forms, geometrical patterns and bright colours.

Le Corbusier publishes *Urbanisme*, his highly contentious but influential vision of a modern city.

Maurice Ravel writes his opera *L'enfant et les sortilèges* to a libretto by **Colette**.

At the Théâtre des Champs-Elysées **Josephine Baker** enjoys a huge and controversial success with *La Revue Nègre*, riding a wave of enthusiasm for black art and artists of which Paris is the centre.

Tennis star **Suzanne Lenglen**, who dominates the

women's game throughout the 1920s, wins both the French Open and Wimbledon championships.

1926 In May Abd el-Krim is captured, though sporadic fighting continues for another two years.

In July, the failure of the Cartel to stop the decline of the franc results in the appointment of the right-wing **Raymond Poincaré** to head a government of national unity with a programme of **financial reform**.

The expatriate generation

For much of the Anglo-Saxon world, the image of France between the wars has less to do with the reality of its social and political life than with the experiences of a few **expatriates**, mostly American, who made a temporary home in Paris. World War I had introduced a whole generation of young Americans to this wonderfully un-American, unpuritanical and, from the perspective of the 1920s, un-Prohibitionist city. Once the war ended, many of them were eager to get back, and the Paris of romantic legend was in part created by writers such as **Ernest Hemingway**, **Scott Fitzgerald** and **Henry Miller** who acted as their chroniclers. This was the world that Hemingway evoked in *A Moveable Feast* – the cafés of the **Latin Quarter** and **Montparnasse**, the lingering walks along the Seine, the encounters with semi-mythical figures such as **Gertrude Stein** and **Ezra Pound**, **Wyndham Lewis** and **Ford Madox Ford**. Three quarters of a century later, the lure of these ghosts still contributes to the appeal of Paris.

But it was not just on the French capital that the expatriates made an impact. Until the 1920s, tourists had thought of the **Côte d'Azur** as a winter destination. It was the expatriate community that turned it into something else. They wanted a summer resort where they could bake in the sun and swim in the warm water, wear espadrilles and sailor shirts and feel that pleasure was theirs for the taking. First one hotel stayed open to cater for them, then more. Before long the **Riviera** in summer had become fashionable. The lifestyle it offered became the basis of Europe's postwar tourist industry.

> **"** There is never any ending to Paris and the memory of each person who has lived in it differs from that of any other. We always returned to it no matter who we were or how it was changed or with what difficulties, or ease, it could be reached. Paris was always worth it and you received return for whatever you brought to it. But this is how Paris was in the early days when we were very poor and very happy. **"**
>
> Ernest Hemingway, *A Moveable Feast* (1964)

The growing extremism of *Action française* leads to its condemnation in December by **Pope Pius XI**.

1927 France undertakes the construction of the **Maginot line** as a defence against German attack.

In May **military service** is reduced to one year.

In November the *Croix de Feu* is founded, an organisation of former servicemen decorated in action. Under the leadership of **Colonel de La Rocque** in the early 1930s, this will become one of the most powerful right-wing groups in France.

Release of **Abel Gance**'s epic, six-hour film *Napoléon*. A romanticized view of Napoléon's early career, the film employs a number of innovative techniques, such as split screen and rapid cutting.

A French team beats the USA in the **Davis Cup** international tennis competition. The French win the competition for the next five years.

1928 Between 22 and 29 April, Poincaré and his centre-right supporters win victory in elections to the Chamber of Deputies. The restored confidence of the financial markets enables him to return the franc to the **gold standard** at about one-fifth of its prewar value.

1929 In June the **Young Plan**, resulting from a second renegotiation of war reparations, recommends reduced German payments, but these new arrangements are soon overtaken by the economic consequences of the **Wall Street crash**.

On 27 July Poincaré resigns for reasons of health. Briand, yet again, forms a new administration.

From 24 to 29 October prices collapse on the **US stock market**.

Louis de Broglie is awarded the **Nobel prize** for Physics for his discovery of the wave nature of electrons, first proposed by him in 1923 and verified experimentally in 1927.

The poet and dramatist **Paul Claudel** publishes his play *Le soulier de satin*, written some years earlier though not performed until 1943. Set in Renaissance Spain, it exemplifies both Claudel's religious preoccupations and his technical mastery.

1930 In April a law on **social insurance** completes earlier steps taken in 1924 and 1928 to provide sickness, invalidity and old age benefits for those with low incomes.

On 30 June, the French end their occupation of the **German Rhineland**.

1931 In January **Pierre Laval** forms a new administration.

On 6 May the opening of the **colonial exhibition** at Vincennes marks the high point of France's colonial fortunes. Designed to boost support for the empire among French citizens, it attracts some eight million visitors during its six-month run.

On 13 May **Paul Doumer** is elected president of the Republic.

On 13 July, under the **moratorium** announced by the

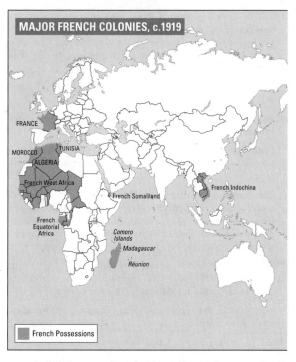

MAJOR FRENCH COLONIES, c.1919

FRANCE

MOROCCO

TUNISIA

ALGERIA

French West Africa

French Somaliland

French Indochina

French Equatorial Africa

Comoro Islands

Madagascar

Réunion

French Possessions

American President **Herbert Hoover**, Germany suspends payment of reparations, damaging the French economy at a time when it is already under pressure from a worsening global situation. Numerous small banks fail and industrial production goes down. The tidal wave from the Wall Street crash has finally reached France, initiating a **slump** that will last for much of the decade.

Completion of **Le Corbusier**'s Villa Savoie at Poissy. With

its clean lines, open plan and lack of ornament, it epitomizes his conception of the house as 'a machine for living in'.

1932 On 7 May President Paul Doumer is assassinated by a White Russian, **Pavel Gorgulov**, who holds him responsible for France's rapprochement with the Soviet Union.

Harsh economic conditions lead to **bankruptcies** in the textile industry and among the farming community.

Louis-Ferdinand Céline publishes *Voyage au bout de la nuit*, which scandalizes as much by its revolutionary use of French slang as by its sombre commentary on social injustice and human malevolence.

François Poulenc writes his *Concerto for Two Pianos*, a work that typifies his witty and eclectic style.

1933 Hitler becomes Chancellor of Germany.

France's national airline, **Air France**, is founded.

1934 On 8 January the body of **Alexandre Stavisky** is discovered at Chamonix. The author of a financial swindle that threatens to implicate members of the government, Stavisky is said to have committed suicide, but there are persistent rumours that he has been killed to stop him talking. Right-wingers seize on the scandal and organize popular demonstrations that culminate in a riot in the place de la Concorde on 6 February in which several people are killed. The affair causes the fall in quick succession of two administrations, posing a threat to the survival of the Republic.

On 9 February **Gaston Doumergue** forms a new government of national union and confidence is restored.

On 5 March, partly in response to right-wing actions at the time of the Stavisky scandal, the *Comité de vigilance des intellectuels antifascistes* is formed. This becomes the basis of the left-wing coalition, the ***Front populaire*** (Popular Front).

On 9 October Croatian nationalists assassinate King Alexander I of Yugoslavia and the French Foreign Minister, **Louis Barthou**.

1935 On 2 May France and Russia agree a **pact** of mutual assistance.

In spite of huge left-wing demonstrations, the conservative government of Pierre Laval pushes through a series of

deflationary measures in the second half of the year which have the effect of cutting wages in the public sector by ten percent and increasing the price of fuel and transport. Their unpopularity paves the way for the left's electoral victory the following year.

Reacting to fraudulent practices in the wine industry, France introduces the system of *Appellation d'origine contrôlée* (AOC) to regulate the origin and quality of its wines.

1936 In January **paramilitary organisations** are banned.

The victory of the *Front populaire* in elections to the Chamber (26 April–3 May) enables Léon Blum to form a new administration, which for the first time includes women. A huge wave of strikes in May reflects a general sense among workers that the time has come for change. Blum's government quickly responds with social reforms. Under the **Matignon Agreements** of 7 June, workers are granted wage rises of between seven percent and fifteen percent two weeks' annual paid holiday and a forty-hour working week. Later in the year, the age for compulsory schooling is raised to 14.

In June the banning of the fascist leagues leads to the creation of the *Parti social français* (born out of the *Croix de Feu*) by Colonel de La Roque and the *Parti populaire français* by Jacques Doriot, both appealing to an extreme right-wing element that will come into its own with the establishment of the Vichy regime (see p.309).

Following the start of the **Spanish Civil War** on 18 July, Blum is instrumental in establishing a **non-intervention pact** among the European powers, which is largely disregarded by Italy and Germany.

On 17 November the Minister of the Interior, **Roger Salengro**, who has played an important part in securing the Matignon agreements and the dissolution of the fascist leagues, commits suicide as a result of a right-wing smear campaign accusing him of desertion and treachery during the war.

1937 In February, in an effort to restore market confidence, Blum announces a 'pause in reforms', but the economy continues to weaken, leading to further devaluations of the franc. When the Senate refuses Blum extraordinary financial powers in June, he resigns and is replaced by **Camille Chautemps**.

BETTMAN/CORBIS

The cabaret singer Edith Piaf rose to fame in the 1930s. She was especially admired for her poignant ballads, such as *La vie en rose*, which she delivered with great emotional force

At the end of August, the railway companies are nationalized to create the **SNCF** (*Société nationale des chemins de fer*), which will be the backbone of France's successful public transport system.

Picasso's *Guernica*, painted as an indictment of the Luftwaffe's bombing of a Basque village, is exhibited in the Spanish pavilion at Paris's **International Exhibition**.

Release of *La Grande Illusion*, **Jean Renoir**'s powerful antiwar film starring the great French film actor, **Jean Gabin**.

The women's magazine *Marie Claire* is launched.

1938 Between 11 and 13 March Germany forces Austria to agree to annexation – the *Anschluss* (Union).

On 10 April **Edouard Daladier** forms a new government when a second Blum administration collapses after four weeks, again brought down by the Senate's refusal to accept Blum's economic plans.

Between August and September Hitler turns his attention to **Czechoslovakia** and presses for the annexation of the Sudetenland. Abandoned by France and Britain under the terms of the **Munich agreement** (30 September), Czechoslovakia is powerless to resist. The French Communists refuse to vote in support of the agreement, bringing about a break with the Radicals and the end of the *Front populaire*.

> " The alarm goes off at 3 am. We walk down to the Dôme; night air very mild. The Dôme and the Rotonde are feebly lit. The Dôme is noisy; lots of uniforms. Out on the terrasse two tarts are sitting with their arms round a couple of officers; one of the girls is singing mechanically. The officers take no notice of them. Inside, shouts and laughter. "
>
> Simone de Beauvoir, *La force de l'âge* (1960), trans. Peter Green

Jean-Paul Sartre publishes his philosophical novel *La Nausée*, which expresses many of the central concerns of **existentialism**.

1939 Following the German invasion of Czechoslovakia on 15 March, France and Britain promise to support Belgium,

Philippe Pétain

The career of **Philippe Pétain** (1856–1951) moves in a classic arc from obscurity to fame to infamy. Born into a family of farmers in the Pas-de-Calais, he attended the élite military academy of St-Cyr and went on to become a professor at the School of War, where he taught until 1907. A colonel at the outbreak of World War I, he had risen more slowly than many of his contemporaries because he favoured, against the prevailing orthodoxy, a defensive rather than an offensive strategy. Once the war had started, however, the mistakes and failures of the senior officers ensured his rapid promotion. Cool under fire and decisive in a crisis, he earned the respect of **General Joffre**, the commander-in-chief. When the situation at **Verdun** looked all but lost, Pétain managed to organize a defence that saved the battle and made him a hero both with the French people and, more significantly, with his own troops.

Raised to the title of **Marshal of France** in 1918, Pétain had an important say in France's military policy during the interwar period, not least in the construction of the **Maginot line**. It was his misfortune not to die before the Germans so easily bypassed it. Old, autocratic, deeply influenced by the right-wing ideas of *Action française*, he imagined that by taking the post of Prime Minister in France's hour of defeat he could help to create a new nation, purified and reborn. As the trucks rolled north and east towards the concentration camps, he seems never to have comprehended that instead he had created a monster. In 1945 he was condemned to death by the High Court, a sentence commuted to life imprisonment. He died six years later, a prisoner on the island of **Yeu**, off the Atlantic coast.

the Netherlands and Switzerland (23 March). Over the next three weeks the same undertaking is given to Poland, Greece and Romania.

In July the National Assembly adopts the '*code de la famille*', a collection of measures, including financial incentives, designed to increase the birthrate.

On 3 September, two days after the invasion of Poland, France and Britain **declare war** on Germany. A brief French offensive to the east of Metz gives way to eight months of the '**phoney war**', during which allied forces await the German attack.

Jean Renoir's cinematic masterpiece, *La règle du jeu*, satirizes the frivolity of a society on the edge of disintegration.

1940 On 20 March the Daladier government falls and is replaced by that of **Pierre Reynaud**.

On 10 May **German forces** bypass the Maginot line and **invade** France.

From 28 May to 4 June French and British troops are evacuated from **Dunkirk**.

On 10 June, in the face of the **German advance**, the government retreats to **Bordeaux**. On the same day, **Italy** declares war on France and Britain. Four days later, the Germans enter **Paris**.

Unable to persuade the Cabinet to fight on from outside France as a government in exile, **Reynaud resigns** (16 June). **Marshal Pétain** becomes prime minister and on the following day declares an end to hostilities. On 18 June **General de Gaulle** broadcasts an appeal from London for France to continue the struggle.

On 22 June an **armistice** between France and Germany is signed at Rethondes in the same railway carriage that had been used for the signature of the armistice at the end of

World War I. France is divided into an **occupied sector** (the north and along the Atlantic coast) and an **unoccupied sector** under French administration; its army and fleet are demobilised; it is obliged to pay the costs of the German occupation.

On 28 June the British government recognises de Gaulle as leader of **Free France**. Through July and August, French colonies – among them the New Hebrides, Chad, the Cameroons, Tahiti and the Moyen-Congo – rally to his standard.

2 July: The government of France establishes itself at **Vichy** and recalls Parliament. On the following day the British destroy the **French fleet** at Mers-el-Kébir in Algeria. The Assembly, whipped in by the deputy Prime Minister Pierre Laval, votes full powers to Pétain, bringing to an end the Third Republic (10–11 July). This is followed by the promulgation of twelve constitutional acts which define *Etat français*, a new France based on right-wing values in direct opposition to those of the Republic. On 24 July Hitler announces the annexation of **Alsace-Lorraine**.

From September to December the growing **resistance** to the German occupation is reflected in the birth of the underground newspapers *Résistance, Combat,* and *Libération.*

On 12 September four teenage boys discover the caves at **Lascaux** (see p.4), which are opened to the public in 1948.

On 23 September the attack of the Free French on **Dakar** ends in failure when local forces fail to support them.

Pétain and Laval meet Hitler at **Montoire** on 24 October to establish the terms of the collaboration. Three weeks later, Germany releases 50,000 French prisoners of war.

Suspicious that Laval is out to displace him, Pétain has his deputy dismissed and arrested (13 December).

Vichy: a puppet regime

Pétain, it seemed, was once again the saviour of the nation. A new *Etat français*, centred on **Vichy**, would rise from the ashes of France's humiliating defeat. By the middle of July 1940 some ten million civilians were on the road, making for the unoccupied *zone libre*. But the shape of things to come was already being indicated by rabidly anti-Semitic denunciations in the newspapers. This was to be the kind of state advocated since the beginning of the century by Charles Maurras and *Action française* – a Catholic France that had no place for Jews, Freemasons or foreigners. **Internment** without trial was one of the earliest measures to be introduced. Under the slogan *Travail, Famille, Patrie* (Work, Family, Fatherland), which replaced the Republican *Liberté, Egalité, Fraternité*, Vichy set a course of social and political repression, designated the 'national revolution'. Central to its programme were a reversal of the Republic's anti-clericalism, a purge of the educational system, and a new emphasis on **traditional family values**. To this end, divorce was made more difficult and abortion punishable by death. Pétainist movements such as the *Chantiers de la jeunesse* and the *cadres d'Uriage* were set up to foster these values among the young.

From November 1942, when Germany took over the unoccupied zone, Vichy's status as a **puppet regime** was increasingly apparent. The growing prominence of Darnand's *Milice* (see p.310), and the eventual inclusion in the Cabinet of **extreme collaborators** such as **Philippe Henriot** and **Marcel Déat** caused popular support to bleed away. Vichy was none the less a regime accepted, whether with enthusiasm or resentment, by the majority of the population for much of the war. Only in the 1970s did France really begin to face the extent to which collaboration had been part of the texture of ordinary life during these years.

1941 **Rationing** of all essential goods gives rise to a **black market**.

The process of collaboration sees the birth of organizations such as the *Rassemblement national populaire* and **Joseph**

Charles de Gaulle broadcasting to the Free French from London in June 1940

Darnand's *Service d'ordre légionnaire*. Darnand's group will become the dreaded political police force known as the *Milice*, specializing in measures against Jews and members of the Resistance. The *Légion des volontaires français*, formed in July to fight bolshevism, is an expression of the deep strain of **anti-communism** that had led many in the previous year to think 'Better Hitler than Stalin'. At the same time, pockets of resistance gain strength, leading to increasingly harsh reprisals. In October, hostages are executed in a number of towns across France.

On 24 September de Gaulle establishes the **National Committee of Free France** in London.

On 7 December the US enters the war after the Japanese attack on **Pearl Harbour**.

Charles de Gaulle

Born at Lille into a cultured upper-middle-class family, **de Gaulle** (1890–1970) graduated from the military academy at St-Cyr before going on to serve under **Pétain** in World War I. His courage under fire – he was three times wounded and spent two and a half years as a POW – was matched by a reflective intelligence apparent in the military books he published between the wars. In particular, he realized the importance that **tank warfare** would have in the future – an insight that benefited the Germans more than his compatriots.

De Gaulle's role during **World War II** can be summed up in the closing words of his address from London on 18 June, 1940, the day after Pétain had announced an armistice: 'The flame of French resistance will not be extinguished.' This speech was the key example of an ability de Gaulle retained throughout his political life to use the media to his advantage at moments of crisis. Despite a turbulent relationship with **Churchill** and the deep mistrust of **Roosevelt**, de Gaulle managed brilliantly to preserve the notion of '*la France libre*' and also to establish himself as its incarnation.

Impatience with the direction of postwar politics consigned him to the political wilderness in 1946, until the war in **Algeria** brought him back to power twelve years later. The architect of the **Fifth Republic**, he pursued policies designed to reinforce France's role on the world stage, among them the acquisition of nuclear weapons. Shaken by the events of **May 1968**, he sought to shore up his personal authority with a referendum, but his proposals for administrative and political reform were defeated. On 27 April, 1969, he resigned. Having retired to Colombey-les-Deux-Eglises to write his memoirs, he died there on 9 November, shortly before his eightieth birthday. With his single-minded dedication to an ideal of the grandeur of France, he had done more than any other figure in the century to shape his country's destiny.

1942 On 1 January **Jean Moulin** is parachuted into France to coordinate the various Resistance movements that have come into existence.

From February to April, **Blum**, **Daladier** and **Gamelin** (former commander of allied forces in France) are put on trial at Riom. Blum's triumphant defence prompts the Germans to have the trial halted.

On 17 March the first convoy of **racial deportees** leaves the unoccupied zone. A month later, on 18 April, Laval returns to government at the insistence of the Germans. From mid-November most of Pétain's powers will be transferred to him.

From 29 May **Jews** are obliged to wear the yellow star in the occupied zone. Between 21 and 22 July, 13,000 Jews are rounded up and held in the Vélodrome d'Hiver sports stadium (the Vel' d'Hiv) before being deported. Of some 75,000 Jews deported in all, only about three percent come back.

On 8 November, after an Anglo-American landing in Algeria, **Admiral Darlan**, the commander of Vichy's army, signs an armistice with the Allies.

On 11 November the Germans move into the unoccupied zone.

General Henri Giraud, having escaped earlier in the year from imprisonment in Germany, is named Civil and Military High Commissioner in North Africa (26 November). Roosevelt, in particular, thinks him a preferable alternative to de Gaulle as the leader of Free France. On 27 November the **French fleet** scuttles itself at Toulon to avoid falling into German hands. On 24 December, Admiral Darlan is assassinated in Algiers.

Albert Camus publishes his first novel, *L'Etranger*. The story of its alienated, enigmatic hero reflects Camus' concern (explored in the same year in his philosophical work *Le Mythe de Sisyphe*) with the challenge of an existence that is perceived as essentially 'absurd'.

Les Editions de Minuit, a clandestine publishing house set

up during the Occupation, brings out *Le Silence de la mer* by **Vercors**, which becomes an underground classic of the Resistance.

1943 Between 14 and 27 January de Gaulle and Giraud attend the **Casablanca conference**, at which Roosevelt and Churchill – meeting to discuss global strategy for the conduct of the war – attempt to settle the leadership of the Free French. De Gaulle does not accept that there is anything to be settled.

On 16 February Laval presides over the introduction of **forced labour** in Germany (STO - *Service du travail obligatoire*). Some 875,000 Frenchmen will be exported to help the German war effort. This hated policy drives many young men into the *maquis* (Resistance groups operating in mountainous or isolated terrain).

On 7 May, German resistance to allied forces crumbles in **Tunisia**. With the tide of war beginning to turn against Germany, the newly formed *Conseil national de la Résistance* (CNR) holds its first meeting (27 May). A week later de Gaulle and Giraud set up the *Comité français de la libération nationale* (CFLN) in Algiers, of which de Gaulle becomes sole president in October. On 21 June Jean Moulin is arrested at Caluire, near Lyon, and dies after torture. The leadership of the CNR passes to **Georges Bidault**.

In September and October **Corsica** is liberated by the Allies.

Antoine de Saint-Exupéry publishes his classic children's book *Le Petit Prince*.

Sartre publishes *L'Etre et le Néant*, his major philosophical work and the principal text of postwar existentialism.

Les Enfants du paradis is released. Set in the world of the theatre in 1830s Paris, the film is the high point of a unique style of poetic romance created by the regular collaborators **Marcel Carné** (director), **Jacques Prévert** (writer) and **Alexander Trauner** (designer).

1944 In January advocates of a policy of **'total collaboration'**, notably Déat, Darnand and Doriot, become part of the Vichy government. In the same month, de Gaulle makes a speech at the **Brazzaville** conference in which he outlines a programme of reform for colonies seeking more autonomy.

The Resistance

Uncoordinated and politically diverse, the initial **Resistance** networks often had little in common beyond a refusal to accept defeat. On 1 January, 1942, **Jean Moulin**, chosen for the job by de Gaulle, was parachuted into France with the task of moulding them into a unified force. By the beginning of 1943 he had persuaded the three main networks operating in the south to form into the *Mouvements unis de la résistance* (MUR). He then turned to the north, where his efforts finally resulted in the formation of the *Conseil national de la résistance* (CNR), which united MUR with the eight principal networks in the northern zone. The historic first meeting of the CNR at a house in the rue du Four in Paris on 27 May was a triumph not just for Moulin but also for de Gaulle, who could increasingly claim to be the one figure recognized by all the resistance groups in France.

As the outlook for Germany darkened, the resistance grew bolder and measures of reprisal, such as the massacre at **Oradour-sur-Glane**, became more savage. In March and July 1944, the networks of the Plateau des Glières and Vercors were crushed by greatly superior German forces. On 17 August, as allied troops approached the capital, the **Paris Resistance** rose against the Germans to play its part in liberating the city. In the end, it is perhaps less easy to determine the practical impact of the Resistance on the course of the war than its immense psychological importance to the process of recovery that followed.

In June the CFLN becomes the **'*Gouvernement provisoire de la République française*'**, with de Gaulle as its president. On 6 June allied forces land in **Normandy** and begin the advance on Paris.

On 10 June, a day after the hanging of 99 hostages in the town of Tulle, the village of **Oradour-sur-Glane**, near Limoges, is set on fire and its whole population of 642 civilians massacred by a detachment of the SS. The men are shot, the women and children burned to death after being herded into the church.

On 16 June de Gaulle receives a rapturous welcome in **Bayeux**, the first town in France to be liberated. On 15 August the American troops and the forces of the Free French land in **Provence**. Three days later the Vichy government falls and Pétain and Laval accompany the Germans in their retreat.

Paris rises against the Germans (19 August). Six days later, by agreement with the Americans, **General Philippe Leclerc**, at the head of the Second Armoured Division, liberates the city. On the following day, 26 August, de Gaulle leads a triumphal parade down the **Champs-Elysées**.

On 9 September de Gaulle forms a government of **national unity**. Having maintained a French government in exile, he can now claim a legitimacy that safeguards France from the American organization set up to administer liberated countries.

> " Practically no one shouted 'Long live France!' but everyone called out 'Long live de Gaulle!' In moments of great distress or great joy, the crowd has a natural tendency to turn to one man and make him the symbol of their need to admire or to be protected. "
>
> Georges Bidault, quoted in Alistair Horne, *The Savage War* (1977)

9
France since the Liberation
1944–2002

The end of the **Occupation** left France facing the need to rebuild itself for a postwar world. **De Gaulle** was important to this but perhaps less so than he had hoped. When he resigned from office in 1946, expecting to be called back, the political parties simply let him go. After initial economic difficulties, which caused a sharp **devaluation** of the franc, France began to climb free of the rubble of war. With the aid of the American **Marshall Plan**, the country entered on a period of economic and social prosperity that was to stretch across the next thirty years. It was known in retrospect, with a wry glance at the *Trois Glorieuses* (the three glorious days of the 1830 revolution), as the *Trente Glorieuses*.

Among France's **colonies** the outlook was more stormy. Violent unrest in **Madagascar** was only one aspect of a colonial backdrop dominated by the long-running conflict in **Indochina**, which came to an end in 1954 with the humiliating defeat at **Dien Bien Phu**. Just six months later, the newly formed **FLN** inaugurated its own war of independence in **Algeria**. This was to be the darkest page of France's postwar history, opening the door to a world of terrorism and torture that left the French people shocked and disorientated. By the time it ended in 1962, France had divested herself of most of her remaining colonial possessions.

The threat posed by France's disaffected generals in Algeria led to the return of General de Gaulle, who now framed a new Constitution for the **Fifth Republic** which shifted the balance of power towards the President. Over the next ten years his policies emphasized France's role as an independent player on the international stage, developing the country's nuclear capabilities and holding aloof from the **NATO** alliance. But social troubles were building an unrecognized head of steam, and the eruption of protests from students and workers in **May 1968** fatally undermined his position.

The post-de Gaulle era was ushered in by **Georges Pompidou**, who presided over the expansion of the **EEC** (European Economic Community) and the last days of relative economic calm before the **oil crisis** unleashed by the Arab-Israeli Yom Kippur War in 1973. It fell to **Valéry Giscard d'Estaing** and **François Mitterrand** to steer France through the awkward years that followed. Both introduced measures of social liberalization, but both were hampered by the economic circumstances. The election of **Jacques Chirac** as president in 1995 brought a form of Gaullism back to power at the end of the century.

The second half of the 20th century saw a dramatic rise in the general standard of living – in 1954 less than sixty percent of French homes had running water – accompanied by large-scale **urbanization**. At the start of World War II, about thirty percent of the population lived on the land; by the year 2000, the figure was less than five percent. As the economic problems of the 1970s took hold and **unemployment** began to rise, so **racial tensions** increased. Although France's immigrant population at the close of the century made up no more than six or seven percent of the total, about the same as in the 1930s, it presented a scapegoat that the politicians of the *Front national* found easy to exploit.

Even before World War II had ended, France, or more specifically Paris, was reasserting its cultural pre-eminence in the west. One after another, **existentialism**, **structuralism** and **poststructuralism** shaped the dominant intellectual trends of the second half of the century. The French *nouveau* *roman* challenged long-held assumptions about prose fiction, while in the cinema the *nouvelle vague* transformed both film-making and film criticism. Architecturally, there were **grands travaux** such as the **musée d'Orsay**, the new **National Library**, the expanded Louvre, the **Bastille opera**, the complex of skyscrapers at **La Défense**, and the Institute of the Arab World, as well as major projects outside Paris such as Rem Koolhaas's **Grand Palais** in Lille. Not all of these were wholly successful but, as the new millennium approached, they expressed a vital confidence in France's future.

THE DÉPARTEMENTS OF FRANCE

1944 De Gaulle heads a provisional government of national unity, created in Algeria the previous year as the *Gouvernement provisoire de la République française*.

On 5 October **women** are given the right to vote.

In the context of moves to resurrect the French press, the newspaper ***Le Monde*** is founded in December.

Female collaborators were often publically humiliated by having their heads shaved, like these women at Chartres

A public controversy between **Albert Camus** and **François Mauriac** highlights the question of how to deal with **Nazi collaborators**. Up to ten thousand summary executions have been carried out in purges ('the purification') across France since June, and now an attempt is being made to introduce a proper judicial framework. It will remain a contentious issue. The application of justice is patchy, tending to fall more heavily on the working classes than on the upper and middle classes, while moves to purge businesses, professions, and administrative hierarchies are selective and often half-hearted. Among those who do not escape is the writer **Robert Brasillach**, shot for collaboration on 6 February, 1945.

Jean Genet publishes his first novel, *Notre-Dame des Fleurs*, written while he was in prison. A thief and prostitute, Genet shocks the literary establishment with his poetic vision of the prewar criminal underworld, but his writing is acclaimed by Cocteau and Sartre.

The painter **Jean Dubuffet** has his first solo exhibition. His deliberately crude works, *art brut*, reflect his interest in the spontaneous art created by children and the insane.

1945 In January the **Renault** automobile company, tainted by its collaboration with the Germans, is nationalized without compensation. Later in the year it launches the hugely popular 4CV model.

De Gaulle is not invited to the **Yalta conference** (4–11 February) where Churchill, Stalin and Roosevelt plan the

> Each time I spoke of justice with respect to purification, M. Mauriac spoke of charity. And the virtue of charity is rather singular in that it seems to make me argue for hatred when what I am really calling for is justice.
>
> Albert Camus, quoted in Olivier Todd, *Albert Camus: A Life* (1997)

closing stages of the war and its aftermath, but France gets a designated zone in the proposed occupation of Germany.

France is one of fifty nations that agree the **Charter of the United Nations** at the San Francisco Conference (25 April–26 June).

Marshal Pétain gives himself up (26 April). In August he is condemned to death, but his sentence is commuted by de Gaulle to life imprisonment.

April–May: The municipal elections, which see women voting for the first time, result in a victory for the left.

On 8 May **Germany surrenders**, bringing the war in Europe to an end.

Anti-French riots in the **Constantine** region of Algeria are harshly put down (8–12 May).

Air France is nationalized (26 June). The **Banque de France** and a number of other large banks follow in December. This is part of a broad strategy of nationalization that in April 1946 will take in the gas and electricity companies as well as the big insurance companies.

De Gaulle is not invited to the **Potsdam conference** (17 July–2 August), where Britain, Russia and America decide the future of Germany.

On the day of the **Japanese surrender** (2 September), which marks the end of World War II, **Ho Chi Minh**, speaking in Hanoi, declares Vietnamese independence. With British help, the French reoccupy Saigon and take control of the south.

In October the *Ecole nationale d'administration* (ENA) is created. This will provide many of the leading figures in France's postwar administrations.

Pierre Laval, Pétain's Vice-Premier, is executed (15 October).

On 21 October **elections** for a Constituent Assembly result in a victory for the left.

The first issue of *Les Temps modernes* appears. Founded by, among others, Jean-Paul Sartre, Simone de Beauvoir, Raymond Aron, Jean Paulhan and Maurice Merleau-Ponty, it becomes one of the most influential literary and political journals of postwar years.

1946 At odds with the prevailing mood of the Assembly, and mistrustful of their ideas for a new constitution, **de Gaulle resigns** (20 January). Instead of being recalled by the Assembly on a wave of public support, he is succeeded by the socialist **Félix Gouin** under the terms of a caretaker agreement between the political parties.

Left-wing proposals for a constitution that would give dominant power to an Assembly are rejected by referendum in May. Revised proposals, increasing the power of the President, are drawn up by a newly elected Constituent Assembly and receive lukewarm acceptance in October. The constitution of the **Fourth Republic** ends up looking much like that of the Third. Elections to the Chamber of Deputies, held the following month, produce another majority for the left.

Earlier in the year, on 13 April, the **Marthe Richard law** makes brothels illegal, bringing to an end a long tradition of tolerance, both in Paris and the provinces.

Opening of the first **Cannes Film Festival** (20 September).

In November **Jean Monnet** introduces a five-year modernization plan, designed to revitalise the **French economy**. Together with the American aid provided by the **Marshall Plan** (agreed the following June), this lays the groundwork for a period of economic growth that, in spite of frequent industrial unrest, will last until the mid-1970s. Accompanying it is a growth in **population** that starts with the postwar baby-boom and continues until the mid-1960s, when the birth rate again begins to fall.

The Swiss sculptor **Alberto Giacometti** returns to Paris and begins the attenuated figurative work for which he is famous.

The popular singer-songwriter **Charles Trenet** achieves his greatest success with *La mer*.

1947 On 16 January the election of **Vincent Auriol** as President marks the start of the Fourth Republic. It begins amid economic gloom. **Bread shortages** are worse than during the war, and from June through to November there are numerous strikes, sometimes violent. In the course of the year a total of over 23 million working days are lost.

Existentialism

Although the development of **existentialism** can be traced back through thinkers such as Jaspers and Heidegger to the Danish philosopher Søren Kierkegaard, its significance in French intellectual life belongs to the postwar years and to one man in particular: **Jean-Paul Sartre**. Between them, *L'être et le néant* (1943, *Being and Nothingness*) and his trilogy of novels *Les Chemins de la liberté* (1945–49, *The Roads to Freedom*) offer an account, in the first case philosophical, in the second imaginative, of what existentialism entailed. Its emphasis on the acts of personal choice by which the individual defines a relationship with a world lacking any transcendent structure of meaning spoke directly to a generation that had experienced the madness of war and the disorientation of its aftermath. **Anti-bourgeois** and hostile to the confident orthodoxies of **Christianity** and **Marxism**, it appealed particularly to the young. The philosophy soon became a style. Associated with the cafés and clubs of **St-Germain-des-près**, existentialism gave a uniquely Parisian flavour to the youthful angst of a black-clad postwar generation whose icons were figures like the singer **Juliette Gréco** and the writer **Boris Vian**.

Jean-Paul Sartre and Simone de Beauvoir in front of Rodin's statue of Balzac

In March a colonial uprising breaks out in **Madagascar**. Over the next 18 months it is savagely repressed, leaving many thousands dead.

In April de Gaulle founds his new political party, the *Rassemblement du peuple français* (RPF).

On 22 November **Robert Schuman** forms a new administration created out of a loose coalition of parties from the centre ground between Communism and Gaullism – the so-called **'Third Force'**.

Towards the end of his career, **André Gide** is awarded the Nobel prize for Literature. Among the works that have built his reputation are *L'Immoraliste* (1902), *Si le grain ne meurt* (1924), *Les Faux-monnayeurs* (1926), *Retour de l'URSS* (1936) and the revealing *Journal* which he kept for most of his life.

Albert Camus publishes *La Peste*. Its account of the struggle against an epidemic in Oran draws a clear analogy with France's recent experience of the German Occupation.

Le Corbusier designs the *Unité d'habitation* at Marseille, a block of flats with an internal shopping street halfway up. Completed in 1952, it incorporates his theories of a '*ville radieuse*' and becomes an influential prototype for postwar housing throughout the world.

The couturier **Christian Dior** brings in his **'New Look'** with the pinched waist and accentuated bust and hips that will become the classic western female outline of the 1950s.

The founding of the Magnum photographic agency, by Robert Capa, **Henri Cartier-Bresson,** George Rodger and David 'Chim' Seymour initiates a new era of photojournalism.

1948 In January the franc is **devalued** by eighty percent.

In April elections in **Algeria** are fixed in favour of government candidates.

Against a background of further economic problems and a new wave of strikes, the Schuman government falls in July.

In December the United Nations Organisation adopts the **Universal Declaration of the Rights of Man**.

Citroën launches its most enduringly popular car, the 2CV, followed in 1950 by the DS.

Olivier Messiaen composes his *Turangalîla-symphonie*, a massive, eastern-inspired orchestral work.

1949 In the first half of the year, **rationing** of bread, chocolate and milk ends, but the franc suffers two further devaluations in April and September.

In July France joins **NATO** (the North Atlantic Treaty Organisation), a military alliance created three months earlier to counter the threat from Soviet Russia.

Simone de Beauvoir publishes *Le Deuxième Sexe*, which will later become a primary text for the feminist movement.

Paris Match, a weekly illustrated magazine modelled on *Life*, is founded.

1950 In May, in a significant move towards **European integration**, Robert Schuman, now foreign minister, proposes a **common market** in coal and steel, an idea rejected by Great Britain.

L'Observateur politique, économique et littéraire is launched. This influential left-wing magazine will later become first *France Observateur* (1954) and then *Le Nouvel Observateur* (1964).

1951 Strikes in the public sector continue, in spite of attempts to check them by increasing salaries and introducing a minimum wage.

A guerrilla conflict in **Tunisia** adds to the burden of the war in Vietnam, while anti-French demonstrations take place in **Morocco**.

Philippe Pétain dies in prison on the island of Yeu (23 July).

In September new laws, sympomatic of a move to the right in the politics of the Fourth Republic, provide for state subsidy of private education.

Robert Bresson's distinctive style of low-key film-making, which focuses on the theme of personal redemption, is established with his third film, *Journal d'un curé de campagne* (*Diary of a Country Priest*).

Indochina

In the course of the 19th century France had acquired control of the area of Southeast Asia that included Vietnam, Laos and Cambodia, collectively known as **French Indochina**. At the end of World War II, Laos and Cambodia were happy enough to accept a relaxed form of colonialism within France's *Fédération indochinoise*, but Vietnam was another matter. Its northern half had been taken over by the nationalist forces of the **Vietminh**, and their leader **Ho Chi Minh** demanded independence for a unified country. An unsatisfactory compromise, worked out at Fontainebleau in September 1946, merely papered over France's basic commitment to regaining control of the whole country.

When the French bombarded **Haiphong** two months later, the touchpaper was lit. Facing a guerrilla army with widespread local support, the French made little headway and settled in 1949 for establishing an 'independent' state under the former emperor **Bao Dai**. It was a solution that owed more to ideological imperatives than to the reality of Vietnamese politics. Aided by the **Communist Chinese**, the Vietminh eroded Bao Dai's precarious hold on the country. Financial assistance from America could not counterbalance the mounting cost in human lives: public opinion in France was turning against the war. By the end of 1953, when Communist insurgency had spread to neighbouring Laos, French forces were concentrated in what should have been an impregnable garrison at **Dien Bien Phu**. But **General Giap** brilliantly outmanoeuvred them, dragging his artillery up to the high ground from which he could subject the French position to a relentless bombardment. On 7 May, 1954, Dien Bien Phu surrendered.

For the Vietnamese, the subsequent agreement at Geneva was no more than a pause in the ongoing conflict – the US was waiting in the wings to defend South Vietnam – but for the French this had been a shocking defeat. It weakened the Fourth Republic and tragically hardened the army's response to the crisis that was on the point of erupting in Algeria.

1952 On 17 January the Tunisian nationalist leader **Habib Bourgiba**, regarded as a threat by the French administration, is kidnapped at Bizerta. His abduction contributes to rising civil disorder.

From January to March **strikes** are violently put down by the police.

The award of the **Nobel prize** for Literature to **François Mauriac** confirms his status as one of France's greatest contemporary Catholic novelists.

1953 **Widespread strikes** take place throughout the summer.

In May **Jean-Jacques Servan-Schreiber** and **Françoise Giroud** launch *L'Express*, an American-style weekly news magazine intended to support the left-wing politics of future premier Pierre Mendès France.

The execution of the Rosenbergs in the US on 19 June intensifies **anti-American** feeling in France.

On 20 August the French depose the **Sultan of Morocco**, thought to be too sympathetic to the nationalists, and replace him with his more amenable uncle. The consequent resentment leads to the formation of a Moroccan army of national liberation.

In November the French begin to dig in at **Dien Bien Phu**.

Pierre Poujade founds *l'Union des commerçants et des artisans* (UDCA). Initially a protest movement of small shopkeepers, it quickly broadens its base to include a core of supporters whose views tend to be anti-Semitic, anti-intellectual and anti-immigrant. Over the next three years **Poujadisme** is a political force to be reckoned with, attracting up to 200,000 supporters. It is here that **Jean-Marie Le Pen**, future leader of the *Front national*, begins his career.

The first performance of **Samuel Beckett**'s *En attendant Godot* (*Waiting for Godot*) is staged at the Théâtre de Babylone in Paris. The play expresses with bleak power the mixture of despair, humour and stoicism characteristic of Beckett's vision.

Jacques Tati's film *Les Vacances de M. Hulot* (*M. Hulot's Holiday*) establishes his particular brand of physical comedy.

Henri-Georges Clouzot's classic suspense film, *Le Salaire de la peur* (*The Wages of Fear*), wins the Palme d'or at Cannes.

1954 In February the **abbé Pierre** begins his crusade on behalf of the **homeless**, turning a spotlight on the casualties of France's economic expansion.

On 10 April France becomes the first country to introduce **VAT**.

The **fall of Dien Bien Phu** (7 May) marks the defeat of France in Indochina.

On 17 June **Pierre Mendès France** forms a new administration and in August is given special powers to manage the economy. In a speech at **Carthage** (31 July) he envisages internal autonomy for Tunisia.

On 1 November a wave of **terrorism** in Algeria, orchestrated by the newly formed *Front de libération nationale* (FLN), heralds the start of the **Algerian uprising**.

In the journal *Cahiers du cinéma* **François Truffaut** publishes what will become the manifesto of *nouvelle vague* cinema when he formulates the *auteur* theory of filmmaking, giving primacy to the role of the director.

1955 In February the crisis in Algeria leads to the fall of the Mendès France government. **Edgar Faure** forms a new administration.

In April a **state of emergency** is declared in Algeria, where violent riots later in the year are met by equally violent repression.

The Algerian War

Of all France's colonial conflicts, the war in **Algeria** was the most savage and left the deepest scars. On 1 November, 1954, the *Front de libération nationale* (FLN) orchestrated a series of attacks on police stations and official buildings. According to the proclamation it issued, its goal was national independence within an Islamic framework. The French government responded by condemning the rebellion and reasserting Algeria's colonial status. Later attempts to soften this response were at odds with the reality on the ground, where cruelty was sharpened by a ferocious racism that drove many more moderate elements among the Algerians into the camp of the rebels. Terrorism and massacres on the part of the FLN were answered by terrorism and massacres on the part of the Europeans. From 1957 the French army under **General Massu** routinely used torture.

The cost to France – human, moral and financial – was steadily turning the tide of public opinion. The return to power of **General de Gaulle** in the wake of the military and civilian uprising in May 1958 was expected by the colonists to produce a hardening of the line against Algerian independence, but de Gaulle recognized that history was against them. In spite of attempts on his life and a terrorist campaign mounted by the **OAS** (*Organisation de l'armée secrète*), he backed a policy that led ineluctably to the referendum which, on 1 July, 1962, confirmed **Algerian independence**. For almost eight years the war had run like a stain through the political life of France, achieving nothing. It had cost many thousands of lives, turned French soldiers into torturers and brought down the Fourth Republic.

In May agreement is reached on the autonomy of **Tunisia**, and Bourgiba returns the following month.

France is hit by **widespread strikes** (June–October).

Claude Lévi-Strauss publishes *Tristes tropiques*, the intellectual autobiography that wins his work in anthropology a degree of popular recognition.

Structuralism

The emergence from the 1950s onwards of the theories associated with **structuralism**, and later **poststructuralism**, confirmed the role of Paris as the intellectual crucible of the west. Drawing on the work in linguistics of **Ferdinand de Saussure** (1857–1913), the anthropologist **Claude Lévi-Strauss** argued that cultures should be understood as systems within which the meaning of individual elements depends on their structural relation to other elements in the same system. It was a theory whose application across a range of disciplines produced a seismic change in the study of society, the arts and humanities. **Roland Barthes** expanded the insights of structuralism into the science of cultural signs known as **semiotics**. Others, poststructuralists as they came to be called, developed and modified aspects of structuralism for different ends: **Jacques Lacan** to theorize the structure of the unconscious, **Michel Foucault** to explore the discursive strategies by which society defines and maintains itself, **Jacques Derrida** to deconstruct the claims of language to represent reality. These have been among the main focuses of academic and intellectual debate in the second half of the 20th century.

1956 In January elections to the Chamber of Deputies result in victory for the centre-left coalition, the *Front Républicain*.

In March, in a move partly designed to prevent the spread of the Algerian conflict, **Tunisia** and **Morocco** are granted independence.

In September the first underwater telephone cable linking **Europe** and the **US** is completed.

On 22 October the French divert an aircraft carrying four Algerian nationalist leaders, including **Ben Bella**, and arrest them.

Following **Nasser**'s nationalization of the **Suez canal** in July, the French and British embark on a disastrous military intervention (November–December). Unsupported by America, and opposed by Russia with the threat of nuclear war, the action ends in humiliation.

Film director **Roger Vadim** celebrates a new popular hedonism when he launches the career of **Brigitte Bardot** with the sexually explicit *Et Dieu créa la femme* (*And God Created Woman*).

The attempt by director **Alain Resnais** and poet **Jean Cayrol** to confront the human implications of the concentration camps in their film *Nuit et brouillard* meets official resistance. Under diplomatic pressure from West Germany, it is withdrawn from the **Cannes film festival**.

1957 In January a series of terrorist acts mark the start of the **battle of Algiers**. On 7 January **General Jacques Massu** is made responsible for the restoration of order. In the course of the next nine months his forces torture and terrorise their way to a temporary victory over the FLN, but the moral battle has been lost, and the cost to France in both money and international standing is immense. By the middle of the year there are some half a million French troops in Algeria, most of them conscripts.

In France **prices increase** and the value of the **franc falls**.

On 25 March the signing of the **treaty of Rome** creates the **European Economic Community** (EEC), of which France is a founder member.

Albert Camus is awarded the Nobel prize for Literature.

Founding in Italy of the **Situationist International**, an anti-capitalist movement that attempts to aestheticize political theory and action. Situationist ideas strongly influence the events of **May 1968**.

1958 In prosecuting the Algerian War, the French bomb a **Tunisian village** just across the border, causing international outrage and hastening the fall of the Fourth Republic (8 February).

On 13 May an uprising of **European settlers** in Algiers is supported by the army under **Generals Salan** and **Massu**. Ten days later, paratroopers from Algeria land in Corsica, positioning themselves for a possible invasion of France.

Having played a waiting game as the pressure builds, General de Gaulle declares himself 'ready to take on the powers of the Republic' (15 May). By forcing a change of political regime, the Algerian rebels have effected a *coup d'état* in all but name. The Communists, as well as François Mitterrand and Mendès France, oppose the recall of de Gaulle, but he is the only figure who can command a broad enough allegiance to resolve the situation. The Fourth Republic is dead.

On 2 June de Gaulle is invested with **full powers** by the National Assembly. His new Constitution, which gives more authority to the President, including the power to appoint and dismiss the Prime Minister, is accepted in a referendum on 28 September. In December, he himself is elected President of the **Fifth Republic** for a seven-year term.

André Malraux is appointed Minister of Culture (27 July).

1959 On 1 January the European **Common Market** comes into force.

Compulsory schooling is extended to the age of 16 (6 January).

André Malraux

Brought up in the suburbs of Paris by his mother and grandmother, **Malraux** (1901–76) always claimed to loathe his childhood. At the age of 17 he turned his back on it, leaving school and moving into the world of book production and art criticism. A journey to **Indochina** in 1923, supposedly for archeological research, ended abruptly with his arrest in Phnom Penh for the theft of works of Khmer art. Released partly thanks to a petition mounted by French intellectuals, he soon returned to Indochina as a vigorous critic of France's colonial policy. Over the next seven years he drew on the Far East for the three novels that made him an international name: *Les Conquérants* (1928), *La Voie royale* (1930) and *La Condition humaine* (1933), the last of which won the Prix Goncourt.

Increasingly engaged by the struggle against fascism in the 1930s, Malraux commanded a squadron of planes for the Republican forces during the **Spanish Civil War**, out of which came his novel *L'Espoir* (1937). A resistance fighter in the final year of World War II, Malraux played only a brief political role in its aftermath, devoting himself to the study of art that resulted in *Le Musée imaginaire* (1947) and *Les Voix du silence* (1951). But when de Gaulle returned to power in 1958, Malraux took on the job of **Minister of Culture** for a ten-year period which saw, among other things, the development of France's **Maisons de Culture** (cultural centres), the cleaning and restoration of numerous historic buildings and the revitalisation of the Marais district in Paris.

In a life sown with personal tragedy – both his sons were killed in a car accident – he managed to combine a speculative intellect with a commitment to individual action that made him a continuingly glamorous figure. His ashes were transferred to the Panthéon in 1996 on the 20th anniversary of his death.

The Fifth Republic is inaugurated under the presidency of de Gaulle, who names **Michel Debré** Prime Minister (8 January).

The film-makers of the French **new wave** burst into prominence with a series of landmark films, including Louis Malle's *Zazie dans le métro*, Jean-Luc Godard's *A bout de souffle* (*Breathless*), François Truffaut's *Les 400 coups* (*The 400 Blows*), Claude Chabrol's *Les Cousins*, and Alain Resnais' *Hiroshima, mon amour*. Their work reacts against the narrative-bound, studio conventions of the past and has a free and improvized quality to it.

A scene from *A bout de souffle* (1960), Godard's radical and nihilistic take on American film noir, starring Jean Seberg (left) and Jean-Paul Belmondo

1960 On 1 January the **new franc** is introduced.

De Gaulle's recall of General Massu provokes violent protest among supporters of a **French Algeria**, leading to the 'week of barricades' in Algiers (24 January–1 February). Failure to win over the army brings the protest to an end and strengthens de Gaulle's hand.

On 13 February France carries out its first **atomic test**, in the Sahara.

In March de Gaulle speaks of an 'Algerian Algeria'. In the course of the year a series of **French colonies** gain **independence**: French Cameroon, Togo, Madagascar, Dahomey, Niger, Upper Volta, Chad, the Ivory Coast, the Central African Republic, Congo, Gabon, Senegal and Mauretania.

On the brink of the great tourist explosion of the 1960s, the first stretch of the *autoroute du Soleil*, leading south to the **Riviera**, is opened. The same year sees the launching of the *France*, the world's largest ocean liner.

1961 A referendum endorses de Gaulle's policy of **self-determination** for Algeria (8 January). This leads to the formation of the **OAS** (*Organisation de l'armée secrète*), headed by **General Raoul Salan** and dedicated to maintaining French control of Algeria. A failed **military putsch** in Algeria clears the ground for a negotiated settlement with the nationalists (21–25 April).

The police run riot in response to a **Muslim demonstration** in Paris, killing numerous demonstrators whose bodies are tipped into the Seine (17 October).

1962 The OAS mounts a **terrorist campaign** in France and Algeria (January–March). At a left-wing demonstration against the OAS on 8 February, brutal police action results in the death of eight demonstrators, crushed against the grill of the Charonne métro.

On 18 March the **Evian agreements** are signed, putting an end to the Algerian War. The agreements win overwhelming support in a **referendum** (8 April).

Georges Pompidou succeeds Michel Debré as Prime Minister (14 April).

Algerian independence (3 July) results in a massive exodus of Europeans, the so-called *pieds-noirs*, most of whom emigrate to southern France.

The visit of the West German Chancellor **Konrad Adenauer** in July marks a thawing in relations between France and Germany and is followed by an official visit by de Gaulle to Germany later in the year.

On 22 August an OAS commando group open fire on de Gaulle's car at Petit-Clamart in a **failed assassination** attempt. Partly in consequence of this, de Gaulle speeds up his plans for **constitutional reform**. The policy of choosing the President by universal suffrage rather than, as before, by an electorate of 'notables' is agreed by referendum on 28 October.

France and Britain sign an agreement to develop the supersonic airliner **Concorde** (29 November).

1963 In January de Gaulle **vetoes** the application by Britain to join the EEC. In the same month, France and Germany seal their reconciliation with a **treaty of cooperation** and friendship.

Alain Robbe-Grillet publishes *Pour un nouveau roman*, a manifesto for the new kind of fiction associated with himself, **Nathalie Sarraute** and **Michel Butor**. The 'New Novelists' reject the traditional conventions of plot, character and chronology, forcing the reader to chart a path through observations and events that often have no clear meaning.

1964 France officially recognizes **Communist China** (27 January).

Jean-Paul Sartre refuses the Nobel prize for Literature, believing that such honours taint the relationship between writer and reader.

Jacques Anquetil wins the Tour de France for the fifth time.

1965 On 29 October **Ben Barka**, the exiled leader of the opposition to the king of Morocco, is **kidnapped** outside the Brasserie Lipp in St-Germain-des-près and never seen again. The affair, in which members of the French police and security services are implicated, leads to a break in diplomatic relations between France and Morocco.

De Gaulle is re-elected President, but **François Mitterrand**, the candidate of the left, wins considerable prestige by taking him to a second round (12–19 December).

The French scientists **François Jacob**, **André Lwoff** and **Jacques Monod** are awarded the Nobel prize for Medicine for their work on genetics.

1966 In February, France, which has has long been suspicious of Anglo-American dominance of **NATO**, withdraws from the organisation's operational structures but remains a member of the alliance.

In a speech in **Phnom Penh** (1 September), de Gaulle condemns American involvement in Vietnam.

1967 **Gaullists** win a narrow majority in elections to the Chamber of Deputies (5–12 March).

On 18 March the oil tanker *Torrey Canyon* runs aground, discharging 31 million gallons of oil and causing widespread pollution along the coast of Brittany – the first of a series of similar disasters that include the wreck of two other oil tankers, the *Amoco Cadiz* in March 1978 and the *Tanio* in March 1980.

On 29 March France's first **nuclear submarine**, *Redoutable*, is launched.

May '68 – Les Evénements

Against the background of the American war in **Vietnam**, explosions of youthful protest, fuelled by miscellaneous grievances, had been taking place across the world. What sparked the events in Paris was a student occupation at the **Nanterre campus** which led on 2 May to the closure of the faculty. The following day a demonstration was held at the **Sorbonne** in the heart of the Latin Quarter. The brutality of the police sent in to clear the courtyard turned a protest into a riot: the *événements* were under way.

The next three weeks brought France to the edge of revolution. The thuggery of the French riot police (*Compagnies républicaines de sécurité* – CRS) helped win public opinion to the students' cause, and on 10–11 May, the **'night of the barricades'**, Paris saw street battles on a scale that had not been witnessed for decades. By this time protest had spread to the workers. Posters, slogans, sit-ins and meetings all contributed to a round-the-clock ferment of **revolutionary activity**. On 15 May the **Odéon theatre** was occupied. Responding belatedly to the crisis, Pompidou's government attempted to buy off the workers with an agreement on wage rises and improvements in working conditions, but by then matters had gone too far.

On 29 May **de Gaulle**, under pressure to resign, flew to Germany to see General Massu and other commanders of the French army of occupation. Assured of their support, he went on television the next day to declare the dissolution of the National Assembly and his own refusal to resign. His decisive resumption of power, aided by a massive **Gaullist demonstration** in the Champs-Elysées, swung the political balance. Within a fortnight the revolutionary euphoria had dissipated, the workers were back in their factories and the university faculties back under the control of the authorities. The events of May had produced few tangible results, but they had changed the social climate irrevocably, paving the way for future reforms and more liberal attitudes.

In Paris rioting students throw stones at police during the upheavals of May 1968

In a speech in Montréal on 26 July de Gaulle proclaims the separatist slogan, 'Vive le Québec libre', thereby upsetting the Canadian government for whom **Québec nationalism** is a sensitive issue.

1968 In May **protests** by students and workers, violently opposed by the police, bring the country to the verge of revolution.

On 24 August France carries out its first **H bomb test**, on **Muroroa atoll** in the Pacific.

> For ten years now demographers and sociologists have repeatedly prophesied the coming of the wave of youth. Well, the wave has reached us, and is beginning to break.
>
> Pierre Viansson-Ponté, in *Le Monde*, 15 May, 1968, quoted in John Getton,
> *Student and Workers* (1969)

1969 On 27 April de Gaulle attempts to reassert his authority through a **referendum**, but his plans to reorganize the regions and reconstruct the Senate are rejected by 54 percent of the voters. He **resigns** the following day, and Pompidou wins the subsequent presidential elections, naming **Jacques Chaban-Delmas** Prime Minister.

The **devaluation** of the franc in August is followed by a wave of **strikes**.

1970 On 9 November **Charles de Gaulle** dies, and is buried three days later at **Colombey-les-Deux-Eglises**.

1971 In June the *Parti socialiste* (PS) is created out of a number of non-communist left-wing groupings and elects **François Mitterrand** as its first secretary.

Max Ophuls' film *Le Chagrin et la pitié* is screened for the first time. A study of French **collaboration** during the war, it inspires a bitter controversy which suggests that France is only now beginning to come to terms with that area of its past.

Work begins on demolishing the 19th-century pavilions of **Les Halles** to make way for an ultra-modern shopping centre.

1972 The **expansion of the EEC** to include the UK, Denmark and Ireland is approved by referendum (23 April).

In June, the parties of the left unite to form a common programme.

Uneasy about a legislative programme that his critics see as too liberal, Pompidou dismisses Chaban-Delmas and replaces him as Prime Minister with the more conservative **Pierre Mesmer** (5 July).

In September **Jean-Marie Le Pen** founds the extreme right-wing *Front national*.

1973 Following the **Yom Kippur War** between Israel and her Arab neighbours, **OPEC** (Organization of Petroleum Exporting Countries) decides on **huge increases** in the price of oil, with drastic consequences for the economies of the west (October–December).

1974 On 2 April **Georges Pompidou** dies in office. In the subsequent Presidential elections **Valéry Giscard d'Estaing** beats François Mitterrand in the second round and appoints **Jacques Chirac** Prime Minister. Supported by the Gaullists, Giscard none the less has a liberal social agenda some of which he manages to fulfil. He names **Simone Veil** Minister of Health, only the second woman minister to be appointed since 1958. **Françoise Giroud** is given the new post of secretary of state for the '*Condition féminine*'. Over the next fifteen months the law on **contraception** is liberalized, the age of majority is lowered to 18, the **Veil law** (promulgated 17 January, 1975) legalizes voluntary **abortion** within certain limits, **divorce** becomes possible by mutual consent, and the first steps are taken towards breaking up the monolithic **state broadcasting system**. But in the end Giscard's presidency falls victim to the economic situation created by the oil crisis. He has come to power just as almost three decades of economic growth, the *Trente Glorieuses*, are drawing to a close.

1975 On 1 August France (along with most other western nations and the Soviet Union) signs the **Helsinki Accords**, which range across a number of issues, including the inviolability of post-World War II frontiers, respect for human rights, and economic and scientific cooperation.

In September the OPEC countries decide on another rise in the price of oil.

1976 The 20th Congress of the **French Communist Party** abandons the doctrine of the dictatorship of the proletariat (4–8 February).

On 25 August Chirac resigns. **Raymond Barre** is appointed Prime Minister and in the following month presents a series of **anti-inflationary** measures – the Barre plan.

In December the Gaullist party is transformed into the *Rassemblement pour la République*, with Chirac as its president.

1977 The *Centre national d'art et de culture Georges-Pompidou* in Paris is opened on 31 January. Designed in a radical 'High-Tech' style (with service ducts and escalators on the exterior), the Pompidou Centre rapidly becomes one of the most visited cultural monuments in the world.

Chirac is elected **mayor of Paris** (13–20 March).

The left makes gains in municipal elections, but internal strains in the **Socialist-Communist alliance** lead to its break-up in September, six months before the elections.

1978 In February the **UDF** (*Union pour la démocratie française*), broadly supportive of **Giscard d'Estaing**, is created out of an alliance of republicans, social democrats and right-wing radicals.

In March, thanks to the disunity of the left, the **right-wing groupings** manage to retain a majority in elections to the Chamber.

French troops intervene in **Zaire** to help crush a left-wing rebellion against the dictator **Mobutu** (19 May–6 June).

1979 Rising unemployment leads to **social unrest**, with strikes in the banking sector, insurance, and the steel industry (January–March).

In March the **ecu** (European Currency Unit) comes into operation. An artificial currency used by member states of the **European Union** as their internal accounting unit, it is the precursor of today's euro.

In a further shock to the western economies, the OPEC

countries decide on another steep increase in petrol prices, provoked by the crisis in Iran, where an **Islamic revolution** led by Ayatollah Khomeini has toppled the Shah.

Following the first elections to the **European Parliament** by universal suffrage, **Simone Veil** is elected President of the Parliament (17 July).

Jean-Paul Sartre

The kind of celebrity enjoyed by **Jean-Paul Sartre** (1905–80) was a peculiarly French phenomenon – England and America do not look for their heroes among the ranks of the intellectuals. Brought up in Paris by his mother and grandparents, Sartre was an outstanding student at Paris's *Ecole normale supérieure* and went on to take up an appointment as a philosophy teacher in Le Havre. By this time he had begun his lifelong liaison with **Simone de Beauvoir**. Despite the impact of the **Spanish Civil War**, his prewar writings, which include his first novel *La Nausée* (1938), were not primarily political. It was during World War II, for nine months of which he was held prisoner by the Germans, that he laid the groundwork of his later fame. Before the armistice was signed, he had published his philosophical work *L'être et le néant* and the first two volumes of *Les Chemins de la liberté*, as well as *Huis clos*. The development of **existentialism** (see p.324) which these works heralded, made Sartre a dominant presence in French intellectual life for the next thirty years.

Inveterately suspicious of institutions and institutional orthodoxies, he was rarely prepared to toe any party line for long, maintaining at best a wary relationship with the **Communist Party**. His role was that of protester, critic and libertarian socialist, whose stands on a range of issues from torture in Algeria to political censorship at home earned him recognition as the moral conscience of the left. His funeral on 19 April, 1980 produced the sort of public demonstration more usually accorded to a head of state. As the procession made its way to the cemetery of Montparnasse, France was marking the end of an intellectual era.

In October the satirical magazine *Le Canard enchaîné* reveals that **Giscard d'Estaing** accepted an undeclared gift of diamonds from **Jean Bedel Bokassa**, self-styled emperor of the Central African Republic.

On 24 December the European space rocket *Ariane* is launched for the first time.

The mathematician **Yvonne Choquet-Bruhat** becomes the first woman to be elected to the Academy of Sciences.

1980 The grim economic situation, reflected in high inflation and unemployment, is aggravated by OPEC's imposition of two further rises in the price of oil in the first half of the year and by yet more rises in October-November as a result of the **Iran-Iraq War**.

Jean-Paul Sartre dies (15 April).

The New Hebrides gain independence as the **Republic of Vanuatu** (30 July).

Marguerite Yourcenar, author of *Mémoires d'Hadrien*, becomes the first woman to be elected to the *Académie française*.

1981 In the presidential elections, the socialist candidate **François Mitterrand** beats Giscard d'Estaing in the second round (26 April–10 May). He appoints as Prime Minister **Pierre Mauroy**, who introduces a range of **social legislation**, including the abolition of the death penalty, a shorter working week, an increase in the minimum wage and state benefits, a loosening of state control over broadcasting, and a devolution of power to the regions. But again the weakness of the economy makes these changes difficult to pay for, forcing a shift towards more conservative policies.

Victory for the *Parti socialiste* in elections to the Chamber confirms the swing to the left (14–21 June).

On 11 August an **amnesty** is declared for **illegal immigrants**.

Parliament abolishes the **death penalty** (18 September).

The first stretch of the high speed train (**TGV**) link from Paris to Lyon is opened (22 September).

From October to December, as unemployment edges towards two million, the franc is devalued and **Jacques Delors**, Minister for the Economy, announces a 'pause in the reforms', but the government pushes ahead with a series of nationalizations that include banks as well as chemical, electronics, arms and insurance companies.

The first performance is given of *Répons* by composer **Pierre Boulez**. It is the summation of Boulez's work at **IRCAM**, the music research laboratory that he set up at the Pompidou Centre in 1977.

1982 In January the **working week** is set at 39 hours and paid holidays are increased to five weeks per year.

In June another devaluation of the franc leads to a four-month **wage** and **price freeze** in an effort to combat inflation.

In July a new law on audio-visual communication opens the way for private ownership of radio and television stations.

An attack on a **Jewish** restaurant in the Marais leaves six dead and 22 injured (9 August). This is one of a number of terrorist attacks through the summer aimed at Jewish targets.

After years of political agitation, elections are held in **Corsica** for its first regional assembly (8–24 August).

1983 In February the Nazi war criminal **Klaus Barbie**, known as the butcher of Lyon, is extradited from Bolivia.

In March, following another devaluation of the franc, the government introduces more **austerity measures** to meet the economic crisis. State expenditure will be cut back and taxes increased.

In June the **Professional Equality Law** seeks to combat discrimination against women.

Armenian Liberationists kill eight people in a bomb attack on Turkish Airlines at Orly airport (15 July).

On 4 December 60,000 people gather in Paris at the end of the **'March of the Beurs'** against racial discrimination.

In this year, **Luc Montagnier** and his team at the Institut Pasteur identify the **AIDS virus**.

Beurs

Derived from *verlan* (slang that inverts letters or syllables) for *arabe*, the term **Beurs** refers to second-generation immigrants from France's former colonies in northwest Africa. In use since the late 1970s, it came to prominence in 1983 when a huge protest march against racism was christened by the media the **March of the Beurs**. Throughout the 1980s, beur culture gained increasing exposure: the music, cinema and literature of the beurs, typically concerned with the problems of mixed French and North African identity, had a conspicuous vitality, and **Radio Beur** (1981–92) was a highly successful competitor in the new wave of private stations that followed relaxation of the state monopoly on broadcasting.

The other side of this cultural profile is a social reality that has confined the vast majority of beurs to suburban housing estates with high unemployment and the full range of associated problems. Efforts to turn the beurs into an organised political force foundered among conflicting interests, and by the mid-1990s the term itself was under suspicion from many who saw it as tainted by the racial and social assumptions of the French media.

 For some, the Algerian War isn't over yet. The presence on French territory of a little less than one million Algerian immigrants arouses their nostalgic hatred, and when they attack an Arab, this inscribes itself in the impossible and intolerable mourning which history demands regarding 'French Algeria'.

Tahar Ben Jelloun, *Hospitalité française* (1984) trans. Anne Donadey

1984 Between January and March, government plans for **private education**, which would have provided for limited state intervention, excite widespread opposition, leading in July to their withdrawal and the resignation of Mauroy. The more pragmatic **Laurent Fabius** is appointed Prime Minister.

Jean-Marie Le Pen's *Front national* wins over ten percent of the votes in the European elections (17 June).

1985 On 10 July the **Greenpeace** ship *Rainbow Warrior* is sunk in Auckland harbour **New Zealand** by explosives planted by two French intelligence agents. The ship has been protesting against French nuclear tests in the Pacific, and the attack, which kills a Greenpeace photographer, has been carried out on orders from the French authorities. The French Minister of Defence, **Charles Hernu**, resigns on 20 September, and **Laurent Fabius** is seriously damaged. Mitterrand, who, unlike Fabius, knew of the order, emerges relatively unscathed.

On 7 December terrorist attacks by **Armenian Liberationists** damage two department stores in the boulevard Haussmann.

The Nobel prize for Literature is awarded to the novelist **Claude Simon**, whose works include *Le Vent* (1957) and *La Route des Flandres* (1960).

Bernard Hinault becomes the second Frenchman to win the Tour de France five times.

1986 On 1 January Spain and Portugal join the **EEC**, bringing the membership to twelve.

On 12 February France and Britain sign the treaty to build the **Channel Tunnel**.

In the same month the media take a further step into private ownership with the launch of the **fifth** and **sixth TV channels**.

Elections in March give control of the National Assembly to the right. The Fabius administration resigns and Mitterrand appoints **Jacques Chirac** Prime Minister, initiating the first period of 'cohabitation' between a President and Prime Minister on opposite sides of the political divide. Chirac sets out to undo some of the recent changes, abolishing the wealth tax, disbanding a short-lived Ministry of Women's Rights, and attempting to unravel some of the nationalizations, but his authority is challenged by industrial unrest and a continuing wave of terrorist attacks in Paris for which the extreme left-wing/anarchist group *Action directe* claims responsibility. These culminate in the murder of **Georges Besse**, managing director of Renault, on 17 November.

In December France is hit by **a series of strikes** that run into the New Year, involving students, transport services and electricity workers.

> " No monument, no facility is to be equated with its use alone. All of them inscribe, in space and time, a certain idea of the useful, the beautiful, of city life and the dealings of men and women among themselves. In this way do we derive the different meanings of the verb *édifier* in French: to build, but also to signify, to advocate … certain values, certain virtues. "
>
> François Mitterrand on France's architectural *grands projets*

Opening of the **Cité des Sciences** at La Villette, and the **musée d'Orsay**, ingeniously housed in the old railway station.

1987 On 21 February the four **ringleaders** of *Action directe* are arrested.

On 11 May the trial of **Klaus Barbie** opens in Lyon. Sentenced to life imprisonment, he dies in custody in 1991.

New Caledonia

A French colony since the middle of the 19th century, **New Caledonia** was one of the first of the overseas French territories to rally to General de Gaulle in 1940, acquiring the status of 'territoire d'outre mer' in 1946. The founding of the *Front de libération nationale kanak socialiste* (FLNKS) in 1984 marked the start of an **independence struggle** that resulted in numerous deaths before an unsatisfactory compromise was reached in 1985. The situation was complicated by the fact that in any test of electoral strength, **loyalist Europeans**, voting together for the *Rassemblement pour la Calédonie dans la République* (RPCR), could outvote the divided indigenous populations. When the question of independence was put to a referendum on 13 September, 1987, a boycott by many of the **Kanaks** gave a sweeping victory to loyalists.

In April the following year, violence again broke out when two gendarmes were killed and hostages taken. The subsequent French operation to free the hostages left nineteen Kanaks dead. A temporary solution was devised by **Michel Rocard**, who brought the leading representatives of the FLNKS and the Europeans together to agree what was in effect a partitioning of the territory, with the prospect of another referendum on independence in 1998. In the event, the Prime Minister at the time, Lionel Jospin, pre-empted the dangers of a second referendum by arranging the **Noumea accord** in April 1998, which gave a large measure of autonomy to the territory, while envisaging complete independence at the end of a long transition period expected to last between fifteen and twenty years.

On 19 September (Black Monday) the **stock market crashes** following the announcement of America's trade deficit.

1988 **François Mitterrand** wins a second term as President, beating Jacques Chirac in the second round (24 April–8 May). He appoints the financial expert **Michel Rocard** as Prime Minister.

Another of France's long running colonial problems comes to a head with conflict in **New Caledonia** between **Kanak guerillas** and **French forces** (April–May).

On 12 October parliament votes for the *Revenu minimum d'insertion* (RMI), a state payment to anyone over 25 whose income falls below a certain level.

Strikes affect the public sector (November–December).

1989 The architect I.M. Pei's **glass pyramid** in the Louvre is officially opened in March.

In November the affair of the *'foulard islamique'*, in which three girls are expelled from a school in Creil for wearing the Islamic scarf, highlights growing racial tensions. The success of the *Front national* in municipal elections in Dreux the following month is a reflection of the controversy.

1990 In May the desecration of the **Jewish cemetery** at Carpentras leads to mass demonstrations against anti-Semitism. In June a law against racism is passed.

On 2 August **Iraq** invades **Kuwait**, provoking an international crisis and an increase in the price of oil.

Demonstrations in Paris by thousands of **lycée pupils** against school conditions force the Education Minister Lionel Jospin to speed up plans for reform (October–November).

Gérard Depardieu's lead roles in *Green Card* and *Cyrano de Bergerac* consolidate his international reputation.

The Arche de la Défense, completed in 1989, commemorates the bi-centenary of the French Revolution. It was designed by Danish architect Otto Van Spreckelsen

1991 France participates in the American-led **Gulf War** to liberate Kuwait from Iraq (17 January–28 February).

In February riots break out on the island of **Réunion**, a French overseas *département* east of Madagascar, following a government ban on a free radio station.

Unrest in the suburbs leads to frequent conflict between police and young members of the immigrant community (March–July).

On 15 May Mitterrand replaces Rocard as Prime Minister with **Edith Cresson**, whose public tactlessness, combined with her unpopularity among the electorate, ensures that she will not be long in office.

1992 The **Maastricht treaty**, signed on 7 February, provides for closer political and economic union in Europe. The French give it their approval in a referendum in September.

On 2 April Edith Cresson resigns, and **Pierre Bérégovoy** is appointed Prime Minister.

In April **EuroDisney** opens outside Paris.

On 24 July the Director of the **National Blood Transfusion Centre** goes on trial for knowingly using blood supplies that had not been screened for the AIDS virus. He is sentenced to four years in prison.

In September **torrential rain** causes flooding in the south of France.

Georges Charpak is awarded the Nobel prize for Physics for his invention of subatomic particle detectors.

1993 On 1 January the **single market** comes into force in Europe.

In March the right-wing **RPR-UDR** coalition wins an overwhelming victory in elections to the Assembly. Pierre Bérégovoy, whose reputation has been damaged by accusations of financial impropriety, resigns and a few weeks later commits suicide. With the appointment of **Edouard Balladur** to succeed him, a second period of 'cohabitation' begins.

Palestinian leader **Yasser Arafat** is welcomed on an official visit to Paris (21 October).

In the **GATT** (General Agreement on Tariffs and Trade) negotiations France finally wins exemption for cultural products, ensuring that its film industry, in particular, will not be swamped by American imports.

1994 On 17 March the trial begins of **Paul Touvier**, arrested in 1989 for his activities as head of the *Milice* in Lyon during the war. Sentenced in April to life imprisonment, he dies in custody just over two years later.

On 6 May the **Channel Tunnel** is officially opened.

1995 On 26 March the **Schengen convention** comes into force. This provides for **free movement** among the populations of Europe.

Jacques Chirac is elected president, beating Lionel Jospin in the second round (23 April–7 May). Chirac appoints **Alain Juppé** prime minister.

On 11 May France signs the nuclear **non-proliferation treaty**. A month later, on 13 June, Chirac announces the resumption of nuclear tests. The first of these takes place on **Muroroa atoll** on 5 September, in spite of international protests.

Algerian **Islamic militants** launch a series of terrorist attacks in Paris and the Lyon district (July–October).

A wave of strikes in the public sector forces Juppé to retreat from plans to reform the **Social Security system** (October–December).

1996 Death of **François Mitterrand** (8 January).

On 29 January, two days after the second test on Muroroa atoll, President Chirac bows to international pressure and ends nuclear testing. In February, he announces a reorganization of military resources to coincide with the decision to end conscription.

Death of **Marguerite Duras** (3 March), whose work, strongly influenced by her childhood in Indochina, has made her one of the most distinguished French women writers of the 20th century.

1997 In March Juppé forces through a measure tightening

the **law on immigration**, against strong opposition.

A victory for the left in elections to the Chamber introduces another period of 'cohabitation' (25 May–1 June). Juppé resigns and is replaced as Prime Minister by Lionel Jospin. It is Jospin's good fortune to come on the scene at just the moment when France's **GDP** begins to rise and unemployment to fall. A number of successful **privatizations**, including Air France, give a further boost to the government's financial position, providing a solid base for limited measures of social reform.

On 8 October **Maurice Papon**, Prefect of Police at the time of the Muslim demonstration in 1961 and the Charonne métro demonstration the following year, goes on trial for crimes against humanity committed under **Vichy**. After a trial lasting six months, he is sentenced to ten years in prison.

1998 **Urban violence** and **protests** by the unemployed lead in March to a three-year government plan that includes job-training schemes and measures affecting healthcare and debt-repayment.

In April the National Assembly votes by a large majority to adopt the **euro**.

For many, the high point of the year is France's 3-0 victory over Brazil in July to win the football **World Cup**, staged in France.

1999 In January, after violent **New Year clashes** between police and rioters, Lionel Jospin announces measures to combat a rise in juvenile crime.

On 28 June the constitution is amended to promote the **access of women** to elected office. Under the new system, political parties must have an equal number of men and women candidates on their electoral lists for municipal, parliamentary and European elections.

France's players, including Zinedine Zidane (centre) and Marcel Desailly (right), celebrate victory over Brazil in the 1998 World Cup

In December Parliament approves a bill for a **35-hour working week**.

Universal health cover is established to ensure medical cover for the long-term unemployed.

2000 In February the introduction of the new 35-hour working week is met with strikes by workers concerned about its implications for their wages.

In April a fatal bomb attack at a **McDonald's** restaurant in Brittany reflects increasing militancy on the part of **Breton separatists** associated with the *Armée Révolutionnaire Bretonne* (ARB).

In June the National Assembly endorses a proposal (agreed by referendum in September) to change the presidential **term of office** from seven to five years.

On 25 July the supersonic airliner **Concorde crashes** after takeoff from Charles-de-Gaulle airport, killing all 109 passengers and crew in addition to four people on the ground.

Corsica

Handed over to France by Genoa in 1768, **Corsica** saw its nationalist aspirations crushed by the French army. It was a troubled start to a troubled relationship, and two hundred years later the tensions are still unresolved. Since the mid-1970s when a number of resistance groups were formed, notably the *Front de libération nationale de la Corse* (FLNC), political violence has been commonplace. The setting up of an elected **Regional Assembly** in 1982 did little to satisfy nationalist organisations. In 1998 the shooting of the **French Prefect** prompted a policy of repression by his successor **Bernard Bonnet**, until Bonnet himself ended up in prison after involvement in a gendarmerie arson attack on an unlicensed beach restaurant.

Two government reports critical of France's past policy led **Lionel Jospin** to propose a new initiative at the end of 1999: Corsica would be given **partial autonomy**, with more independent powers of administration and taxation, and special provision for the **Corsican language**. Supported by the Corsican Assembly and approved by the French National Assembly in May 2001, the proposals were attacked both by those on the mainland who argued that they undermined the integrity of the French state and by many Corsican nationalists who saw them as an inadequate compromise. In January 2002 they received a further setback when France's highest court, the Constitutional Council, ruled that the bill to give Corsica limited self-government was unconstitutional. The island's future relations with France remain uncertain.

Following years of unrest, the **Corsican Assembly** votes on 28 July in favour of government proposals for a **gradual devolution** of political power to the island, but terrorist groups respond with a sharp increase in violence.

In September protests against **high fuel prices** bring much of the country to a standstill. In November fears of a deepening **BSE** (bovine spongiform encephalopathy) crisis lead to a government ban on the sale of beef on the bone.

2001 Even for France, this is a year rich in high-profile **political scandals**. The former Foreign Minister **Roland Dumas** is sent to prison for misusing funds of the state-owned Elf Aquitaine company. An investigation into political party financing results in moves to **impeach** President Chirac for involvement in criminal corruption. Further scandal arises from disclosures about the President's use of a secret cash fund accumulated while he was Prime Minister. Meanwhile, the son of the late President Mitterrand goes on trial for his part in **illegal arms trafficking** in Angola.

In June, the government announces that **national conscription** (introduced in 1905) will cease at the end of 2001, a year earlier than scheduled.

Following a terrorist attack on the **World Trade Centre** in New York on **11 September**, France aligns itself with other European powers in support of what America presents as a **'war against terrorism'**. President Chirac declares, 'France knows that terrorism can be combated only by resolute, collective action, and she will do what must be done.'

2002 In February the **franc** ceases to be a legal currency.

After a lacklustre presidential campaign, in which neither **Jacques Chirac** nor **Lionel Jospin** address the issues of immigration and rising crime that are on the minds of the electorate, the extreme right-winger **Jean-Marie Le Pen** stuns the nation by beating Jospin in the first round. The

French are left with a choice between the incumbent Chirac, deeply compromised by allegations of corruption, and the leader of the *Front national*. The alarm caused by Le Pen's showing in the first round creates a series of unprecedented political alliances that give Chirac a land-slide victory on 5 May. He names Jean-Pierre Raffarin Prime Minister.

The swing to the right is confirmed in the **parliamentary elections** the following month, when the centre-right sweep to power with a programme of tax cuts, pension reform, liberalization of the labour market and initiatives on crime.

books

books

T he range of books on French history is vast – writings on Napoléon and his period alone run to some quarter of a million volumes. This is a highly selective list, restricted to works written in English or available in English translation. Many of the titles listed below are in paperback and in print. Those that aren't (marked 'o/p') should be available in secondhand bookshops, or via online retailers. Publishers are detailed with the UK publisher listed first, separated by an oblique slash from the US publisher where both exist. When a book is available only in one market, 'UK' or 'US' precedes the publishing information; if the same publisher handles both, it is simply listed once.

General histories

Fernand Braudel, *The Identity of France* (2 vols., trans. Siân Reynolds, HarperCollins). Braudel sets out to put the history of France in its geographical context before going on in the second volume to relate this to social and economic developments.

Peter Burke, *The French Historical Revolution: The Annales School 1929–89* (Cambridge University Press; Stanford University Press). Burke's survey of the hugely influential Annales school of French historians (notably Lucien Febvre, Marc Bloch, Fernand Braudel, Georges Duby, Jacques Le Goff, and Emmanuel Le Roy Ladurie) provides a useful way to get one's bearings in the field.

Alfred Cobban, *A History of Modern France* (Penguin o/p). Published in three volumes between 1957 and 1965, this clear and accessible history, which covers the period from 1715 to 1962, is out of print but relatively easy to find.

Albert Guerard, *France: A Modern History* (University of Michigan Press). Although slightly dated now, Guerard's well-written survey from pre-history to the 1960s is still an engaging introduction.

Colin Jones, *The Cambridge Illustrated History of France* (Cambridge University Press). This excellent short history is well served by an imaginative range of illustrations.

Roger Price, *A Concise History of France* (Cambridge University Press). Price's salutary insistence on the social context of political events involves a certain loss of narrative drive, but this is a reliable one-volume history.

Gordon Wright, *France in Modern Times: From the Enlightenment to the Present* (Norton). Wright traces the evolution of France's political and social structures, adding a helpful bibliographical chapter to each section.

Ancient and medieval France

Barry Cunliffe (ed.), *The Oxford Illustrated History of Prehistoric Europe* (Oxford University Press). Cunliffe brings together a series of authoritative essays on the development of civilization in Europe from the earliest inhabitants to the barbarian tribes that superseded the Roman empire.

J.F. Drinkwater, *Roman Gaul: The Three Provinces, 58 BC–AD 260* (Croom Helm; Cornell University Press). This is a brief, scholarly introduction to the period of Roman rule up to the establishment of the Gallic empire.

Georges Duby, *France in the Middle Ages 987–1460: From Hugh Capet to Joan of Arc* (trans. Juliet Vale, Blackwell). This first volume in Hachette's Histoire de France considers both the defining structures of medieval French society and the course of France's political history, focusing primarily on the earlier part of the period.

Gregory of Tours, *The History of the Franks* (trans. Lewis Thorpe, Penguin). As a historical record, Gregory's account needs to be approached with caution, but it gives an unrivalled feel for the texture of life in early Merovingian France.

Friedrich Heer, *Charlemagne and His World* (Weidenfeld and Nicolson). An attractive and relatively undemanding introduction to the history and culture of the period, with plenty of illustrations.

E. James, *The Franks* (Blackwell). James provides a useful guide to the complexities of the Merovingian period, looking at social structures and cultural life as well as political history. His earlier *The Origins of France: From Clovis to the Capetians, 500–1000* (Macmillan) follows the story through to the Carolingians.

Emmanuel Le Roy Ladurie, *Montaillou: Cathars and Catholics in a French Village 1294–1324* (trans. Barbara Bray, Scolar Press). Ladurie uses inquisition documents to build up a vivid picture of peasant life in a Cathar village.

Jonathan Sumption, *The Hundred Years War, Vol. I: Trial by Battle, Vol. II: Trial by Fire* (Faber; University of Pennsylvania Press). In its depth of research, grasp of detail and ability to command the reader's attention, Sumption's work is a feat of narrative history.

From Renaissance to Revolution

Norbert Elias, *The Court Society* (trans. Edmund Jephcott, Blackwell; Random House). Elias examines life at Versailles to produce a fascinating study of the nature and meaning of court society.

Robert Darnton, *The Great Cat Massacre and Other Episodes in French Cultural History* (Basic Books; Random House). Darnton's oblique approach to 18th-century modes of thought yields intriguing insights.

R.J. Knecht, *The Rise and Fall of Renaissance France* (Blackwell). Knecht's informed account of 16th-century France keeps the historical narrative firmly rooted in its social and economic context.

Emmanuel Le Roy Ladurie, *The Royal French State 1460–1610* (trans. Juliet Vale, Blackwell) and *The Ancien Régime 1610–1774* (trans. Mark Greengrass, Blackwell). These two volumes, which are part of Hachette's Histoire de France, present a nuanced and persuasive study of the period, marked by Ladurie's characteristic concern with the social evolution of France.

Louis de Saint-Simon, *Memoirs* (3 vols. trans. and abridged Lucy Norton, Prion). Acerbic, biased, full of scandalous detail, the memoirs offer a wonderful glimpse of the human and political realities behind the magnificent façade of Versailles.

The Revolution

Richard Cobb, *Reactions to the French Revolution* (Oxford University Press). Cobb brings an absorbing concern with individual lives to this study of aspects of the Counter-Terror.

William Doyle, *Origins of the French Revolution* (Oxford University Press). Doyle provides a brief, lucid analysis of the causes of the Revolution and of the ways in which modern research has affected prevailing views on the subject.

William Doyle, *The Oxford History of the French Revolution* (Oxford University Press). This detailed study traces the course of events from the accession of Louis XVI, paying particular attention to the impact of the Revolution on the rest of Europe.

Antonia Fraser, *Marie Antoinette: The Journey* (Weidenfeld and Nicolson; Doubleday). Fraser's dramatic narrative, which makes a good case for seeing its subject as more unfortunate than blameworthy, gives a colourful picture of the last years of the *ancien régime*.

François Furet, *Interpreting the French Revolution* (trans. Elborg Forster, Cambridge University Press). Furet's landmark analysis, published in 1979, set out to challenge the prevailing Marxist view of the Revolution as driven by the interests of an increasingly powerful bourgeoisie. See also his volume in Hachette's Histoire de France,

Revolutionary France, 1770–1880 (trans. Antonia Nevill, Blackwell), which argues that it was only with the republican electoral victories of 1876–77 that the principles of 1789 finally became established in French political life.

Pieter Geyl, *Napoléon: for and against* (Jonathan Cape o/p). Written in the early 1960s and out of print for some time, Geyl's useful book compares representations of Napoléon from Chateaubriand onwards, demonstrating the extremes of adulation and abhorrence he has inspired among historians.

Christopher Hibbert, *The French Revolution* (Allen Lane). Hibbert's clarity of presentation and sharp eye for telling detail make for a highly readable work of popular history.

Simon Schama, *Citizens: A Chronicle of the French Revolution* (Viking; Knopf). Schama writes with a flair for combining scholarly detail and lively narrative, though his account takes us only to the fall of Robespierre.

D.M.G. Sutherland, *France 1789–1815: Revolution and Counter-Revolution* (Oxford University Press). With considerable subtlety Sutherland emphasizes the differing effects of the Revolution on various social and regional groups, insisting on the importance of counter-revolutionary movements in shaping the history of the time.

Alexis de Tocqueville, *The Old Regime and the Revolution* (trans. Alan S. Kahan, University of Chicago Press). De Tocqueville's classic mid-19th-century study remains a vital contribution to the understanding of this period of French history.

Jean Tulard, *Napoléon: The Myth of the Saviour* (trans. Teresa Waugh, Methuen). Tulard attempts to separate the more ambiguous reality from the legend.

France in the 19th century

Jean-Denis Bredin, *The Affair: The Case of Alfred Dreyfus* (trans. Jeffrey Mehlman, Braziller; Norton). Bredin analyses the Dreyfus affair and its background in scrupulous detail.

Stuart L. Campbell, *The Second Empire Revisited* (Rutgers University Press). Campbell's survey of the changing assessments of Napoléon III provides an object lesson in the slippery nature of historical judgement.

Louis Chevalier, *Labouring Classes and Dangerous Classes in Paris during the First Half of the Nineteenth Century* (trans. Frank Jellinek, Routledge). Chevalier's provocative, idiosyncratic work of social history focuses on the underside of early 19th-century French society.

Michael Howard, *The Franco-Prussian War: The German Invasion of France, 1870–1871* (Routledge). Howard's outstanding work of military history is still the best account of this crucial episode in the emergence of modern France.

André Jardin and André-Jean Tudesq, *Restoration and Reaction, 1815–1848* (trans. Elborg Forster, Cambridge University Press). The first volume in the *Cambridge History of Modern France*, this study of the Restoration and the July Monarchy usefully redirects attention from Paris to what was going on in the provinces.

Theodore Zeldin, *France, 1848–1945*, (2 vols., Clarendon Press). Zeldin never loses sight of the individuals behind the events, and his brilliant analysis of the human realities underlying this century of French history has rightly become a classic.

For anyone interested in the development of French social life, the writings of the great 19th-century novelists are an endless resource. Among the most illuminating are Victor Hugo's *Les Misérables*, Honoré de Balzac's series of novels *La Comédie humaine*, Gustave Flaubert's *L'Education sentimentale*, Emile Zola's Rougon-Macquart novels and Marcel Proust's *A la recherche du temps perdu*.

Modern France

Maurice Agulhon, *The French Republic 1879–1992* (trans. Antonia Nevill, Blackwell). This final volume in Hachette's Histoire de France is a measured survey of the period by one of France's most distinguished historians.

John Ardagh, *France Today* (Penguin). Over the years this social study has established a well-earned reputation as a standard introduction to the changing face of contemporary France.

Robert Gildea, *France since 1945* (Oxford University Press). Gildea offers a balanced and informative assessment of France's political, social and cultural life in the second half of the 20th century.

Robert Gildea, *Marianne in Chains: In Search of the German Occupation, 1940–1945* (Macmillan). Focusing on the Loire valley, Gildea uses national and local archives to explore the reality of ordinary French responses to the Occupation.

Alistair Horne, *A Savage War of Peace: Algeria 1954–1962* (Macmillan). Horne's classic study of the Algerian war makes grim but compelling reading.

Maurice Larkin, *France since the Popular Front, Government and People 1936–1986* (Oxford University Press). Larkin sets the French experience within a wider European context in this lively, well-written account of the period.

Robert Paxton, *Vichy France* (Columbia University Press). Paxton's study demonstrates convincingly the extent to which Pétain's government embraced and exploited the Nazi agenda.

Charles Sowerwine, *France since 1870: Culture, Politics and Society* (Palgrave; St Martin's Press). A breezy, up-to-date survey that covers the ground with assurance, giving welcome prominence to the role of women during the period.

Art and culture

Peter France (ed.), *The New Oxford Companion to Literature in French* (Oxford University Press). An indispensable work of reference that includes francophone literature from France's former colonies as well as a range of broader cultural entries.

Denis Hollier (ed.), *A New History of French Literature* (Harvard University Press). Hollier's collection of essays, each accompanied by a bibliography, charts the development of French literature from the Oaths of Strasbourg to the 1980s, giving due emphasis to the social and political background.

Alex Hughes and **Keith Reader** (eds.), *Encyclopedia of Contemporary French Culture* (Routledge). This useful volume, focused on the last half-century, defines culture to include topics as diverse as food, politics, education, transport and technology.

Michael Kelly (ed.), *French Culture and Society* (Arnold, Oxford University Press Inc.). Kelly tends to sacrifice detail for coverage, but this is another useful reference book on aspects of French culture since World War I.

Edward Lucie-Smith, *A Concise History of French Painting* (Thames and Hudson o/p). Out of print at the moment but easy to obtain in libraries, Lucie-Smith's lively, well-illustrated account surveys French painting from the Middle Ages to the 1960s.

Whitney S. Stoddard, *Art and Architecture in Medieval France: Medieval Architecture, Sculpture, Stained Glass, Manuscripts, the Art of the Church Treasuries* (HarperCollins). With separate chapters on the great cathedrals, this is a scholarly but readable study of the Romanesque and Gothic periods, covering a wide range of artistic production.

Theodore Zeldin, *The French* (Collins; Kodansha International). Zeldin's wry view of the intricacies of French society is anecdotal and light-hearted but full of beguiling insights.

index

Entries in **colour** represent feature boxes

b

n

o

t

W

Y

Z

around the world

Alaska ★ Algarve ★ Amsterdam ★ Andalucía ★ Antigua & Barbuda ★ Argentina ★ Auckland Restaurants ★ Australia ★ Austria ★ Bahamas ★ Bali & Lombok ★ Bangkok ★ Barbados ★ Barcelona ★ Beijing ★ Belgium & Luxembourg ★ Belize ★ Berlin ★ Big Island of Hawaii ★ Bolivia ★ Boston ★ Brazil ★ Britain ★ Brittany & Normandy ★ Bruges & Ghent ★ Brussels ★ Budapest ★ Bulgaria ★ California ★ Cambodia ★ Canada ★ Cape Town ★ The Caribbean ★ Central America ★ Chile ★ China ★ Copenhagen ★ Corsica ★ Costa Brava ★ Costa Rica ★ Crete ★ Croatia ★ Cuba ★ Cyprus ★ Czech & Slovak Republics ★ Devon & Cornwall ★ Dodecanese & East Aegean ★ Dominican Republic ★ The Dordogne & the Lot ★ Dublin ★ Ecuador ★ Edinburgh ★ Egypt ★ England ★ Europe ★ First-time Asia ★ First-time Europe ★ Florence ★ Florida ★ France ★ French Hotels & Restaurants ★ Gay & Lesbian Australia ★ Germany ★ Goa ★ Greece ★ Greek Islands ★ Guatemala ★ Hawaii ★ Holland ★ Hong Kong & Macau ★ Honolulu ★ Hungary ★ Ibiza & Formentera ★ Iceland ★ India ★ Indonesia ★ Ionian Islands ★ Ireland ★ Israel & the Palestinian Territories ★ Italy ★ Jamaica ★ Japan ★ Jerusalem ★ Jordan ★ Kenya ★ The Lake District ★ Languedoc & Roussillon ★ Laos ★ Las Vegas ★ Lisbon ★ London ★

in twenty years

London Mini Guide ★ London Restaurants ★ Los Angeles ★ Madeira ★ Madrid ★ Malaysia, Singapore & Brunei ★ Mallorca ★ Malta & Gozo ★ Maui ★ Maya World ★ Melbourne ★ Menorca ★ Mexico ★ Miami & the Florida Keys ★ Montréal ★ Morocco ★ Moscow ★ Nepal ★ New England ★ New Orleans ★ New York City ★ New York Mini Guide ★ New York Restaurants ★ New Zealand ★ Norway ★ Pacific Northwest ★ Paris ★ Paris Mini Guide ★ Peru ★ Poland ★ Portugal ★ Prague ★ Provence & the Côte d'Azur ★ Pyrenees ★ The Rocky Mountains ★ Romania ★ Rome ★ San Francisco ★ San Francisco Restaurants ★ Sardinia ★ Scandinavia ★ Scotland ★ Scottish Highlands & Islands ★ Seattle ★ Sicily ★ Singapore ★ South Africa, Lesotho & Swaziland ★ South India ★ Southeast Asia ★ Southwest USA ★ Spain ★ St Lucia ★ St Petersburg ★ Sweden ★ Switzerland ★ Sydney ★ Syria ★ Tanzania ★ Tenerife and La Gomera ★ Thailand ★ Thailand's Beaches & Islands ★ Tokyo ★ Toronto ★ Travel Health ★ Trinidad & Tobago ★ Tunisia ★ Turkey ★ Tuscany & Umbria ★ USA ★ Vancouver ★ Venice & the Veneto ★ Vienna ★ Vietnam ★ Wales ★ Washington DC ★ West Africa ★ Women Travel ★ Yosemite ★ Zanzibar ★ Zimbabwe

also look out for our maps, phrasebooks, music guides and reference books

ROUGH GUIDES TWENTY YEARS